228548

786
N
Norman, Herbert.
    The organ today [by] Herbert Norman and H. John Norman. New York, St. Martin's [1967, ©1966]
    ix, 212 p. illus., 46 plates. 22 cm.

SAN MATEO PUBLIC LIBRARY
SAN MATEO, CALIF.

    1. Organ.   I. Title

ML555.N67   1967   786.6   67–14488/MN
                                6/67   750
Library of Congress   [5]

THE ORGAN TODAY

The Organ Today

HERBERT NORMAN
F.I.S.O.B., F.I.M.I.T., F.R.S.A.

and

H. JOHN NORMAN
B.Sc., A.R.C.S., F.I.M.I.T., A.I.S.O.B.

ST. MARTIN'S
NEW YORK

First published in the United States of America 1967
© 1966 BY HERBERT AND JOHN NORMAN
Published in Great Britain by
Barrie & Rockliff (Barrie Books Ltd.)
Library of Congress Catalog Card Number 67-14488
Manufactured in Great Britain

Contents

	Page
Preface	ix
1. A Brief Historical Survey	1
2. The Instrument	16
3. The Mechanism of the Organ	26
4. Tracker Action	30
5. Pneumatic Actions	39
6. Electro-pneumatic Actions	46
7. The Windchests	58
8. Raising the Wind	76
9. The Swellbox	89
10. The Console	96
11. The Stops a. flue pipes	112
b. flue-pipe voicing	122
c. reed pipes and their voicing	127
12. Glossary of Stop Names	139
13. The Organ-case	175
14. The Placing of the Organ	181
15. Buying an Organ	187
16. Organs and Organ-builders—the future?	193
Appendix: Stop-lists	199
Index	207

Plates

(*between pages 116 and 117*)

Plate 1. One Manual organ in Carisbrooke Castle Museum.
Plate 2. Cambridge, Pembroke College Chapel.
Plate 3. Germany, St. Lamberti, Gladbeck (Johannes Klais).
Plate 4. Portugal, Braga Cathedral.
Plate 5. Signature of Snetzler.
Plate 6. London, The Hyde Park (Mormon) Chapel.
Plate 7. Organ pipes in their ranks.
Plate 8. An organ of 1602 now in Carisbrooke Castle Museum.
Plate 9. Heptonstall Church (Hill Norman & Beard).
Plate 9a. Tone cabinet casework.
Plate 10. A typical arrangement of knobs, keyboards and pistons.
Plate 10a. An alternative-stop control system.
Plate 11 and 11a. An ultra compact two manual console
Plate 12. Two manual stop-key console.
Plate 13. Three manual stop-key console.
Plate 14. A concert organ four manual stop-key console.
Plate 15. Two manual stop-tablet console.
Plate 16. Two manual plain stop-knob console.
Plate 17. Three manual stop-knob console.
Plate 18. Three manual stop-knob console.
Plate 19. Three manual stop-knob console.
Plate 20. Stop-knob console designed to Canadian requirements.
Plate 21. Norwich Cathedral.
Plate 22. Marlborough College Chapel.
Plate 23. A four manual designed to be low enough to see over.
Plate 24. Moosejaw, Sask, St. Andrews.
Plate 25. Foot controls.
Plate 26. Precision engineered relay.
Plate 27. Studied simplicity.
Plate 28. Flue pipes.
Plate 29. A reed voicer's workshop.
Plate 30. The mounted cornet.
Plate 31. The revised use of Trompette-en-chamade.
Plate 32. Holbrook Royal Naval School, Suffolk.
Plate 33. Bass pipes for a simple functional screen.
Plate 34. Open display of pipework.

LIST OF PLATES

Plate 35. London, Royal Albert Hall, Willis.
Plate 36. 17th-Century British classical.
Plate 37. Norwich Cathedral, S. Dykes Bower.
Plate 38. Bradford Cathedral—Sir Edward Maufe.
Plate 39. The two manual 'werk-prinzip'.
Plate 40. Dunster Church—Norman.
Plate 41. The Denham—NP Mander.
Plate 42. The Quintet—Norman.
Plate 43. Trinity College School Chapel, Port Hope, Ont.
Plate 44. P. Q., St. Lambert, St. Barnabas Church—Norman.
Plates 45 & 46. Heptonstall Parish Church, McGuire & Murray. H.N. & B.

Figures

1. Pan Pipes	.	.	.	1
2. The hydraulus	.	.	2
3. King's College Chapel	.	9
4. Nag's head and louvred swells	.	.	.	12
5. Keyboard notation	.	18
6. Sekkau (end plate)	.	25
7. Tracker action	.	.	31
8. Pin action	.	.	32
9. Tracker action	.	.	33
10. Backfall action	.	.	36
11. Backfall action (Sydney)	37
12. Tubular-pneumatic action, basic form	.	39
13. Tubular-pneumatic action, charge type	42
14. Tubular-pneumatic action, exhaust type	.	.	43
15. Hope-Jones's magnet	.	47
16. Electro action, chest actions	.	.	.	48
17. Electric action transmission	.	.	.	51
18. Action diagrams	.	52
19. A slider windchest	.	59
20. The Roosevelt chest	.	63
21. The pouch-pallet chest	65
22. Windchests. Pallet-valve positions	.	.	.	68
23. Bass note chests	.	72
24. Bellows	.	.	.	77
25. Fan blower	.	.	79
26. Wind regulators, tremulant etc.	82
27. Swellboxes	.	.	90
28. Radiating pedal board	.	99
29. Console dimensions	.	100
30. Tablet stop-controls	.	103
31. The parts of the flue pipe	113
31a. Wood pipe parts	.	115
32. The parts of a reed pipe	129
33. Diapasons	.	.	.	140
34. Dulcianas	.	.	.	142
35. Mild strings	.	.	144
36. Orchestral strings	.	146
37. Inverted conical pipes	.	147
38. Open flutes	.	.	153
39. Open wood flutes	.	155
40. Hohl flutes	.	.	155
41. Harmonic flutes	.	157
42. Tapered pipes	.	.	159
43. Stoppered wide scale pipes	161
44. Stopped wood pipes	.	161
45. Stoppered pipes narrow scale	.	.	.	163
46. Pierced stoppered pipes	164
47. Trumpets	.	.	168
48. Oboes	.	.	.	170
49. Cor anglais	.	.	170
50. Clarinets	.	.	172
51. Rohr Shalmey		172
52. Vox humana	.	.	173
53. Rankett	.	.	.	173
54. Heptonstall Parish Church	180

Preface

WE are persuaded that we write this book for students, players and admirers of the organ. We suspect that in doing so we may have recorded a craftsman's eye view of the designing and building of the instrument. However, we hope it will appeal to all who wish to know how and why organs are made in the diverse ways that to many is their charm. We like to believe it contains views and arguments which could be helpful to those who, in the course of church duties, wish to be able to exercise some discernment as to quality and good design.

The organ as a musical instrument or as a fascinating mechanical edifice has so much of history, of craftsman-like endeavour and changing fashion built into it, that it is impossible to write about it and avoid historical details. It is the built-in history that is our theme.

We write about the traditional pipe organ. Those instruments with electronic tone generation belong to another field and a different industry, that has had surprisingly little impact on pipe organ building, except on occasions to generate a new interest in the traditional that was not there before.

No excuse is offered for the space devoted to near obsolete action forms. Existing records are scanty and undetailed. It is typically British to be interested in near lost causes, be it locomotives, Georgian architecture, tramcars, or obsolete organ designs.

The absence of organ stop-lists or 'specifications' is deliberate: they take a lot of space and in practical terms tell much less than they pretend to do. Because they leave so much room for interpretative skill they are not useful when put forward as model or ideal schemes. Nevertheless we have included a short appendix containing stop-lists with which we have been associated. In the last analysis they may be not quite perfect, but they may be of interest.

It is our hope that what we write may lead to a better understanding of what inspires one of the few remaining art crafts, one that survives and flourishes because it is still creative.

Acknowledgements

The authors are grateful to and acknowledge the obligation to H.M. Ministry of Public Buildings & Works for permission to reproduce the photographs used for plates which are Crown Copyright, and to the expertise of the photographers, Frederick Watson (Muswell Hill), and M. Marney (Ilford) and to the many others whose work in our collection goes unidentified. The line drawings of figs. 3 & 6, are from the works of the late Dr. Arthur Hill, M.A., F.S.A., in whose art we remain aspiring students. To our colleagues on the Board of Directors of Hill Norman & Beard our thanks for allowing us to express our personal points of view and for the use of some technical illustrations.

I
A Brief Historical Survey

THE organ, as a musical instrument, is descended from primitive flutes or panpipes. These consisted of a number of transverse flutes strapped together, each capable of giving one note only (Fig. 1). This of course is a principle basic to the organ in distinction from the wood-winds of the orchestra, each of which is but one pipe adapted to play many notes.

The transition from transverse flutes to direct or endblown ones is not recorded, but the next step, blowing the pipes by mechanical means, was reputedly due to Ctesibius, a Greek barber living in Alexandria about 250 B.C. This enabled larger pipes, sounding lower notes, to be used, that were beyond the capacity of one person's lungs. In this instrument the 'wind' was stored in an inverted bell-jar standing in

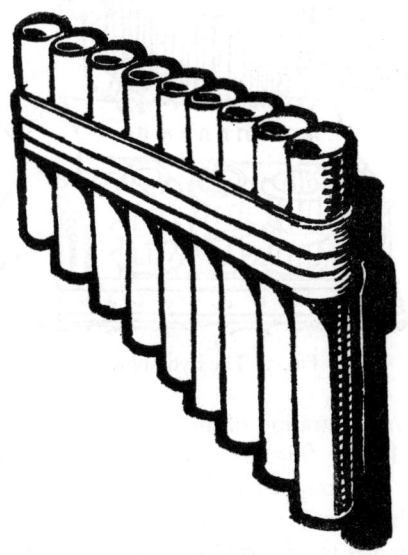

FIG. 1. Pan pipes

water (the water being displaced by air), hence the Roman name for the instrument, the 'Hydraulus'.

Sometimes organ pipes would be arranged to sound automatically in a statue or some other ornament, and some of these were considered minor wonders of the time. The instrument itself was used for leading choirs at festivals, and as a musical accompaniment to feasts, and, it is said, the Emperor Nero played on the Hydraulus. In a portable form they were carried into battle to demoralize the enemy!

Towards the end of the Roman Empire, organs were also constructed with diagonal bellows similar to an old-fashioned blacksmith's bellows. After the collapse of Rome, knowledge of organs survived only in the Middle East, little more being heard of them until the eighth century, when they were being made in Byzantium (Constantinople). After that, the knowledge of organ-making spread quickly across Europe, and Charlemagne imported an organ of Arabian manufacture to Aachen in 812.

The Church, as patron of the arts, took up the organ and many early organ-makers were monks. There were organs in Glastonbury Abbey and Winchester Cathedral before the Norman conquest.

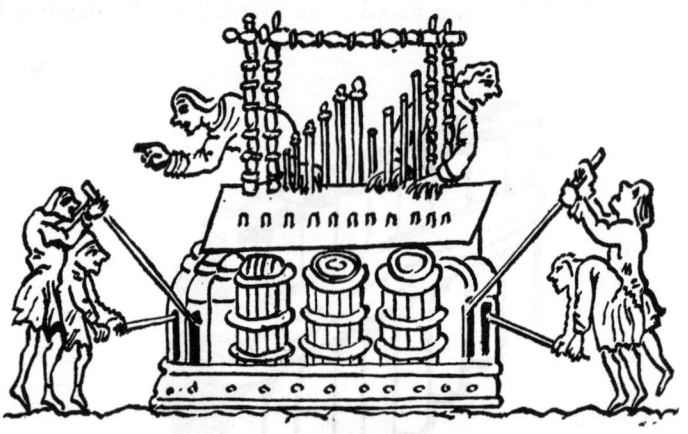

FIG. 2. The hydraulus

The well-known illustration of an hydraulic organ from the sixth century Utrecht Psalter (Fig. 2) shows four men pumping air into receivers wherein it is trapped under water pressure. Two organists stand behind a table from the top of which air gushes through several holes. A rack supports ten assorted pipes which they could grasp and thrust into the gushing air jets. We can readily accept that with the

A BRIEF HISTORICAL SURVEY

unavoidable legato style the results were truly described as a terrifying roar.

The earliest organs had but one pipe per key, just as a clavichord has but one string per key. However, the power that can be obtained from a single pipe is limited, particularly with wind pressures light enough to be easily blown by human muscle-power. Louder organs were needed to lead larger choirs. The ear is not uniformly sensitive to changes in intensity of sound, for two similar pipes sounding together do not sound twice as loud as one. In fact it would need ten similar pipes to produce a sound apparently twice as loud. Organ-builders surmounted this difficulty by making the second set of pipes an octave higher in pitch. This increases the brightness of the tone as well as increasing the power, just as other musical instruments give a brighter tone when played more loudly. The higher pitched pipes also use less wind than additional pipes of unison pitch.

In their quest for power and brilliance, the early organ-builders carried this process further, developing what today we call the diapason chorus, ranging in pitch from the unison, or even the sub-unison; to almost every conceivable harmonic multiple of the foundation pitch up to several octaves above the unison.

It was soon realized it was not necessary to have all the pipes in use all the time. A mechanical arrangement to 'stop-off' a group of higher pitched ranks when not required not only had musical advantages, but also saved wind that had to be generated by human muscle-power. This arrangement of 'stops', to cut out unwanted ranks from speaking, became quite comprehensive; each rank having its individual control. The higher pitches were and still are an exception, being generally controlled in groups of two, three, or more ranks, known as mixtures.

Control of individual stops made possible a wide dynamic range. Today the organ has a wider dynamic range than any other instrument; from near inaudibility to sounds sometimes approaching in intensity the threshold of pain.

Individual stop control also makes it possible to combine stops of particular pitches, to produce combination-tones, such as unison and two octaves above, or unison and one octave and fifth above, in organ terminology 8 ft. and 2 ft. or 8 ft. and $2\frac{2}{3}$ ft. respectively.

It is customary for organ (and harpsichord) pitches to be expressed in terms of the nominal length of resonator of an open pipe sounding the bottom C on the organ keyboard, which is two octaves below middle C, i.e., manual unison pitch is 8 ft.

Up to this point we have been considering only pipes of normal proportions producing normal organ tone, known as diapason or principal tone. Organ-builders, however, discovered that the tone could be varied by using a wider scale, giving a flute-like tone, or a narrower scale, giving a more edgy tone. They discovered also that a pipe with the top closed by a stopper, would sound a note at approximately one octave below its open pitch, and that the tone so produced had a distinctive timbre, consisting only of the odd numbered harmonics, particularly useful in colouring flute-toned stops.

As in the drone note of the bagpipe, wind instruments consisting of a vibrating reed (its tone generally modified and amplified by a resonator) have been known for many centuries. Some medieval keyboard reed instruments known as regals still survive today. Incorporated as part of the organ, reed-stops rapidly acquired an important place in the tonal design.

At first the crude buzz of regals (without resonators) and the raucous blare of early trumpets (with conical resonators) together with the technical difficulties of making them even in tone and power, restricted their use to musical climax stops, adding 'clang' to the rather pure sound of the diapason chorus. Later, refinements in tone and improvements in voicing technique made possible reed choruses usable on their own, without support from a flue-pipe (diapason) chorus, and ultimately to solo reeds, useful as distinctive tone colours in their own right.

In medieval times organs existed in a very wide range of sizes. There were small 'portable' organs with a basic pitch corresponding to 2-ft. stop, which could be carried in procession and played at the same time. Larger, and only semi-portable, were the 4-ft. pitch 'positive' organs (Plate 1), and finally there were the large organs of 8-ft. pitch, some with 16 ft. drone basses which were the wonder of their day. It may be surmised, that owing to the very limited flexibility of the early instruments, a small instrument was used for small sounds, and a large instrument for a large sound. When a greater range of control was possible, so that large instruments could be played softly, the small 4-ft. and 2-ft. organs ceased to be made.

It has been argued that musically something was lost when this happened and there have been occasional attempts to revive interest in tiny organs, particularly in Germany in the 1930's.

Although the 8-ft. organ (generally with a 16-ft. bass) has been the norm for many centuries now, what has actually happened is that the smaller organ has been assimilated into the larger ones as separate organs, but under the control of one player. Thus we have the evolution of the two- and three-manual organ, for all the early instruments had but one keyboard.

Frequently organs were set on galleries, and the 4-ft. toned positive organ would be bracketed over the gallery edge (Plate 2), behind the player and hiding him from public view. Such organs were known as Rückpositives in Germany and Choir or 'chayre' organs in England, in distinction to the main organ known as the Haupt-orgel or Hauptwerk in Germany, and as the great organ in England. A 'double organ' of 8-ft. great and 4-ft. based choir was in fact the standard size of a good organ in England throughout the seventeenth century. The Choir organ, though based on the 4-ft. principal was, however, a modification of the earlier positives, in that an 8-ft. flute was provided to give a bass to the chorus.

In Germany the development of the organ was more rapid than in other countries, and in the middle of the sixteenth century, organs existed with three-manual divisions, including a 2-ft. pitched 'Brustwerk' set in the main organ just above the player, and a pedal division based on the 16-ft. pitch, the action to which was considered too heavy for operation by the fingers.

The classic design, the 'werk prinzipl', culminated in the organs built by Arp Schnitger (1678–1718) and considered by some as the zenith of the Dutch and North German school of organ-building.

As was perhaps natural, organs developed along slightly differing lines in different countries, and national characteristics of organ-building became apparent. These differences survive in varying extents to the present day and extend to mechanical and architectural details as well as musical matters.

The chief characteristic of the Dutch and North German school of the so-called 'Baroque' period was the adherence to the 'werk prinzipl'; that is, that all divisions were based on a different pitch and generally, each in a separate case. Another common feature was the presence, particularly on the Hauptwerk, of two independent choruses. There was a narrow scale chorus of diapason or principal tone in unison and quint pitches topped by a trumpet, and a wide-scale chorus of stopped pipes and open flues (generally tapered) which might include a tierce-sounding rank as well. Players were discouraged from mixing the two groups by the placing of the stop-controls on opposite jambs either side of the console.

After the time of Schnitger, and particularly after the death of Silbermann, this school of organ-building gradually gave up its principles and became a pale imitation of other schools, but in the last thirty years there has been a revival of interest in and a return to the 'Baroque' Schnitger organ (Plate 3).

These neo-Baroque instruments show surprisingly few modifications of the original forms, and seem as well suited to the music of Bach and his predecessors as the original instruments for which the music was written. Frobenius and Marcussen in Denmark, Flentrop in Holland and Von Beckerath in Germany are among the leaders of this revival today.

Somewhat after Schnitger, the South German school came into prominence. The greatest works of Gabler and Riepp were for the large abbey churches and the organs were both large and extravagant in specification. The famous Gabler organ at Weingarten, with its flamboyant rococo cases distributed between the windows of the west wall, has stops ranging from a principal-toned Kontra Bass 32 ft., with the larger pipes in the case, to a twenty-rank mixture. These organs depart from the strict principles of the North German school and show early romantic influences such as mild-toned string stops. The voicing is more refined, less forceful, and with a less precise attack, but, combined with the favourable acoustical surroundings, the effect of the best of these organs is unequalled in grandeur and power.

Italian organs, though they developed quite early, tended to remain smaller than their counterparts in Germany, frequently being of one manual only and with the pedals permanently coupled to the manuals rather than provided with pipes of their own. The Renaissance cases of some of these sixteenth-century instruments are remarkable for their stately architectural qualities, disciplined in form yet with great freedom of detail. Musically the organs were refined and slightly fluty in tone and of moderate power. Reeds, if any, were not an important part of the tonal scheme, and there were no mixtures, but each pitch (sometimes as high as the thirty-sixth or ¼ ft.) was provided with independent stop-control.

Beating stops, now commonly called Celestes, were known to the early Italian builders, though they were not, of course, soft stops or string-toned stops as we know them today, but ordinary diapasons or flutes. Perhaps the best known of the early Italian builders were the Antegnati family on whose instruments Fresobaldi played.

In Spain and Portugal the organ developed somewhat later—and on very different lines to those of Italy, the best instruments being contemporary with the great instruments of South Germany. Though many small or medium-size churches in Spain have no organ to this day, large churches are not restricted to one organ only; Toledo

Cathedral having three, and Mafra Monastery in Portugal, having six. Their large instruments are particularly magnificent in both appearance and sound (Plate 4).

The outstanding feature of Iberian organs, however, is the remarkable development of the reed-stops. In the German organ, the reeds are voiced to blend with the flue choruses, indeed, frequently they are unusable alone, owing to their irregularity. The Spanish reeds, however, are of great power, for use by themselves, or antiphonally against the fluework, rather as an English tuba is used. Both the regularity and the power of these reeds is achieved by placing the pipes outside the organ and projecting them horizontally from the case. This both keeps the dust and dirt out and nearly doubles the power. The effect on the appearance of the organ is also quite striking.

This feature, of reeds *en-chamade*, has in recent years spread to Denmark, England and America, though the climax nature of such stops make them relatively rare specialities. The organ-builder is also faced with the difficulty and expense of enabling them to defy gravity without making the means too evident. Although Marcussen in Denmark and Hill in England have made *en-chamade* reeds which are in fact normal trumpets for use with the flue chorus, their natural power and directional sound make them normally a solo reed.

Early French organs were characterized by somewhat fluty diapasons (known as 'Montres' as they frequently are on show in the case), and a well-developed set of flute-toned mutations (the French names Nazard, Tierce and Larigot having now become almost universal). The general predominance of the Grande Orgue over other departments was a further distinguishing feature. The best known early French organ-builders were Thierry and Clicquot, but in the nineteenth century these were overshadowed by Cavaillé-Coll, a great master craftsman who in his day led the world in organ-building.

Cavaillé-Coll pioneered most of the better features of the Romantic organ. He had had experience in Spain, and the reed tones he developed were renowned for their small scale, prompt speech and fiery brilliance. They also have a marked tendency to go out of tune, but perhaps not as badly as the regals and other short-length reeds of the North German school. The reeds always had a more important place in the French organ than in the German. The organ of Cavaillé-Coll was in a sense an orchestral organ, i.e., an imitative organ; but unlike the later imitative organs, it had a reed and mixture chorus which in its way was as effective as anything that had gone before.

Possibly the greatest tribute that can be paid to the Cavaillé-Coll organ is, that a whole school of composition was founded on, and inspired by it. César Franck, Guilmant and Widor are perhaps the best known composers of this school.

In England the organ developed in a less ambitious way than it had in Germany. In general, organs were small, generally of one manual without pedals, and with manual choruses developed up to the fifteenth, or at most the twenty-second; without mixtures. Early two-manual organs were referred to as double-organs and were rarities until after 1600. The only builder of this period whose work survives to the present day was Thomas Dallam. The case of his organ in King's College Chapel, Cambridge still stands after 350 years (Fig. 3). Dallam's fame also rests upon the organ he built as a present from Queen Elizabeth I to the Sultan of Turkey, his journey to Turkey to erect it and the diary he wrote of his adventures there.[1]

This organ which had a clockwork operated barrel mechanism and sundry automata, was of course a purely secular instrument. Although this, and many other such instruments have not survived, it is as well to remember that then, as now, the organ was by no means exclusively a sacred instrument. Small barrel-operated organs playing jigs and dances were being made up to one hundred and twenty years ago. Their successors, the French fairground organ and the Dutch street organ are still in circulation.

One secular instrument of very early seventeenth-century build is the richly ornate three-stop organ (dated 1602) now preserved in Carisbrooke Castle, Isle of Wight (Plate 1), and another, larger and better-known example is the 1612 Compenius organ built for the King of Prussia's Banqueting Hall and now in Frederiksborg Castle, Denmark. Incidentally, both these organs retain their original mean-tone tuning.

During the Commonwealth, organs were banned, and many were taken down or destroyed. Following the Restoration, there was a great revival of organ-building. Bernard Schmidt, later known as 'Father' Smith, was the first of the three famous Anglo-German organ-builders to come on the scene. Smith, Snetzler and Schultze appeared at about 100-year intervals. Each made a lasting impact on English organs by his new ideas and executive skill. Yet the curious fact remains, that with the possible exception of Schultze, their instruments are more English than German. Schmidt (or Smith) built a great many organs in England, a few of which remain. He is perhaps best known for his organ in St. Paul's Cathedral, later added to and enlarged by Willis. The case of this organ, split in two halves and altered, covers the

[1] See *An Organ for the Sultan* by S. Mayes, London, 1954.

FIG. 3. King's College Chapel, Cambridge c. 1610 (Dallam)

present instrument which includes some of his pipes. This case is to the design of Sir Christopher Wren and is much more rococo in style than the more disciplined classical cases which were the rule in England right up to the Gothic revival. The case was much too small for the organ Smith wanted to build, and his complaints led to Wren's celebrated remark about 'a damned kist o' whistles'.

Smith had a great rival in Rene (or Renatus) Harris, a grandson of Dallam, brought up in France during the Commonwealth. His (very) public rivalry with Smith was carried to great length culminating in the famous 'Battle of the Organs' in which each builder constructed an instrument for the Temple Church, and the Benchers were left to choose which they preferred to keep. Smith's organ remained and Harris removed his to use it elsewhere.

Smith's organs were larger than those of his predecessors, but still small by continental standards. The St. Paul's organ was of two manuals, great and choir of 21 stops, the great with two mixtures and a cornet and the choir with one mixture. It stood upon the screen. His German contemporaries would have thought in terms of three manuals and pedals, some sixty stops and would probably have put it on the west gallery. Indeed Renatus Harris wanted to build just such an organ there after Smith's death.

The most remarkable feature about Smith's organ is that the great organ compass ran from 16-ft. C (omitting C♯) instead of the more usual 8-ft. C and the choir organ from F in the 16-ft. octave. It was the late adoption of this long compass that caused the trouble over Wren's organ-case, the figures above the case being added to hide the tops of the necessarily longer pipes. All this was in lieu of a pedal organ which did not become at all general in England until about 1800.

The use of the 'long compass', usually down to G below 8-ft. C, continued until about 1850. It had also been in use in Italy. Thus most of the works of Bach and his German contemporaries could not be performed on English organs until more than 100 years after they were written. It is recorded that Handel used to practise on the St. Paul's organ because it had some pedals. They were added in 1720, although they were only 'pull-downs' acting on the manual keys and without pipes of their own. Almost all Handel's organ music was in fact originally written without pedal parts. They have been frequently added by later editors.

When it did come, the pedal organ was no more than an octave or so of open wood pipes, or bourdons, in the case of small instruments (both flute tones). Adequate pedal organs were slow to emerge, and even now are not universal. The last protagonist of the long compass, S. S. Wesley, insisted on it for the 1854 Willis organ in St. George's Hall, Liverpool, until being convinced otherwise by the dust gathering on the extra keys on his own organ. Very few examples exist in England today.

After Father Smith's death, the rather mild character of the English organ began to show the first Romantic characteristics. The art of voicing soft stops of small scale was unknown and from about 1680 three-manual organs appeared with the pipes of the third manual enclosed in a light wooden box to soften the tone. In order to keep the size of the box down these 'Echo' organs were often of only middle C upwards compass. The idea of a box with a movable panel seems to have originated in Spain and was introduced to England by Abraham Jordan in 1712. His family was in the wine business and he probably borrowed the idea from Spain. Its popularity was immediate, and all the old 'Echos' were soon converted into 'Swells'. The swell organ remained with its short compass, a very subsidiary department. During the eighteenth century it grew in size and importance, displacing the choir as the second manual of the two-manual organ.

John Snetzler, a German-speaking Swiss, emigrated to England around 1740, some years later setting up his workshop in Rose Court, Soho, now known as Manette Street, a turning off London's Charing Cross Road. This district was then the centre of the musical trade. As 'Tin-pan Alley' it remains to this day. Snetzler's organs, following his German training, had a more decisive, brighter, sound than his predecessors, and it is believed he built the first organ in England to have a separate pedal organ. Some of his chamber organs survive to this day, identified by his signature on a paper stuck inside the windchest, 'John Snetzler, fecit Londini (date)' (Plate 5). Perhaps his real importance lies in his introduction of the dulciana. Nobody in England before him had been able to voice pipes smaller in scale than a small diapason, but by applying to the mouths of open metal pipes the box mouth used to steady the speech of stoppered wooden pipes, he made practical the voicing of soft-toned small-scale stops. His first dulciana is reputed to have been in St. Margaret's Church, King's Lynn, but the examples now therein are probably late nineteenth-century copies.

Snetzler's successor as organ-builder to the King, was Samuel Green, who reverted to the mild-toned delicate quality of pre-Snetzler times. His organs contain large-scaled pipes of relatively thin metal, and were lightly blown to give a delicate fluty quality which is most successful in the only moderately reverberant neo-classical churches for which many of his organs were built. His organs for the reverberant cathedrals of Salisbury and Canterbury were relative failures and have long since been removed.

Green furthered the development of the swell organ, constructing larger and heavier swell boxes, extending the compass downwards, and fitting venetian type *louvres* as used today. They had been developed by harpsichord makers and were adapted to the organ by both Green and Avery. They fitted and closed more tightly than the sliding panel of the 'nags-head' shutters, and rapidly became universal (Fig. 4). Despite the

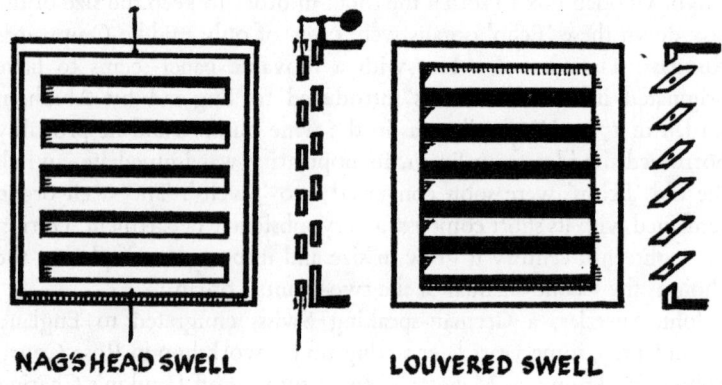

NAG'S HEAD SWELL   LOUVERED SWELL
FIG. 4

comparative failure of Green's experiment of enclosing the entire organ at St. George's, Windsor, his developments undoubtedly assisted in taking the swell organ out of the 'toy' category.

The swell organ as we know it, despite its affinity with the Recit of Cavaille-Coll is the most specifically English department of the organ today, and most of its final development after the time of Green was due to Henry ('Father') Willis who came upon the scene about 1850. Willis introduced the idea of the swell, not as an enclosed and therefore anaemic flue chorus, but basically as a reed chorus, in power an equal partner with the great organ. This was largely made possible by his improved technique of reed voicing with its greater accuracy in manufacture of critical parts, the application of higher wind pressures and with loaded tongues in the basses giving great stability of speech and of tuning.

Heavier wind pressures and loaded tongues were not new, however, having been used by William Hill twenty years previously. Later, Hill and others broadened the swell chorus to include the flue upperwork, the swell organ also became the home of mild romantic stops such as warm-toned strings, celestes and lieblich flutes which benefited by being under swell-box expression. Willis was responsible, with S. S. Wesley, for the introduction of two important playing aids, the combination thumb piston, and the concave pedalboard with radiating keys.

By the middle of the nineteenth century changes in musical taste, which had been moving slowly away from the classic forms for some time and was now approaching the era of Wagner and Debussy, began to affect the organ world. The organ, not really being a naturally romantic instrument had been left musically high and dry. Little organ music of any merit was being written at this time, and many recital programmes consisted of transcriptions of orchestral works. In conformity with the current taste for refinement was the general toning down and a reduction in mixtures and upperwork. This, of course, had to be balanced with a compensating increase of power in the unison stops, which at first caused organ-builders some difficulty.

About this time the Oxford Movement in the Church of England made its influence felt by the introduction of surpliced choirs in chancel stalls, demolition of galleries and screens and the removal of many organs from west gallery positions to a chancel side chapel. Acoustically this was unfavourable and the lightly voiced instruments often seemed inadequate in the new position. The conventional way out of this difficulty coupled with the demand for more power/unison voices, was to increase the basic scaling. This was the solution adopted by Schultze, who used very large scales for the open diapasons, copiously winded and with very wide mouths. With characteristic German boldness, the chorus right up to mixture was similarly treated. This gave a magnificent great organ, but left the other departments nowhere, and was really only successful in reverberant buildings. A number of other builders copied his ideas, notably Lewis. Schultze also left his mark in a romantic flute stop which he introduced from Germany; the delicately toned lieblich gedeckt.

An alternative approach, by Willis and others, was to increase the wind pressure. Willis made his flue pipes of comparatively heavy metal, blowing them hard, but retaining fairly small scales, relying on a reed chorus, on great as well as swell to provide the intensity and weight.

Other builders, notably Hill, depended less on reed choruses, combining rather large diapason scales with the heavier pressures, to give bold results. All this, and the introduction of the climax reed tone, the tuba, was made possible by using mechanical methods of providing the 'wind'; steam engines for very large organs, hydraulic power for medium and small ones. This increased wind pressure, however, caused the action to be heavy and difficult to play, and in larger instruments, pneumatic power assisted the mechanical action, i.e., the pneumatic-lever system, leading eventually to tubular pneumatic transmission, coupling, and action.

The English choir organ had changed from its original 'Positive' department origins, to a mild collection of delightful but often insipid, *mezzo-piano* stops, generally without a diapason in any pitch, and with an imitative clarinet as its only reed. Surprisingly, it was not until the end of the nineteenth century that enclosed choir organs began to appear. Enclosure of a Victorian choir organ, however, robbed the division of what little vitality it had left, and it was realized, that bolder sounds were needed for enclosure to be effective, and so was born the solo organ as a department in its own right, incorporating keen string tones, large-scaled harmonic flutes, and reeds imitative of orchestral tone-colours.

Mild string tone had been developed first in Germany and later in England, but owing to the difficulty of attaining prompt speech without over-blowing, such stops never extended either below Tenor C, or 4-ft. tone. The invention of the 'beard' or 'bar' by the voicer William Thynne about 1880, revolutionized the technique of string-stop voicing, making the use of very small scales, and consequent keen tone a possibility. For some years, voicers vied with one another to produce the smallest scale and most acid-toned string stops with results rarely musical or even bearable for long. Fortunately the fashion has now passed.

It was about this time that organ designers, who had in the past named some stops after their nearest orchestral equivalent as a convenient description, now began to look at the matter the other way round, and tried to make the organ stops resemble as nearly as possible the orchestral tones after which they were named. Since at that time transcriptions of orchestral works were more popular and abundant than real organ music, this policy was not as silly as it sounds. It led to the organs built by Robert Hope-Jones, consisting almost entirely of solo and orchestral tones, ranging from the tibia, a grossly overscaled flute, to the phoneuma, string-toned pipes of ridiculously narrow scale, aptly described, by tuners burdened with them, as 'stair-rods'. Quite large organs built on this concept often had only one stop above unison pitch and that a mild 4-ft. Lieblich flute. They relied entirely on the mechanical effect of the octave coupler to add any brightness. This inevitably leads to individual stops having their own octave and sub-octave couplers and extended compass. Thus was born the Unit-extension System. The development of Hope-Jones's ideas, avoiding its extremes, but pursuing the one-man-band idea to its logical conclusion, led to the theatre organ of the nineteen twenties and thirties as pioneered by Smith-Unit and by Wurlitzer in America.

It may be appropriate at this point to digress into tracing the development of the organ in America. Snetzler exported instruments to both Canada and the then American colony, and all the early American builders had learnt their craft in England or Germany. Casavant Frères of Canada were of course Frenchmen and built organs much as they would have done in Europe. However, a native style began to emerge in the 1850's. The early development of romantic styles of voicing combined with the predominance of the great organ, the latter a characteristic of the English organs of about thirty years earlier. Some of the organs of Johnson, Simmonds and Jardine survive to this day. However, the wide-ranging climate and the need for heavy winter heating played havoc with tracker actions and slider-chests and relatively few of the old instruments have survived.

The American organ-builders of the end of the nineteenth century, notably Roosevelt (a close relative of the first President of that name), and later Skinner, also Casavant in Canada, designed and built successful sliderless windchests and later, electric actions. These were especially suited to their climate and commercial production conditions. The romantic organ of Hope-Jones caught on much more thoroughly in America, the romantic instrument was pushed to its limit, aided perhaps by the low reverberation of their carpeted and generously upholstered churches.

A striking development, both visual and to some extent aural, in quite recent years, has been the organ arranged in functional display, i.e., without a case. Although this had been treated tentatively by Willis in the Royal Albert Hall, London, and in the Alexandra Palace, this system has been pioneered by Holkamp in the U.S.A. some of whose designs have been most striking. In this deceptively difficult form, all the pipes are displayed in natural length and massed array, with the smallest pipes and highest pitch pipes in front and the largest at the rear, all without screening or casework. A recent (1961) London example is in the Mormon Hyde Park Chapel (Plate 6).

In both England and America there has been a swing away from the romantic organ, starting gently in the middle 30's but gaining rapidly since 1950. One of the early leaders of this movement in America was the late G. Donald Harrison of Aeolian-Skinner who, incidentally, was an Englishman. German influence has made itself felt recently in the U.S.A. to the extent of the reintroduction of tracker action in some cases. In England, just as the romantic was not carried to the extremes found in the U.S.A., the trend towards the classical has, so far, been more moderate, and although a considerable change has taken place in organ design, relatively few instruments have been built which can be described as wholly neo-classical.

2
The Instrument

To some the organ is known as the 'King of Instruments', the largest of all musical instruments, commanding the widest pitch and dynamic range, and by others derided as the most mechanical, costly and unexpressive means of music-making. It commands a vast following of musician players, enthusiasts and friends, for whom it alone can reach the sublime in massive and musical sound. Its ancient distinction among keyboard instruments was in the production of sustained musical sound of constant tone-colour, a distinction now shared with the reed-organ or harmonium and their younger cousin the electronic or pipeless organ, and this fascinating quality of sustained sound has not lost its appeal to this day.

The interior of an organ is understandably something of a dusty mystery to many people, but it is surprising how many are amazed that there are a great many more pipes beyond those displayed in the frontal case. The stop-knobs, pulled out or pushed in as changes of tone are reqired are commonly referred to as stops, probably because at first they were used to shut off, or stop unwanted tones. Technically speaking a 'stop' is today a rank of pipes of similar shape and construction, but each sounding a different pitch, from the lowest to the topmost note of the keyboard (Plate 7). Stops differ from each other in timbre or tone-colour and/or in difference of pitch. Every rank of pipes, except mixtures which have multiple ranks, has a stop control, usually a draw stopknob. Every note in the stop has a key by which, through connecting mechanism, it may be sounded. Only by drawing a stop and pressing a key will a note sound.

To every key of the manuals and pedalboard there is at least one pipe. A complete stop, one pipe for each key of the compass, usually has 61 pipes but 54, 56 or 58 are also commonly found, especially in older instruments. Each additional stop means another pipe to each key, so so that in instruments of quite modest size, having 6 to 12 pipes per note, and between 400 to 800 per manual, are quite usual. As some stops have 2, 3 or more pipes per note, quite considerable totals for the whole instrument will result.

THE INSTRUMENT 17

Since the perfection of electro-pneumatic mechanisms at the turn of the century, this simple relation of stops and keys is occasionally disturbed by the use of the unit-extension system, wherein for space or cost saving, a rank of pipes is so connected that it may play independently in two or three pitches, besides the fundamental. This system is described in more detail elsewhere.

The varied voices of the organ fall roughly into broad classifications: diapason, flute, string-like tones, trumpets, and the organ equivalents of orchestral woodwind reed tones.

The first three are produced from 'flue' pipes having a construction based upon the common whistle. The latter two have air-vibrated reed tongues, simulating sound akin to orchestral brass and woodwind. In each of the two main classes, there are many hybrids producing useful musical sounds of subtle distinction. This is dealt with fully in the chapters on pipes and tones.

No organ can be truly representative of the instrument unless its ranks give examples of the five tone-groups, and at least some in several pitches as a chorus. Nevertheless, a useful instrument capable of solo performance need only have principal (or diapason) and flute tone. The former in at least 4-ft., $2\frac{2}{3}$-ft. and 2-ft. pitches and the latter in 8 ft.

The pitch range of the organ covers the entire audible range of the human ear, and even beyond, as most organ-tuners know when coping with an aged player's complaint that the top notes have been tuned to dumbness. An indication of the range can be given as follows. From the low CCCC of the pedal 32-ft. stops at about 16 cycles per second (cps) to the top note of the manual fifteenth 2 ft. at 8,371 cps exists a range of nine octaves. An octave above this top note is possible but extremely difficult to make and voice, as few can define pitch at frequencies above 10,000 cps. Young people can detect sounds up to 20,000 cps or over, and these frequencies are heard as part of the harmonic make-up of principal pipes, but most people have top limits of about 12,000 cps, and this tends to decrease with age, so that top notes tend to sound fluty and dull.

As explained in Chapter 1, the organ-builder's pitch notation of 8 ft., 4 ft., $2\frac{2}{3}$ ft., 2 ft., etc., is based upon the nominal tuning length of a pipe sounding the lowest note of the rank and having a plain cylindrical body open at the top, a principal or diapason. Pipes of other construction differ markedly in length of pipe but the same pitch notation is still used.

Keyboard notation, as now generally used, CC, tenor C, treble C to top C, is superior to the Helmholz notation occasionally encountered, which while accurate in written form, is less precise in spoken use. An 8-ft. stop of tenor C compass is without its low octave, but has 8-ft. pitch, the lowest pipe being played from tenor C key being only 4 ft. in pitch length (Fig. 5).

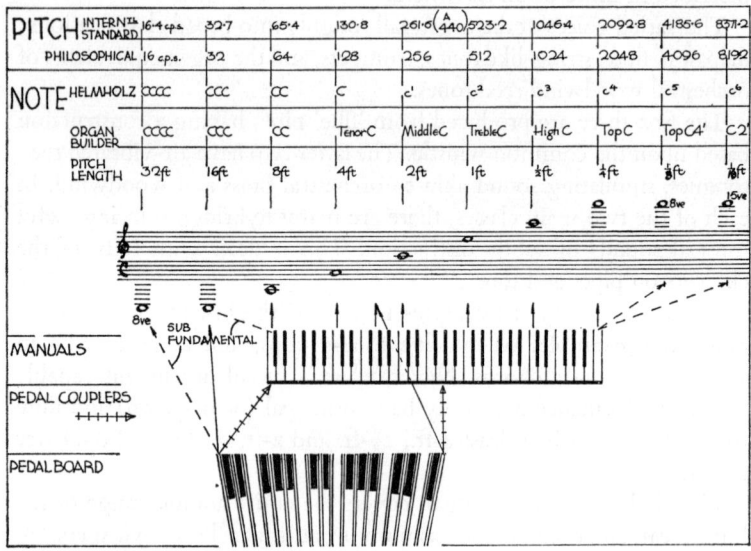

FIG. 5

The vibration frequency of the note varies inversely as the nominal pitch length of the resonator of the pipe, an 8-ft. CC pipe has a note frequency of 64 cps. Doubling the length to 16 ft., halves the frequency to 32 cps. Halving the 8 ft. to 4 ft. doubles the pitch frequency to 128. This doubling occurs at each octave above the fundamental, up to the limits of audibility.

In outlining the nature of the instrument it is necessary to describe, briefly at this stage, its essential polyphonic character based upon tone-colour families of diverse pitch. A single manual with but one or two 8-ft. tones of contrasting power or tone is scarcely an organ, though accompanimental music of a sort is possible. But make one stop an 8 ft. and the other of 4-ft. pitch, different but having complementary harmonic emphasis, and the elements of the organ chorus are there, and in it a means of musical expression. Some very successful examples exist of this basic form by master builders, and when in the hands of imaginative performers, often deceive critical listeners, unaware of the limited resources in use. The 'Willis-on-Wheels' in St. Paul's Cathedral is a well-known example.

The harmonic structure of musical sound is also the underlying structure of the organ-tone chorus and the principle of combinational tones. Cutting an 8 ft. pipe in half to 4 ft. length produces an octave sound of twice the vibration frequency. Halving again produces a sound two octaves above the 8-ft. fundamental and having four times the fundamental frequency. The next octave has eight times the frequency and so on through the audible range. The 8-ft. fundamental frequency ×2, ×4, ×8, ×16 ×32, ×64, ×128, etc. producing 4 ft., 2 ft., 1 ft., ½ ft., ¼ ft., ⅛ ft., and $\frac{1}{16}$ ft., the latter being top C of the manual fifteenth 2 ft.

Adding these sounds in turn to the fundamental, each octave adds further intensity and brightness, but does not change the tone-colour; very much as in mixing paint colours, each octave is a whiter tint of the basic hue and in consequence, lightens the whole. This rule applies only when the note frequency doubles at each stop, i.e., the additions are successive octave sounds.

The other multiples of the basic frequency are also musical sounds, producing the important tone-colouring mutation intervals, the 12th or quint 2⅔ ft. (×3), 17th or tierce 1⅗ ft. (×5), 19th or larigot 1⅓ft. (×6) and so on through ×10, ×12, ×20, ×24, etc. When added to the fundamental or any of its octaves, these mutation sounds change the tone-colour, adding but a modicum of brightness by virtue of higher pitch, while adding subjective lower-pitch frequencies as a result of beat-frequencies with the other harmonic components. These fill out the tone, welding the component parts together in a subtle and complex manner. This is well demonstrated on any complete great organ chorus, when a well-balanced twelfth 2⅔ ft. is added to 8-ft., 4-ft. and 2-ft. diapason. It is the basis of the organ chorus, of mixture stop design and of solo tone synthesis.

What of the other multiples of the fundamental represented by ×7, ×9, ×11 and so on? These exist naturally as harmonics or partials in musical sounds, but are unsuitable for emphasis, being disagreeably dissonant with the tempered intervals of our twelve-note octave. Occasionally, ×7, the flat 21st is provided, but only very limited power is tolerable except for quite bizzare effects.

The classical organ tonal chorus is built up from a stop of the manual fundamental pitch, commonly 8 ft. to which is added stops of the same broad tone family representing multiples of the fundamental frequency, in octaves and mutation intervals expressed as pitch lengths 4 ft., etc.,

4 ft., 2⅔ ft., 2 ft., 1⅗ ft., 1⅓ ft., 1 ft., ⅘ ft., ⅔ ft., ½ ft., ⅖ ft., ⅓ ft. and ¼ ft. The last nine are usually combined as ranks of a multi-rank mixture stop for reasons explained elsewhere. To add weight of tone, a sub-fundamental can be added. When correctly proportioned, voiced and musically adjusted, these many voices become welded into a sonorous whole, the organ tone.

This tone-chorus is musically most satisfying when produced from pipes having the form and tone of the diapason or principal, a tone in which no one constituent harmonic is over emphasized, but the principle is equally effective when applied to reed tones of the trumpet class. However, because of the already considerable harmonic richness generated by reeds, the constituent pitches are usually limited to 16 ft., 8 ft. and 4 ft. and without mutations and upper pitches.

A chorus can also be built up on flute tones, but unless it is exceptionally well designed, voiced and balanced, the sound is thick and cloying on the ear. The so called 'Baroque' positif, or choir division, ideally requires such a flute chorus, complete with mutations, in contrast to a principal chorus usually of unison and octaves only.

The tonal chorus is also applied to the pedal organ in modern design, indeed in many antique continental instruments of earlier times, this principle was known and followed. It serves not only to provide degrees of definition and intensity, but by inter-chorus combination, produces tone-colour contrasts for pedal solo parts.

In large accompanimental instruments, it is not unusual to have two or more diapason choruses of differing power, and one of them under swell box control. In the best examples, these choruses differ subtly in colour, and only slightly in power; so that inter-chorus mingling produces tonal shades, and together, sound louder than the louder of the two alone. Too often this is not so.

The organ's multiple keyboards are a peculiarity shared only with the harpsichord until recent times. However, as stated above, a single manual instrument with but two stops is in essence an organ and much real music is available for such limited resources.

In an instrument lacking expressive touch, another manual offers a convenient means to command contrasting tones or different accents, and in the course of time there has come about an association of particular tone choruses of major or minor intensities, with particular manual divisions. National designs differ in detail, but the general form is traceable in them all.

Universally, the great organ manual division has always contained the fundamental tone of the organ; the diapason or principal in a chorus of pitches, ranging from the simplest minimum of 8 ft. and 4 ft., to the full chorus based on 8 ft. and with stops of all the consonant harmonics up to ¾ in. and not infrequently the sub-fundamental 16 ft. as well. Additionally some quiet accompanimental voices and one or more reed-tones of a chorus character may be provided.

Usually the second manual is the swell, all stops being enclosed in an expression chamber with an adjustable louvred opening; a swell box. They fall easily into four broad groups, an alternative principal chorus of lighter tone texture to that of the great; some soft string tone and a flute group; and an assertive reed chorus often of trumpets in 16-ft., 8-ft. and 4-ft. pitches. The latter, in the best work, embraces the upper work of the flue chorus to form the rich vibrant thrill of the English full swell. The Recit of continental European organs follows closely on these lines in outline, but with differing emphasis in the content of the differing tonal groups.

In England, the choir organ has wavered between a minor great chorus of diapasons and flute, and a motley collection of pianissimo accompanimental or pallid imitative orchestral solo tones, tending more to the latter alternative when enclosed in a swell box. In more recent years comparison with the classical remnants has lead to an increasing appreciation of the musical utility of a major and minor chorus, composed of principal and flute tones, including mutations, and non-imitative reed tones of orchestral woodwind flavour. All at a power level approaching say four-fifths of that of the great chorus.

Where a fourth, and usually uppermost manual is provided it is usually to control a range of strong tone colours of solo power and mainly under swell box expression. The rare fifth manual almost always provides separate keys to an echo or antiphonal division.

The pedal organ provides a bass to the manual tones and choruses and so in general, pedal stops are an octave lower than manual stops of the same timbre. Thus the pedal pitch is usually 16 ft. with 32 ft. tone as the sub-fundamental.

Formerly it was thought in this country that one or more dull-toned 16-ft. stops was all that was needed, and needs for higher pitches could be met by use of the manual to pedal coupler. Gradually an appreciation of the value of a substantially independent pedal tonal range, especially for solo performances, has led to even quite small two-manual instruments having a chorus of four pitches, mutations and even mixtures, to the great advantage of definition and colour in the pedal line.

Pedal compass has become standardized at 32 notes CCC–G but many remain at 30 notes CCC–F with an occasional rarity of

c

twenty-seven or twenty-nine notes only. In this matter the electronic organ designers exercise remarkable freedom, some producing only thirteen notes and placed unrelated to any conventions as to correct position.

Classical and neo-classical instruments are generally arranged on what has come to be known as the 'werk-prinzip' wherein each has a basic principal pitch, on which the tonal structure is built. These basic pitches are generally arranged each an octave apart. Thus a small instrument may have basic pitches of pedal 8 ft., great 4 ft., and positiv 2 ft., which are the pitches of the principal (or lowest pitch diapason stop) on each manual. A larger organ may have pedal 16 ft., great 8 ft., positiv 4 ft. and brustwerk 2 ft., and a still larger one be based on pedal at 32 ft. In each case, however, it is usual for the wide scale or flute chorus to be based on 16-ft. pitch on pedals, or 8-ft. pitch on any manual, even if the pitch of the principal is higher than this.

The principle is also carried into the layout of the organ, each department having its own case, or its own readily distinguishable part of the main case, with the principal of its basic pitch in display. See illustration (Plate 3). Thus the physical disposition of the different departments is visually evident, and because of the effect of the individual cases with their sound-reflecting tops, aurally evident also.

This sort of layout is of course only possible when the organ is arranged against a wall, and there is sufficient height for one department to be mounted above another. Acoustically and musically it is very satisfactory when this can be achieved. So often, unfortunately, an organ must be arranged on a floor with one department behind another. Under these conditions, the 'werk'-prinzip cannot be fully carried out, and all that can be done is to arrange adequate space over the instrument to allow the sound from the rearmost division to pass over the one in front.

Some critics claim that the organ lacks expression in terms of subtle shading of volume, colour and attack. At first this may appear to be true. Indeed, in too many indifferently produced instruments of common pedestrian design, the criticism can be accepted, but as in most art-forms, art lies in the successful overcoming of the apparent limitations of the medium. The music of past and present composers for the organ lacks for little in artistic expression and subtle nuances. With the exact playing of the music under the hands of a master player, the subtle addition or subtraction of a stop to a balanced chorus, and their arrangement in easy access from two or more manuals are the real means of musical expression in the organ.

The introduction of mechanical aids in the form of pneumatic or electrical transmission action made possible an individual action to each pipe and this brought about the unit-extension system, the old classical form usually being referred to as the 'straight' organ.

By this means a rank of pipes could be made playable in several pitches at will, one pipe serving as both CC, tenor C, and middle C, for example in 2-ft., 4-ft. and 8-ft. pitches respectively. In this way a substantial-looking stop-list can be contrived from but three or four stops of extended compass.

The system when applied to modest instruments used mainly for church service accompaniment, and when derived from a sufficient diversity of basic tone-colours, undoubtedly provides variety of a sort. This is because of the greater flexibility of control compared with the same number of pipes under 'straight' control. This combined with economies in space and cost saving can in some circumstances outweigh the loss in accurate balance and augmentative combination that are so important in a solo instrument intended for critical listening.

Serious artistic objections arise when classical choruses are attempted by this 'borrowing' system. The true complementary 4-ft. tone to an 8-ft. fundamental is not its octave tone but one differing slightly in colour within the tonal class and free to be adjusted as to intensity at any point in its compass. A further disadvantage is the relative lack of chorus effect when a few pipes are made to do the work of many. The resulting sound lacks 'freshness' much as an amplified violin would do in place of the string section of an orchestra. Electronic instruments using a single set of tone generators suffer from the same defect, though to a very much greater degree as the chorus effect is then entirely absent.

Nevertheless, some musically attractive instruments have been built on the unit-extension principle, but it requires a helpful building and considerable skill and knowledge of the economics of the system, to devise, voice and finish an organ that justifies the method. A merely clever stop-list is all too easy to manufacture.

So much for extension on the manuals, but the majority of pedal organs in England use the 'borrowing' principle to obtain 8-ft. and 4-ft. tones from the 16-ft. bass tones. Sometimes the compass is also extended downwards and 32-ft. pitch is obtained. While the same criticisms apply as with manual unit-extension borrowings, they do so with less weight here because, with but one or two notes played at any one time, and with careful tapering of the tone and intensity throughout the compass, an acceptable balance is usually obtainable, and valuable resources provided with economy of cost and space. It is a useful combination of engineering and artful artistry.

The borrowing to the pedals of manual 16-ft. stops, is preferably called 'duplexing' and amounts in effect to a selective manual to pedal coupler, so that pedal combinations can be augmented without drawing on the manual by the use of the coupler.

Completely straight pedal stops when mounted together as far as possible, have a synchronous speech and fullness of tone that is easily recognized, and when they can be afforded they are certainly the ideal.

The very size and bulk of all but the simplest organ introduces another factor that sets it apart from most other instruments of music; their dependence upon thoughtful and advantageous placing in the building. This aspect can make or mar almost any organ. It is true that an indifferent designer-craftsman's work, when well placed in reverberant surroundings, may well have greater appeal than that by an acknowledged artist, saddled by an indifferent architect, or an unadventurous client, with an organ chamber that is little more than a kennel abutting on to a carpeted auditorium.

The average church organ, tightly fitted into its organ chamber is lacking in a quality that distinguishes instruments spaciously laid out on open sites. Lacking not only the superior blending speech-quality from unforced pipe speech and the possibility of audible articulation, but also another influence that imparts an individual character to each instrument. As mentioned above, in many continental organs well placed in open positions in reverberant buildings, the groupings of the pipes associated with particular manuals results in an audible space relationship, which is heightened by the semi-enclosure of surrounding tone cabinets that impart a distinctive bloom and subtle tonal contrast. This is a feature largely lost in British organ-building or possibly never really developed, because of our smaller buildings and differing liturgical uses, but it is now being more widely appreciated by thoughtful designers and practised where opportunity offers (Plate 9).

It will be seen that there are two fundamental aspects of organ-design and building. The architectural and acoustic planning, coupled with sound engineering skill in providing appropriate mechanism, and the design, provision and musical trimming of the tonal sources. The former is not only comparatively easy but only justified when the essential tonal artistry that follows is the best that an experienced and imaginative tonal craftsman can create. The former must serve the latter.

Regretfully, this is often not the case, and those who buy organs, by all the procedure of competitive tender, are often successful only in buying their moneysworth in mechanism and material, because artistic imagination and musical good taste with integrity of design, do not show on paper.

In subsequent chapters of more detailed description we endeavour to keep a balance between these two essential aspects, and if our details of mechanism seem extensive, it is that in a better understanding of it and what it can do, it may be the better servant of organ music-making.

Fig. 6

3
The Mechanism of the Organ

SINCE the building of the earliest and crudest keyboard organ, every instrument has had a system of mechanism linking the keys to the air release valves within the windchest under the pipes. It transmits the player's finger movements and so commands the speech of the pipes as rapidly as mechanical ingenuity can devise.

As engineering science developed, new systems were invented and developed to a high degree; each new method nearly but not quite eclipsing the earlier ones. Such is the longevity of organ craftsmanship, that many examples of almost every system are still extant and in regular use.

Until the last quarter of the nineteenth century nearly all organs had purely mechanical or 'tracker' action, wherein the player through his fingers on the keys exerted sufficient force on a system of mechanical traces to open directly the pipe-valves or pallets. The effort required is directly related to the number of pipes and the wind-pressure applied to them so that in large and necessarily powerful instruments playing was a considerable physical as well as musical feat.

In the early organs, wind-pressure, while selected by the voicer, was also limited to the muscular effort and endurance of the usually one-man-power hand blower. About the middle 1800's the application of hydraulic or gas engine power to supplant manual effort, began the end of this limitation on wind-pressure. The heavier wind thus made possible, was at first used as pneumatic power to aid the key action; and later, to aid the voicer to create louder individual voices, when thus relieved of consideration for the player's digital strength.

At first, pneumatic power was used as an aid to a conventional tracker action transmission and was usually applied in England to the swell manual only. This relieved the excessive weight of touch when that manual was coupled to the great. Soon this system was further developed, and the pneumatic power was triggered by air impulses through lead tubes connecting keyboard and organ action. From this development of 'Tubular Pneumatic' action sprang many big changes in the control of the instrument. Intermanual coupling, with

THE MECHANISM OF THE ORGAN

simultaneous playing of octaves above and below the unison, became effortless. This device greatly increased the volume and variety of sound available, if not always with musical artistry.

The difficulty of accurately judging the balance of an accompaniment when the player is too close to, sometimes almost within the instruments, led to attempts to detach the keyboard. Despite the obvious physical limitations to the length of tracker actions, some remarkably long and successful tracker actions were made, and a few of them still exist in rural churches. At least one entirely new one was made in 1964.

Tubular pneumatic action, even in its crudest forms, freed the designer from the traditional internal layout of the tonal divisions; at least to the extent of the practical tube length of about 50 ft. at the extreme of tolerable time lag. No longer did the limitation of the player's physical powers require the windchests of manual and pedal divisions to be closely planned. Now they could be disposed in odd shaped spaces or divided and dispersed. They could be made larger, and the stops more numerous, until almost inevitably, for architectural tidiness, they were banished to confining organ chambers. This was much to their musical degradation, for higher wind-pressures were then demanded to force tones from these unsympathetic acoustical surroundings. Nevertheless the facility of a detached console was soon found to be a valuable improvement when applied with discretion and strictly for a musician's advantage.

It was but a short step from tubular pneumatic to the substitution of simple electrical transmission. As simple in fact as any ordinary doorbell mechanism and at first, by similar components. It overcame the mechanical time-lag inherent in even the best of tubular systems. This action is correctly called electro-pneumatic, because in essence, it is an instantaneous electrical transmission from key to organ, triggering a responsive compressed-air powered action at the windchest. It allows distances between console and pipes, limited only by the extent of acoustic time-lag tolerable in the particular circumstances. In the best systems it has inherent instant coupling, duplexing or borrowing action.

Inevitably, the relative ease and compactness of the switching mechanism, the low costs that economical volume production of components made possible, together with the lower installation costs, led to it superseding the tubular pneumatic after 1939.

Electric action offers a temptation to place various sections of an instrument in any available or even widely dispersed places. Clever exploitation of the new-found mechanical freedom, led to large instruments of great internal complexity and too often indifferent musical capacity. Such instruments are almost as remote as can be conceived from the musical and structural unity that centuries of craftsmanship had developed in the classical square-built, free-standing, low-pressure tracker-action instrument. Nevertheless, electro-pneumatic action, in its wide and versatile use by the best designers, has conferred the blessing of the most responsive, reliable and durable action; and in many circumstances it is the only really practical system.

The unit extension system was born early in the electrical-action development period. True, it was conceived in tubular pneumatic days, but now it was given lusty life that reached its maturity in the theatre organ. Later, accomplished practitioners of this system, applied it with skill to more serious instruments. It is still used in economical space-saving and serviceable small organs, and some miniatures that owe little in their design to the traditional or classical pipe organ.

Lastly, there is the direct or all-electric action in which the use of compressed air, as the power means is eliminated. Here substantial electro magnets directly open individual pipe-valves. It has limited use and only one builder (in the U.S.A.) is known to use it exclusively and consistently. There are at present a number of highly technical limitations to its general adoption for the traditional organ, but as design improves in it and in its associated components, its wider use seems probable. Some very advanced designs are on the drawing-boards.

It need not be a matter for surprise, that in the past fifteen years, the wheel of fashion, or appreciation, has turned full cycle, and many sensitive players are re-discovering artistic values and interpretative aids, in a well-designed and perfectly made tracker action. The sense of crisp direct finger control over the precise moment of speech of the pipe is enjoyed, together with actual control of the intonation or speech attack, though this is a subject of much controversy.

The characteristic touch of tracker actions arises from the pallet-valve under the pipes being naturally held closed by the wind-pressure in the surrounding windchest. This produces a marked resistance to the initial movement of the key mechanically connected to it. In large instruments, or with high wind-pressures, this initial resistance is considerable. Once the pallet has opened and compressed air has filled the windway to the pipe, this resistance is rapidly reduced almost to nil, producing at the key, the sensation of breaking through a crisp crust. Besides giving a very pleasant definition to the key movement, it gives control of phrasing and the synchronization of notes in a chord, as on the pianoforte.

This sense of direct control, leads to claims by sensitive players, that they can control, not only the timing, but also the rate of opening of the pipe-valve, and hence the degree of 'attack' in the pipe speech. Those who reject this claim, contend that the effect is solely subjective, sensed only by the player, and is inaudible to listeners. They support this view with data from highly organized experiments with seemingly convincing conclusions. Nevertheless, sensitive musicians with wide experience of antique or modern tracker-actioned instruments, are equally convinced that there is this inherent musical advantage.

Probably the explanation lies in one aspect, neglected or overlooked in the opposing arguments and experiments, and that is, the style and voicing technique applied to the pipes used in the tests. Pipes voiced in the best manner, on medium wind-pressures, in the style common in the last hundred years, have firm and relatively 'slow' speech, which is comparatively insensitive to small wind-pressure differences and attack qualities, and thus are irresponsive to variation by slow or rapid opening of the key valve.

On the other hand, those experienced in voicing pipes on classical low wind-pressures in the range of $1\frac{1}{2}$ in. wg. to $2\frac{1}{4}$ in. wg. using the antique lip-regulation and open-tip method, know how sensitive such pipework is to quite small pressure variations arising from the qualities of the windchests used. Considerable power and quality change is possible with $\pm\frac{1}{8}$ in. wg. pressure. With that type of pipe speech, there is no doubt that some control of intonation is possible by sensitive keyboard touch. This could explain the charm of some of the ancient and historical continental instruments, and the musical satisfaction they give the player.

Contemporary design in Denmark and Holland is almost wholly with direct mechanical action. Some small new instruments in this country are so built, but the chancel organ position usually required, does not often allow the best layout for good or economical tracker action. Good tracker action requires the best of craftsmanship in its design, in making and setting up. Modern production techniques have only limited application, because the numbers required do not permit cost-saving volume production. Indeed, today, good tracker-action work by acknowledged competent practitioners, costs a significant percentage more than first-class electric coupling and transmission.

In the following chapters the different systems of organ key action are examined and explained in greater detail.

4

Tracker Action

A BRIEF study of basic forms of tracker action will help a student to grasp the general nature of organ action design. In its simplest forms (Fig. 7) and (Fig. 8) the key is contrived as a lever, hinged at its rear end. The pallet-valve within the windchest is similarly hinged and held to the closed position by a light spring. Between them, a simple tracker or push-rod of wood or metal transmits finger movements; depression of the key forces the pallet-valve open against the spring and surrounding air-pressure, which then causes air flow to the connected pipes. This ultra-simple form is only practical in tiny cabinet organs, as clearly the pipe-valves would have to be as closely spaced as the keys in the manual, and follow precisely the chromatic order.

The commonest device to overcome this rigid association of keys and pipes is the double-lever or backfall. In this form, the key is also a double-lever, 'balanced' about its approximate centre (Fig. 9). A vertical trace or sticker transmits a thrust motion to a similar backfall, having a flexible connection passing into the windchest to the pallet-valve. It will be seen that pressing the key will open the valve as in the first example, but with the advantages of detachment from the windchest. By splaying the backfalls, that is, fanning-out the pallet-valve end, the windchest can be made much wider than key spacing—so long as the splay is not so sharply angled as to cause the backfall to be excessively long, and introduce 'spring' which is fatal to a good 'touch'. This is an elegant form, but it still requires the pipes to be planted on the windchest in chromatic order and risking some uncertain tuning arising from acoustic interference between voices tuned only a semitone apart.

A very useful alternative was found by adapting a component familiar as a part of the old style domestic mechanical door-bell system and so called a 'bell-crank' or 'square'. It has an equal simplicity in most respects and the added advantage that by the use of two squares the horizontal part of the action could be extended and when required, splayed beyond the limits of backfalls by the use of traces consisting of light wooden trackers. It is an easy step, to pick out alternative bass notes for instance, arranging the squares at a different level and splaying

TRACKER ACTION

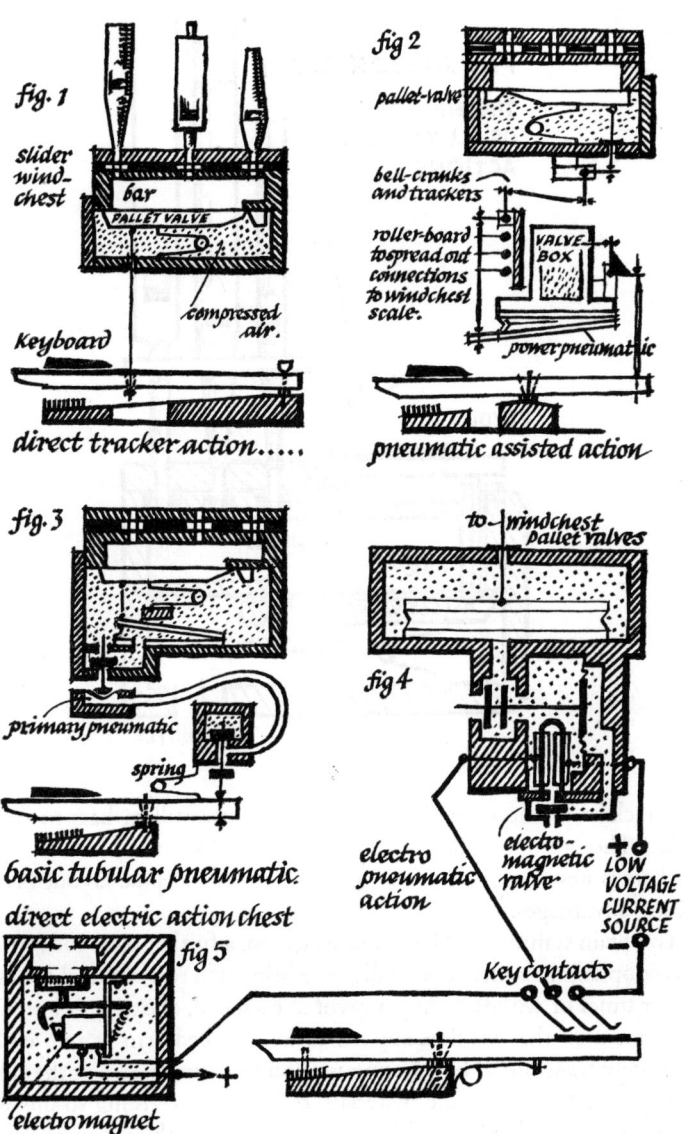

Fig. 7

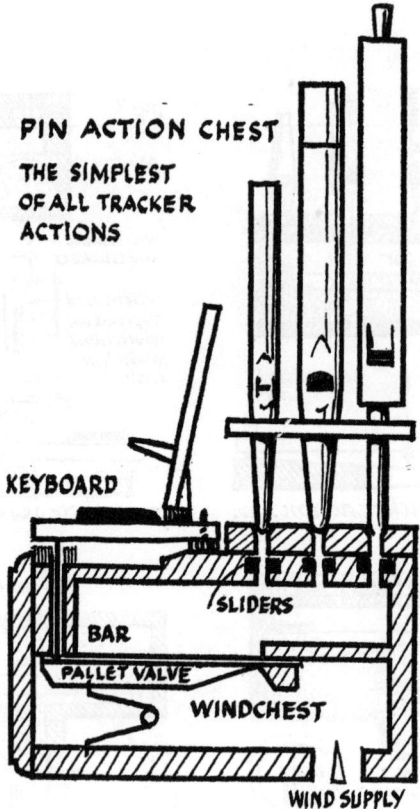

Fig. 8

the trackers to the opposite end, but of course still in bass to treble order. Though practical in mechanical detail this latter use of splayed trackers is never seen now, as a more symmetrical pipe layout brings tuning advantages.

To obtain symmetrical layout or nearly so, a further basic movement was adopted, the roller or 'trundle' consisting of a rod of metal (or as in earlier times of wood) having a pivot at each end, allowing it a rolling movement so that motion applied to an attached arm at one end is accurately transmitted by twisting motion to a similar arm at the other end, or as accurately as the materials' resistance to twisting strains will allow. This twisting 'spring' is the factor limiting the practical length of a 'roller board', as the group structure is called. The illustration shows how readily the pipe layout is freed from the rigid order of the keyboard.

TRACKER ACTION

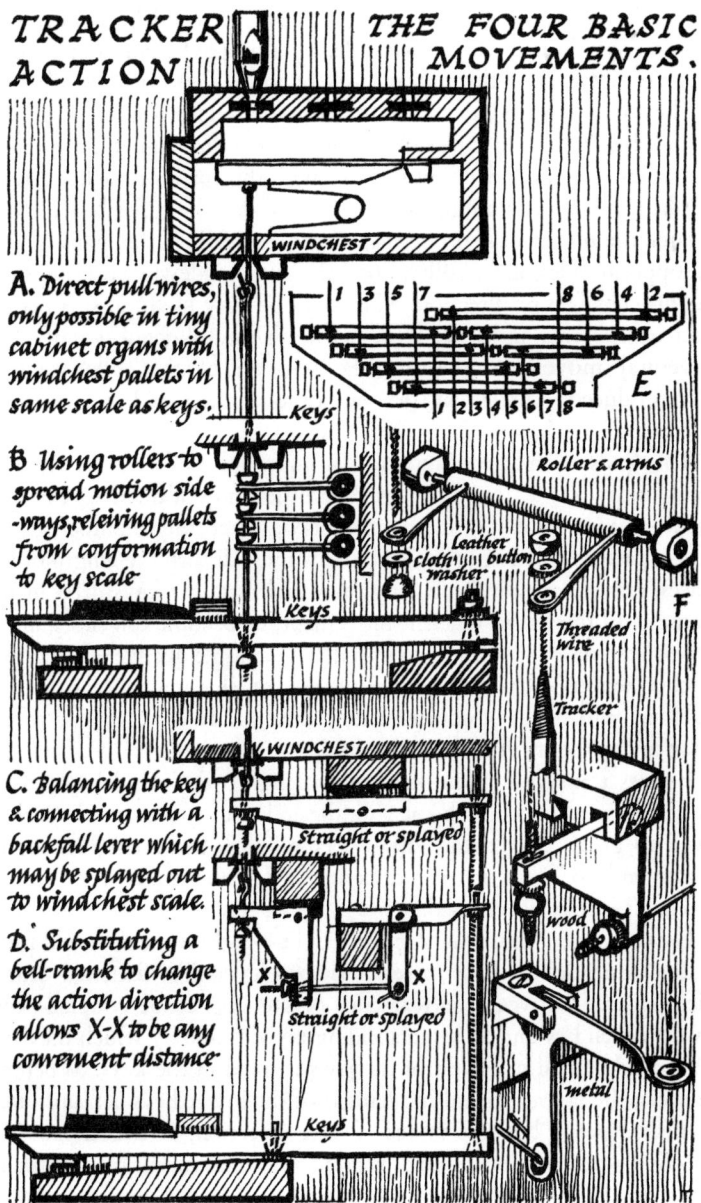

FIG. 9

The roller board has other important uses. It can give a complete sideways shift to the line of action allowing the windchest to be other than directly in line with the console. By a simple variation in its form it can turn the action through an angle of 90°, at the same time adapting the key scale to the windchest, as may be required for a pedal-stop chest, or as when a console is placed at one end of an instrument, a position not often recommended, but possible with this form of tracker action.

The mechanically minded reader will see that the roller board could assume the mechanical properties of the backfall, if the arms are set on opposite sides of the roller, not only giving sideways transmission, but also changes of direction. This could be very useful in small compact instruments and is so used, but needs careful detail design. Any structural movement affecting the position of the roller centres, is reproduced doubled at the end of one arm, with troublesome effects.

This leads to an appreciation of the importance of a rigid and stable frame in tracker-actioned organs. As a little study of the diagrams will show, any movement of the windchests or supporting members of the action parts in relation to the keyboards must disturb the length of the traces, either becoming too long, in which case the keys drop in the frame until there is insufficient movement, or become too short, and a note once pressed, continues to sound. The durable quality of many old tracker actions often depends very much on this matter of structural stability, which can of course include the rigidity or otherwise of the floor under the instrument and console.

Besides transmitting the key movements to the windchests, there must be means for coupling at will, the action of two manuals, such as swell to great. Fortunately, the upper requires to be coupled to the lower and to work in one direction only, and some very simple mechanisms have been used.

For the smaller instrument, having light-weight 'touch', an old form is the 'drumstick' coupler, a set of shaped levers like flattened drumsticks, placed between the rear ends of the keys to be coupled—one lever to each key and all set in a sliding pivot frame by which they can be moved at will in or out of the jaws formed in the keys. When set between the jaws, upward movement of the lower keys is transmitted to those above, but not in the reverse direction. It is compact and effective when the detail design is good and some means of adjustment is provided.

A basically similar but unsatisfactory form has 'stickers' secured to the ends of the lower keys, collectively moved in or out of engagement with the key ends to be coupled. This form has a major disadvantage, in that engagement is nearly impossible while a key is depressed, and if attempted will cause breakage.

A much more elegant piece of mechanism is fortunately available; positive in action, low in friction, and much more versatile in application. This is the 'backfall coupler'. It can be used to couple intermanually in unison and in octaves up and down. The basic principle is illustrated in Fig. 10. The method of engagement, or release, is to raise or lower the centre beam. As the backfall is secured to the action at one end, the free end must move in or out of engagement. A fascinating example of this system actually applied to a crude pneumatic action of a very large instrument in Sydney Town Hall, N.S.W., Australia, is illustrated (Fig. 11).

This device can be used for octave coupling, the backfalls are then splayed one octave in the required direction, but in this case it is important to design the connections in such a way that the octave key is not also depressed, or the coupling would continue in a cascade of octaves to the limit of the keyboard.

The detail parts retain their traditional form; the buttons or leather nuts threaded on to 'tapped' wires formerly of iron but now of phosphor-bronze, the light-weight wooden traces, called trackers or stickers according to whether they pull or push, and the squares and rollers, have been developed and refined in centuries of use. They are still perfect for their part when applied correctly with understanding, despite the ridicule of engineers. However, modern materials are being incorporated; aluminium or plastic sheet for squares and backfalls, laminated plastic strip for trackers, moulded plastics as mounting parts. Nylon as silent bushings and formed metal angle sections as rigid and durable framing are all coming into use.

False movement in the many working centres causes spongy touch or noisy working and must be avoided, if crispness of touch is to be achieved. If noise were no problem, the designer's task would be easier as soft buffing washers or bushings to avoid metal to metal contacts would not be necessary. A successful tracker-action design has the minimum of compressible working points, and the fewest points of adjustment.

The action to the pedal organ can be tracker, but there is little to commend this as the characteristic synchronous speech can be obtained with care by other ways. The demands of pedal playing inflict heavy impact strains, and wear and noise soon result. In large modern examples, electro-pneumatic is used, and manual to pedal coupling is

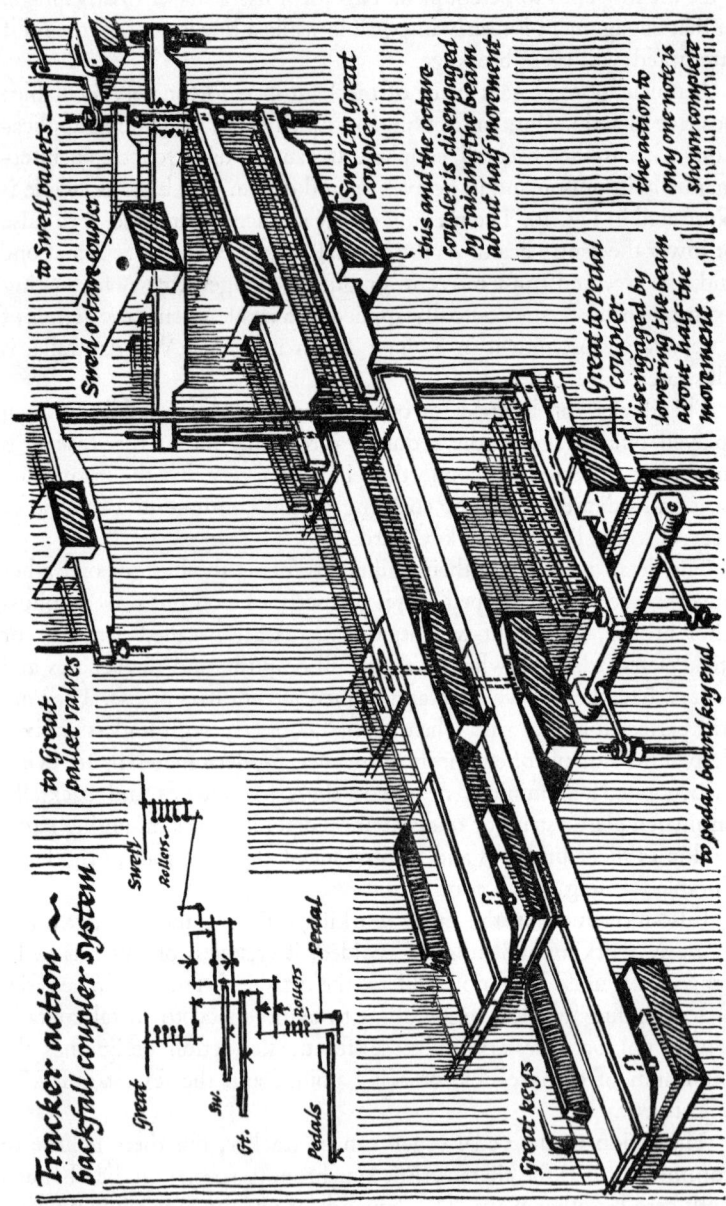

Fig. 10

TRACKER ACTION

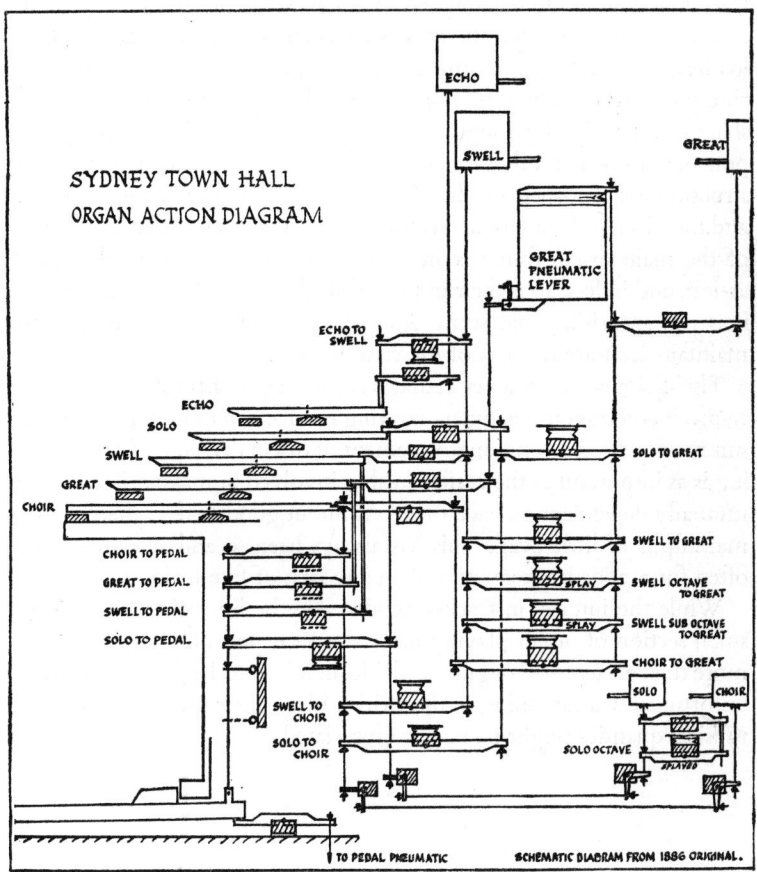

Fig. 11

done by attaching an electro-pneumatic action to the tracker division with which it is desired to couple.

One of the commonest ills of tracker-action organs in poor condition is 'shallow' touch, the key movement having decreased from between $\frac{3}{8}$ in. and $\frac{1}{2}$ in. to such a small amount that the transmitted movement is prevented from being enough to open adequately the windchest pallet-valve. The restricted wind supply results in poor uncertain speech and severe out-of-tuneness. This condition usually arises because of expanding or shrinking movements within the organ frame, resulting in movements of the action parts relative to each other. Climatic changes bringing an excess of damp or of desiccation can cause this. A tracker action should be designed to absorb some of this movement. In a common way to keep the action connections taut and ready, a lead loading strip called a 'thumper' is placed just behind the key ivories, riding on the keys. In good regulation each key is set up to take just its share of the weight; enough to bring the key level, but not enough to pull the windchest valve open. Thus, small movements in the action structure are absorbed by slight variation in the general touch depth, and the action is kept taut and crisp to play. As shown above, the design of the main organ frame is an important element in a good tracker action, and indeed so is the rigidity of the floor on which it stands, and it is not surprising that some designers now use metal structures to maintain accurate relation of the critical parts.

The designer of a tracker action has command of these basic devices to produce a responsive, quiet-working mechanism of pleasant touch to suit many varied layouts and placement of organ divisions. This designing is as important as the craftsmanship involved in making it, each are mutually dependent on each other. Without good design, mere craftsmanship is of little avail. This has always been so and accounts more often for a poor tracker action than any lack of fine making.

While the interest in tracker actions may be limited to a relatively small section of organ-playing musicians, it is possible that were there more tracker-actioned organs available, in mint mechanical condition—unfortunately a rare thing in the British Isles—their music-making and musical qualities might be better appreciated.

5
Pneumatic Actions

THE majority of church organs in England have tubular pneumatic action, and examples of almost every variant of the system are still working, even a few pre-tubular pneumatics using pneumatic action power to assist heavy tracker actions—the 'pneumatic-lever' action. This latter form was applied mainly to reduce the excessive weight of key touch of coupled manuals, with tracker action. Figure 7 (2) shows the system in outline and Fig. 11 a more elaborate application.

Compressed air from the organ bellows-reservoir, under control of a miniature pallet-valve operated by the keys through trackers, inflates a pneumatic bellows-motor which pulls open the windchest main pallet-valve. Considerable design ingenuity was displayed in devising

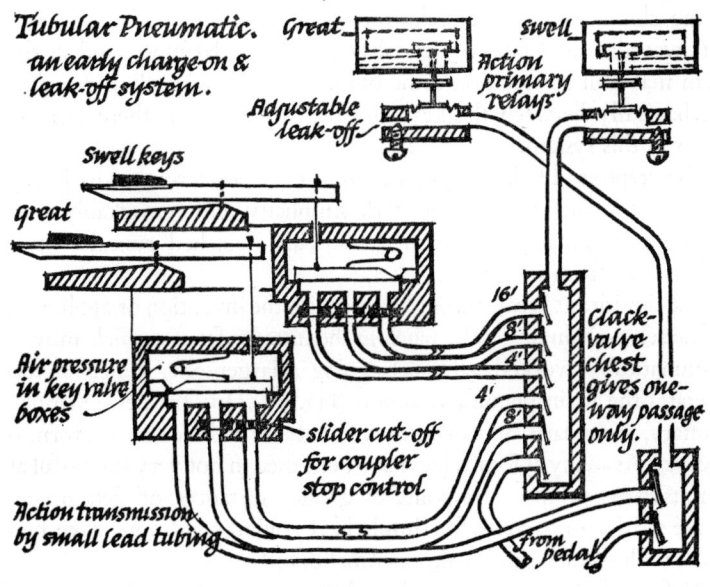

Fig. 12

quick-acting primary valves to offset the ponderous movements of the clumsy pneumatic parts.

Crude and noisy as many examples now seem, the system combined the good features of both tracker and the later tubular pneumatic systems. It retained the crisp direct tracker-action touch to the great manual, and a not dissimilar touch to the swell, as the primary valves had a miniature windchest-pallet form, and yet a minimum increase of weight when manuals are coupled. It also allowed the increased wind-pressures that encouraged the development of more sonorous reed tones in the swell organ.

The tendency to comparatively noisy working, and the costliness of repairs to the miniature bellows-motors, discourages restoration, and it seems likely that soon there will be no examples in playing use. A modern variation of it is applied to contemporary European tracker-actioned instruments, wherein it pulls on the manual bass notes at the instigation of the pedal couplers.

The next step was the devising and development of tubular connections; at first not the small pencil-size tubing now associated with tubular-pneumatic, but a plumber's 1 in. heavy outside diameter lead pipe, stretching from a valve in a miniature soundboard windchest at the keyboard to an inflatable bellows attached to, and pulling open the spring-closed pallet-valve under the pipes.

It was also used between pedal board and pedal pipes, and in that form may still be found in some old instruments. Coupling was done mechanically between the keys and the key valve, as there were no relays in this system.

The response of this action was almost as ponderous as its heavy-weight construction, but for stark simplicity and remarkably quiet working it was a great advance, allowing detached consoles up to twenty feet from the organ.

The significant break-through came with the invention or application of the relay-chain principle, wherein the impulse from a quick-moving pneumatically worked valve sets going a larger one, which in turn operates the main pneumatic action (Fig. 7 [3]) in the best examples, primary, secondary, and main movements are included in one form or another. As many as four relays have been used in not very successful attempts to get prompter response or greater distances of detachment. Quite satisfactory actions for simple heavy wind conditions have been made with primary and main pneumatics only.

At first, this introduction led to the use of much smaller tubing of only pencil thickness, and with the gain in compactness, to pneumatic coupling. At last, the key touch was of constant weight whether coupled or not. An obvious if somewhat crude application of the slider soundboard principle, to cut off unwanted connections until required, formed the simplest coupler-control system (Fig. 12).

The problem of making the connection of say, swell to great, and avoiding it also working backwards as great to swell, or an octave continuing to octave couple the whole length of the key compass, was crudely solved, by provision of a clack-valve at the point where each tube joined another. This was crude, because, to get a quick enough release when the applied air-pressure ceased, a leak-away hole had to be made near the primary pneumatic, nevertheless, some quite effective action systems in big organs were built like this as late as the early 1920's. Great reliability, but rather blurred repetition, is characteristic of this action type.

By introducing a pressure release, or exhaust valve at the key, the responsiveness was greatly improved, and much longer tubular connections became practical.

Now that the air in the tube was no longer uni-directional, but pulsed to and fro as the key was depressed and released, the simple little clack-valve no longer filled requirements, and various forms of 'vee-valves' or 'reel-valves' were introduced (Fig. 13). These moved on receiving a charge, closing the ventilated connection and allowing a to-and-fro air passage in the air connection in use at the moment. An alternative form, was to apply two or more primary motors to the same primary valve.

Tubular pneumatic systems using these details were so successful that they made possible an increased range of manual and intermanual octave and unison couplers. This in turn led to the early attempts at duplexing and borrowing of extended compass stops on both manuals and pedals. All the foregoing actions worked on the impulse of a charge of compressed air, hence the trade terms 'charge', 'drive' or 'pressure action'.

Parallel with these developments, another tubular-pneumatic system, having rather different features, had by the turn of the century been brought to a high state of effectiveness. This system, known as the 'exhaust pneumatic', has several distinctive differences (Fig. 14). The tubular connections are charged with air in the normal note-off state, *all* the pneumatic bellows-motors or pouches are contained within the compressed air in the action windchests, and there are no moving parts in the coupling mechanism. In the better examples of this action, there are two stages of pneumatic relay before the main pneumatic movement.

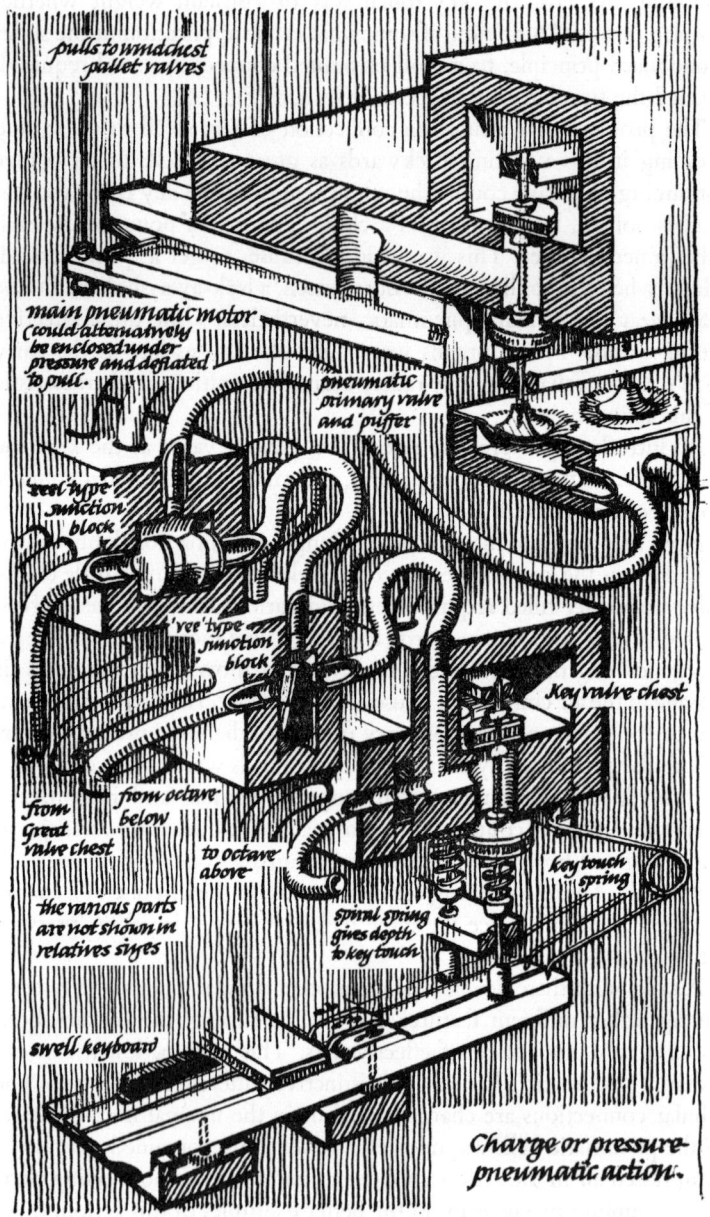

Fig. 13

PNEUMATIC ACTIONS

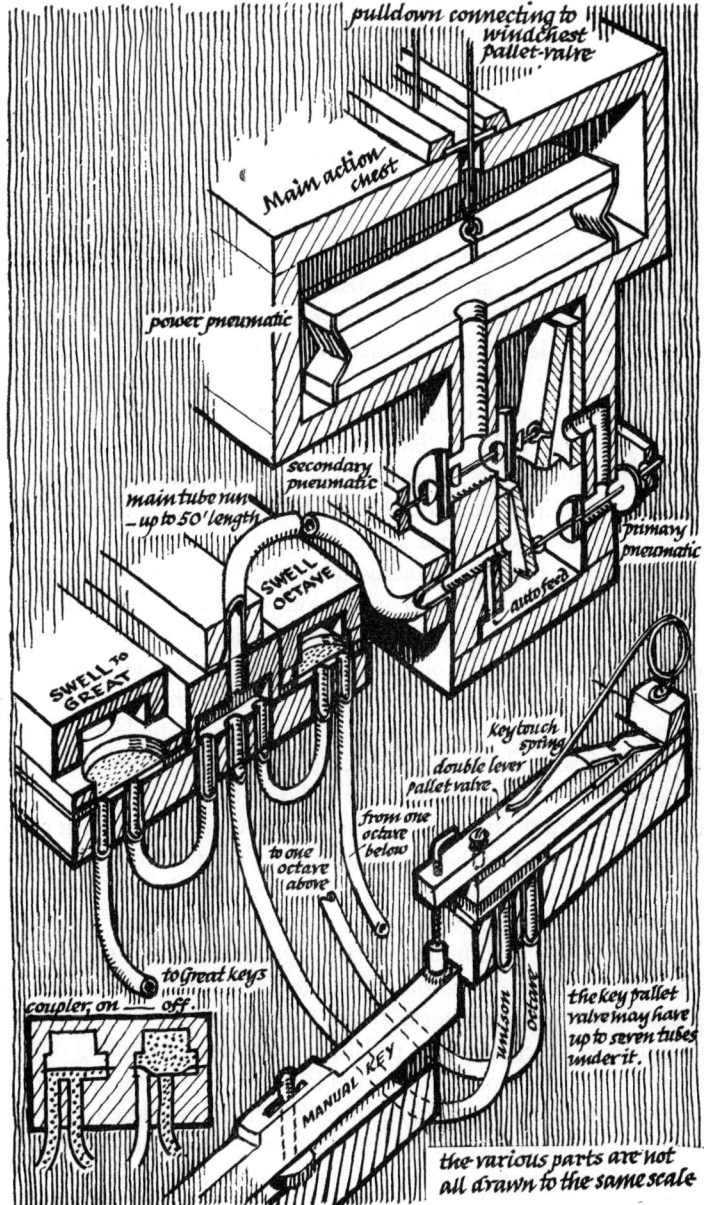

Fig. 14

In all cases, the key lifts a simple pallet-valve, uncovering the end of the transmission tube and allowing the air-pressure inside it, and therefore inside the connecting primary pneumatic, to fall to near atmospheric level. When this happens, the compressed air in the chest collapses a pneumatic bellows moving the primary disc-valve and setting in motion a chain of similar movements of increasing size resulting in the main pipe pallet-valve being opened promptly. Because the wind-enclosed primary pneumatic and valve can be made quite small and sensitive, movement occurs with but a slight fall of pressure in the action tube, resulting in prompt attack even on as much as 50 ft. of tube. Acceptable results by the standards of the day were achieved with as much as 80-ft. length in each tube. When the key is released and the tube-end abruptly closed, pressure is built up again by the 'water-hammer' effect of air momentum in the tube assisted by a small and accurately gauged leak, or 'bleed-hole' in or very near the primary motor. This fills rapidly, assisted partly by the pull of gravity or a spring, plus the air-pressure on the attached valve disc, and so triggers the chain of relay movements to the 'off' position.

Some makers provide an adjustable 'bleed-hole' having a screw choke to the leak-hole. This is an illusion of design refinement as an action needing such precision adjustment is lacking in working margins essential to durability. The only cause of a need to have service adjustment of the leak, is variation in soundness or air tightness of the tube run, and in a reliable design this cannot be tolerated. Simple, unjointed, one piece tubes, with flanges swaged on to the ends, can ensure air tightness, and is a feature of all successful designs.

It was this feature, coupled with the non-moving couplers, that made this action universal in North America and South Africa, until the coming of electro-pneumatics; as it was better able to resist wide atmospheric and temperature changes. Nevertheless, in the heyday of pneumatic actions, British firms were ranged into pro or anti 'exhaust action' groups, and contentious correspondence filled the columns of the popular musical press in the 1920's.

Coupling between manuals, pedals, and for octave coupling on this system is simple and noiseless. To couple a manual, an additional tube-hole is uncovered by the key-pallet. This tube is jointed into the desired manual-action tube. To cut the connection when unwanted, the connecting tube runs through a small leather choke diaphragm or 'membrane' which, when inflated from outside, blows down and closes the tubeway to the action. Releasing the membrane pressure allows the membrane chamber to form a connecting channel.

As many couplers can be provided as there is space for tube holes under the key-pallet. The entire coupling system is contained in a stack of key-pallets, 'membrane couplers' and tubed junctions compact enough to be accommodated within a detached console.

Such was the sensitiveness of attack, that in the best designs, means was provided to give 'false touch', a slight safety margin in the key movement without which it was impossible to play cleanly, and avoid unwanted notes from accidently flipped keys. Such 'exhaust pneumatic' as they were erroneously called, were acceptable with up to eighty feet run in each tube. Unlike the pressure type actions they were best on relatively low wind-pressures and rarely was more than 5 in. wg. used, a great consideration in years before power blowing.

Probably the last three-manual exhaust pneumatic actions to be made in the U.K. is that applied in 1958 to the instrument in Brighton Parish Church by that most able designer-craftsman in that system, the late Frank Sands, F.I.S.O.B.

Suction, as an alternative to air-pressure, was used quite early but only in isolated examples, although developed to a high level of effectiveness in the paper roll piano-player action in the 1920s. If any examples exist, it is probably only as part of a stop action of early design, wherein, to obtain enough power, pressure was used in one direction, and suction for return. Hill built several instruments incorporating this mechanism. Suction needs special generation, whereas air-pressure is already available. In some quarters, there was a fallacious idea (of which one occasionally hears echoes) that suction is more powerful than pressure. A little consideration will show that 10 in. wg. of pressure, exerts the same force as 10 in. wg. of suction. If it were otherwise, it would belie the principle of the water-gauge.

Although tubular main transmission and pneumatic coupling are no longer made, the basic forms of the pneumatic action are retained in modern electric actions, which in the main are more correctly described as electro-pneumatic; pneumatic triggered by electric transmission, which is the subject of the next chapter.

6

Electro-pneumatic Actions

THE early applications of electricity to the organ were in the transmission medium, applied to pressure-type actions in which a crude electro-magnet, not unlike that in an electric door bell, pulled or pushed a pneumatic primary valve which was returned on release by a spring or gravity. At first the electro-magnets were large and clumsy, but the early skill of Italian electrical engineers developed very small light-weight units which had some success, but current consumption was heavy, battery-power sources uncertain and contact material inadequate. Father Willis's action on these lines in Canterbury Cathedral was highly successful but much trouble was experienced elsewhere until a Birkenhead telegraph engineer, Robert Hope-Jones, himself a competent organist, applied his professional experience to the designing and making of an electric action for organs. His basic forms were so fundamentally sound that sixty years or more afterwards, they are still the basis of almost all good action designs[1].

The key to Hope-Jones's success was the small soft iron wire hairpin-shaped magnet (Fig. 15), and the tiny, almost weightless disc-valve armature. Making very small demands on current supplies these allowed the use of durable, light, semi-precious metal wire contacts. At first gold and platinum were used, later it was nickel and bronze.

He applied his electro-magnet to trigger on and off, what in essence was the pneumatic relay chain of an 'exhaust pneumatic action'. His little disc-armature, being equivalent to the key-pallet, connected the internal pneumatics to the outside air, when drawn towards the excited magnet.

The basic principles and working of all electro-pneumatic actions in successful use today are similar. Depressing a manual or pedal key closes an electrical switch, consisting usually of a pair of standard silver wire contacts, that connect a supply of low-pressure electrical current to a wire running from it, to an electro-magnet in the distant organ action. Often there are several contacts, one additional contact for each

[1] The development of electric organ action designs is dealt with in an extensively illustrated paper by J. I. Taylor, *I.S.O.B. Journal* of June 1951 (No. 2. Vol. 1).

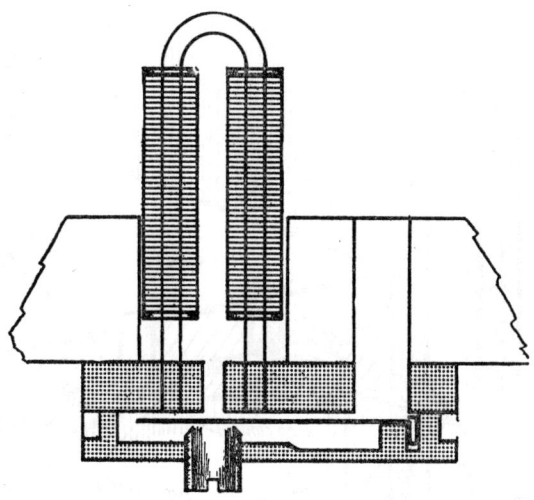

Fig. 15

coupler required to be worked from that key. The electrical charge causes a current to circulate through the windings of the electro-magnet attraction instantaneously occurs at its ends or poles, drawing to them a small disc of magnetic material.

This disc armature is contained in a chamber connected to the compressed air, or 'wind' via a passage between the pole-ends, and also via another air passage to the first pneumatic movement, which is thus inflated at rest, in the 'off' position. The disc when at rest also covers and seals a windway or port to the outside atmosphere.

Exciting the magnet attracts the armature disc to the pole-ends, closing the wind-supply port, opening the chamber and connecting the pneumatic to the atmosphere. This movement is $\frac{1}{20}$ in. or less, and almost instantaneous. Air-pressure around the pneumatic bellows forces air out, collapsing it, and pulling over a valve and in turn setting in motion a similar but larger scaled pneumatic movement, which results in the opening of the desired pipe-valve. Release of the key opens the electrical circuit, de-energizes the electro-magnet, and reverses the chain of pneumatic events (Fig. 16).

An alternative and simpler application of electro-magnets of more recent design, uses larger magnets having lever-armatures working directly on the valve of the main pneumatic, halving the number of movements in the relay chain and yet giving a very responsive mechanism. This development is in line with the trend to use more electricity,

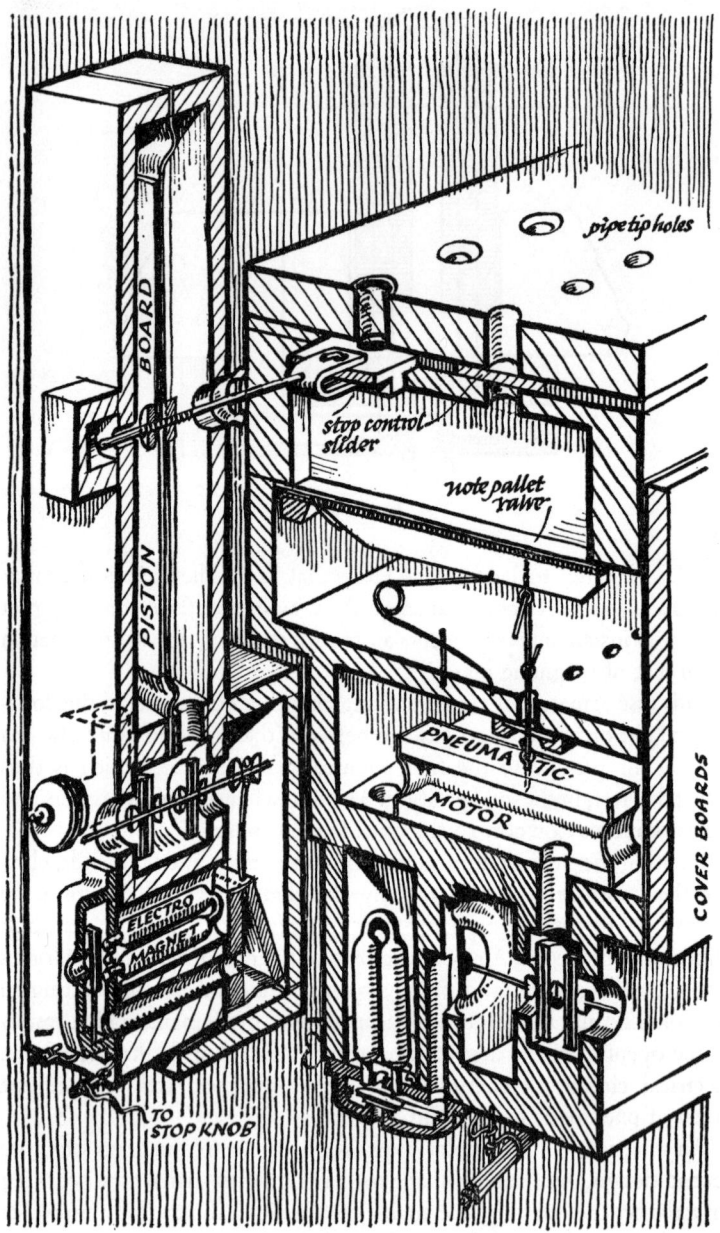

Fig. 16

ELECTRO-PNEUMATIC ACTIONS

as sources become more reliable, and contact systems capable of handling larger currents.

Opening the circuit produces, by induction in the magnet windings, a momentary electrical charge of considerable pressure. This is discharged as it jumps the opening contacts, and can be seen as a minute spark. In well-designed actions, it is very small and does no harm, but should the applied voltage be excessive or the windings and contacts be inexpertly matched, local intense heat is caused, contacts are damaged and result in dumb notes. There are now several means in use for suppressing sparking, involving condensers, carbon resistors or miniature rectifiers.

To couple another manual to that being played, an electrical connection is made to the desired circuit, via an additional key contact which is then wired through a multiple circuit or gang-switch of the required number of notes, and connected into the circuit to be coupled. Octave-coupling or unit organ borrowing is done in the same way. The provision of a separate contact per coupler, is usually a circuit necessity—for the avoidance of (*a*) electrical overloading and (*b*) the creation of a back-circuit that would result in the coupling working both ways, or in the case of octave-couplers, continuing, until it ran out of octaves.

A variant of the foregoing basic circuit requires both separate contacts and separate wipers to each circuit per key, by which switching is simplified and can be self-contained within the key assembly.

In American design and in some early Hope-Jones designs, the key contact was mechanically moved in or out of range of the key-operated wiper; thus combining key contact and switch contact in one. Early and less satisfactory examples affected the weight of key touch, ranging it according to the number of couplers in use, but good modern examples made to precision standards avoid this defect.

The most common form in these systems is a roller with a cranked end engaging the back end of the key. Usually the touch weight spring is incorporated with the roller to provide engagement pressure. The roller, of an insulating material, has running along its length a contact wire or plate which is connected to a source of action current. The contacts lightly rest against the non-conducting roller, or are drawn just clear by the stop-action mechanism. Rotation of the roller by depression of the key brings the electrically charged part into rubbing and rolling contact with the movable wire contact or contacts, completing the required electrical circuits.

Pedal-action circuits are precisely similar to those of the manuals, but the contact systems must take account of the relatively rougher usage.

A wide range of difference of practice is encountered; from contacts on levers at the pedal toe end where movement is great, to positions under the pedal keys, either midway, or to the rear, where it more nearly equals manual keyboard conditions.

In large instruments where there is much coupling and borrowing, a relay may be substituted to replace or augment the multiple key contacts. There are many forms, from a simple repeater-relay feeding gang-switches, or on the separate wiper-contact method; to highly developed switch-relay systems. In the latter the number of electrical contacts is greatly reduced by electro-mechanical control over the actual relay contacts, they being moved in or out of range of the relay-operated wipers. These relay systems are practically essential on unit-extension instruments of any size.

As has already been pointed out, many requirements of coupler connections involve circuit forms that prevent back-running, i.e. swell to great must not result in great to swell at the same time. In most systems, this is achieved by each coupler circuit being initiated by a separate contact as the key or relay. A reference to the basic circuit drawing (Fig. 17) will show how this is effected. But, when a duplex control of a stop, maybe a major chorus reed, is required to play, say from great and from choir, by which it is subject to sub- and octave-pitch control as well; very complicated and elaborate relays would be required to avoid back circuits. Fortunately, the basic shape of chest magnets allows space enough to receive two separate windings, each electrically sufficient in itself to excite fully the magnetic core. By connecting each winding to one manual circuit, no back circuit is possible. Up to four windings have been quite successfully applied in this way, and the student of electrical circuits will find that many interesting variants and combinations are possible, and most have been used in one way or another.

In recent times, benefiting by components developed to commercial requirements of the electronics industries, small rectifiers have become available. One of these tiny units incorported into each circuit line, will make it undirectional, as it allows a useful current to flow in one direction only; blocking any back circuit flow very much as a clack-valve does in the early pneumatic designs. Working diagram (Fig. 18) illustrates this. Combined with more robust key contacts, new systems of organ-action circuitry are being developed.

In some action designs, the main chest pneumatic has its surplus effort put to use to move a wiper engaging contacts, repeating its movement by means of fresh electrical circuits to off-note chests, and

ELECTRO-PNEUMATIC ACTIONS

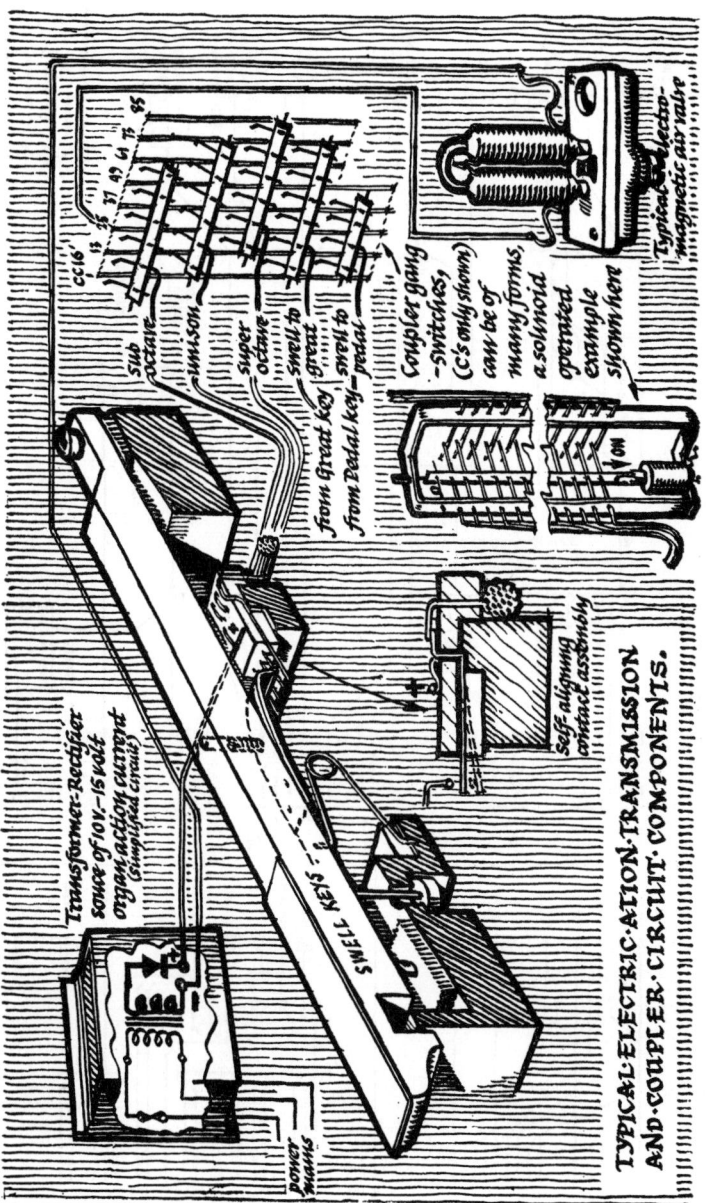

Fig. 17

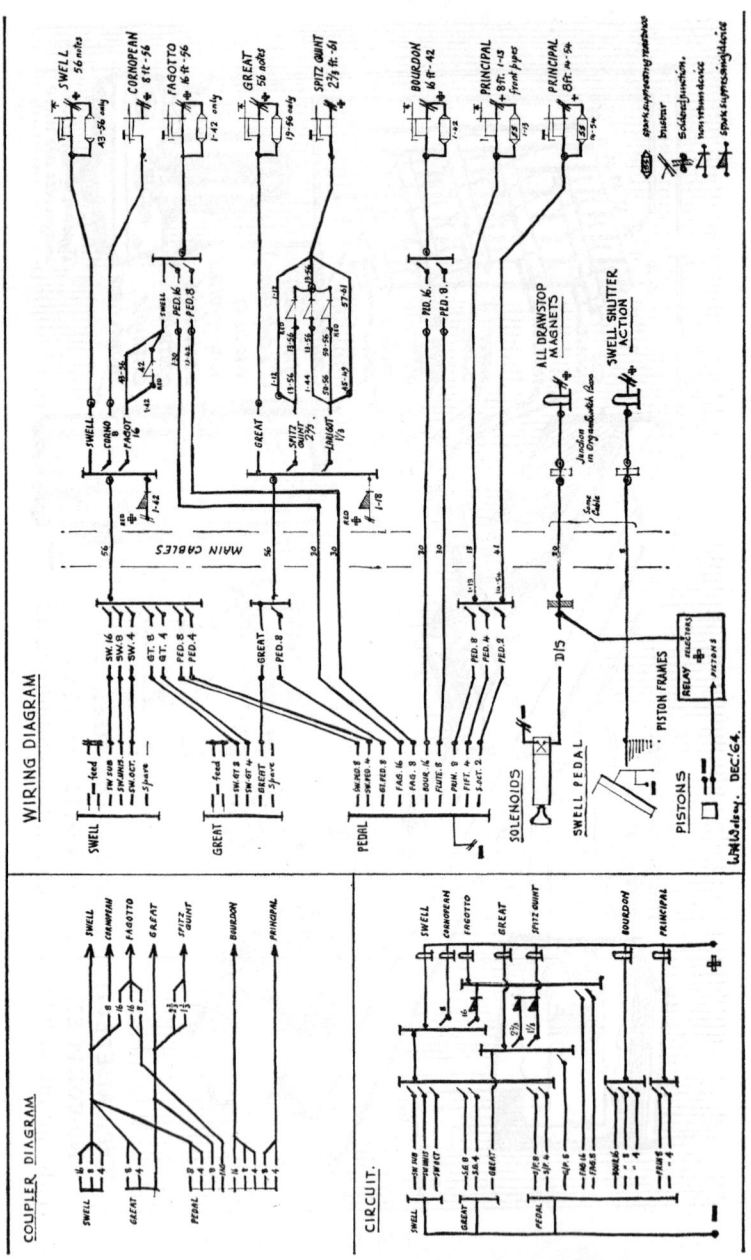

Fig. 18. All Saints Church, Crowborough. Action diagrams

borrows or duplexes. This is simple and convenient, but unless well designed and regulated, the pneumatic relay introduces a tiny time-lag that could appear as lack of synchronization between main and borrowed notes. This non-synchronization is very evident when as in some rather commercial designs, a contact device is placed on the windchest, in place of the off-chest pipe.

Probably before these words are in print, the components of the world of electronics and the computer, will have made some of the foregoing outdated. Action circuits comprising rectifiers, resistors and semi-conductors are off the drawing-board and in the prototype stage. Greater reliability, compactness and in the long run, lower costs are the goal. In this development United Kingdom designers are leading.

The direct-electric action

The direct electric action is the only system truly described as electric, though electro-pneumatic is most commonly so called. In direct electric, not only coupling and transmission is without intervention of any other form of power, but also, the action of opening the pipe-valve is electro-magnetic. This has not been over widely used, but Wicks (U.S.A.), Compton, and to a lesser extent, Austin (U.S.A.), Mander and Hill have used it for particular applications, if not as standard.

It might be supposed that the apparent simplicity of the system would result in it superseding all others, but complications and limitations are revealed in actual practice. Electro-magnets large enough to pull the main pallet-valves of bar and slider windchests cannot be readily built into the narrow spacing between the treble notes, and the heavy iron armatures have considerable inertia, both mechanical and electrical. More successful applications have been made with the more compact single pipe-valve units in a sliderless-type chest, for unit-extension organs, where a pallet-per-pipe action is an essential requirement.

Except for the very small pallet-valves required for small treble pipes on low wind-pressures, the direct magnet pull of any ordinary horseshoe magnet is quite unsuitable. The initial 'pluck' caused by the chest air-pressure, which is diminished as the pipefoot becomes charged, demands a magnet having a high initial pull; the very reverse of a direct-pull magnet which is strongest when the armature is almost on to the pole-ends. The required characteristic is obtained by the 'hook-lever' magnet form. The greatest pull, is when the armature is just beginning to cover the pole, then, as it continues, the pull decreases, so matching the lessening work to be done.

These direct electric pallet-magnet units must of necessity, require much more electric current than the small chest-magnet actions. The considerable number involved in even a modest-size instrument will require much larger low-voltage current sources; generous cable sizes to match, and a system that avoids overloading and burning of the key contacts. Not an easy matter except in the smaller instruments.

Direct electric action has a special advantage in small churches and auditoria in its relative quietness in working, arising from its complete enclosure within a stoutly constructed windchest, and by the fact that only as many units work as there are stops drawn. Thus unlike pneumatics, the action is least quiet when the organ is being played loudly. The reduction in the number of moving parts as compared to pneumatics is a useful contribution to troublefree working and a stimulant to further development.

When viewed from the highest quality standards, these electro-magnet units still leave room for care and know-how in their application. Development is directed particularly to electrical efficiency, towards reducing the weight and inertia of the magnetic parts to give more rapid repetition, and also to reduce coil heat, which may in the aggregate raise the pipewind temperatures to the detriment of fine tuning. These factors are of small account where low power, low wind-pressure units are used, but they do limit their use on normal or high wind-pressure stops on large instruments.

The availability of air-pressure, and the light weight of pneumatic parts leading to quick and quiet working will remain a powerful competitor for direct electric actions. This despite the latter's possibility of attractive low cost arising from highly standardized components in large quantity production by specialists.

Contacts and Cables

Much of the present-day reliability of electric actions is due to the successful development of electrical contact materials and design details suited to the exacting conditions and the inevitably infrequent servicing.

Organ key contacts have presented the biggest design problem, they must be as near as silent in working as metal to metal impact allows; have good air corrosion resistance; and withal, no sensation of mechanical working should be felt when depressing a key. Early examples attempted to meet these conditions with cups of mercury, wires of gold, platinum or dental silver, extruded tungsten filaments or phosphor-bronze spring contacts. Today, wire contacts in a self-aligning and self-adjusting mounting, often in plastics, are of standard silver, a pure silver alloyed with a tiny percentage of copper to give it the necessary resilience while retaining a fair degree of tarnish resistance and low electrical resistance of the oxidized surface. A few builders still use phosphor-bronze, but it is not generally suitable unless unusually high contact-tension is possible and it is quite unsuitable where salt laden or chemically tainted air can be expected to condense on the wire. Owing to the relatively light contact tension that is possible in organ actions, some self-cleaning frictional movement is desirable. Also careful consideration of the electrical polarity of the different contact elements has to be taken into consideration in durable and dependable design; a matter too complex to go into here.

Organ action cables have much in common with telephone cables; indeed much that is used is of the same specification. In early days, double cotton covering was the insulation, but the wax binding made it attractive to hungry rats in under-floor runs. Enamel covering and lead casing later made it tougher for rougher conditions. More recently, tinned copper, which facilitates good soldered joints, is covered in brightly code-coloured P.V.C. (Polyvynyl-chloride, a tough thermoplastic) and sheathed overall again in P.V.C. This is proof against rough handling, vermin, damp, and the pernicious chemistry of the church cleaner's soapy water, seeping down under floors to the cable running out of sight.

The possibilities of the use of printed circuits for durability and simplification by compactness, are being examined. Already they are in use in the electronic organ field for nearly similar uses.

The length of an electric organ action cable has no practical limit and it does not detrimentally affect the action response, any delayed response experienced is due to the speed of sound.

Drawstop Action mechanisms

When considering manual and pedal actions we should include stop control or drawstop actions, as in essence they are the same as the key actions, except that they are more powerful and less critical as to speed of working. The action to drawstop-sliders of a bar and slider windchest, requires a powerful pneumatic, triggered by a tubular or electric transmission, and equipped with a relay chain to step up to requisite power and pace.

In the early days of electrical transmission, the sustained current flow when a stop was drawn 'on' caused a serious drain on the limited current capacity of the primary batteries then commonly used. To avoid this, not too reliable cut-out circuits were contrived, cutting off current flow after the required movement had been made. This device offers an opportunity to provide a 'stop-switch' registrational aid, a valuable facility where the combination controls were sparsely provided. Examples may still be encountered. When the 'stop-switch' was put into operation, no current flowed in stop action circuits for either 'on' or 'off'; therefore while the original setting shown on the stop keys was held in use, a new setting could be prepared and held inoperative until the 'stop-switch' was returned to normal, and current flowed to affect the new combination.

More recently, designs for powerful electric solenoids have been developed, that can move a soundboard slider unaided by pneumatic power. These are useful when, for instance, a tracker-actioned organ requires barely 2 in. wind-pressure, too weak for power purposes and it is wasteful and sometimes noisy to raise a small volume to a more useful level. These will almost certainly be used more in the future.

Current trends

At the time of writing, actions are being made tracker, tubular-pneumatic, electro-pneumatic and direct electric, but mostly electro-pneumatic.

If one's approach to the organ demands simplicity of playing aids, no more than the minimum of unison couplers, a sense of expressive touch and intimate control, and with all that, the playing skill to match, then tracker action could be the answer, as is so widely the case in Denmark and Holland today. But we cannot expect low cost. It demands planning skill, and craftsmanship of the highest order. Inevitably it must very largely be made to measure. If this is not to be wasted, the pipes and voicing must be on an equally imaginative and creative level. Tracker action is not the answer to the quest for a low-cost organ.

For even weight of touch, a wide choice of couplers, a detached console position and a freedom of layout, for ease of duplexing and, unit-extension control where required—then electro-pneumatic it must be. Some parts, however, could be direct electric. The economies possible with volume production of electrical parts ensures competitive cost with other systems.

Tubular-pneumatic is still made, usually where a very simple action replacement or extension is required, such as replacing a worn tracker pedal action, but some complete actions have been made for special circumstances which seem to justify its use. In most cases, cost is as much, or more than electric, and higher standards of timber craftsmanship are essential. It is also more sensitive to faulty working in climatic extremes arising with modern church heating.

For most purposes of general church service accompaniment and where non-professional players must be considered, modern electro-pneumatic mechanisms most often meet the practical needs and the economics of the situation.

7

The Windchests

WINDCHESTS, or in organ-builders' parlance, soundboards, are in essence a table, upon which the pipes of a stop or stops are arranged in an orderly manner, having regard to acoustic considerations and to the technical requirements of individual air supply. It must provide control by note and an over-riding control by rank or stop.

In Roman times, it was a table, with a few holes in it, from which air continuously gushed and into which the organ-players thrust pipes as required. Devising means to control the air flow from crude keys, lead to the fist-playing 'organ-thumper'. This terminology prevailed for a long time; as much later even J. S. Bach described himself in all seriousness as 'Pulsator Organorium'. In time the bar and slider windchest was developed. It has been the most widely used, and is still being produced with a renewed appreciation of its qualities.

The bar and slider chest

This is a complex piece of joinery, requiring matured, high quality timbers, and craftsmanship of a high order. Essentially it is a timber grid, having as many interstices between the timber bars as there are notes in the compass of the stops to be mounted thereon, i.e., 58, 61, 68 or 73 pipes per stop (Fig. 19).

On the top side of the grid, a slab of timber or 'table', seals the interstices, that thus form windways; it is similarly made airtight on the underside, except where an air inlet valve or 'pallet' is placed. All the pipes required to be sounded by the CC key are placed upon the table with holes communicating with the CC windway, and so on with each note of the compass. A windchest encloses the pallet-valves. So much for the 'bar' part of the bar and slider chest. When the CC pallet is opened, by any convenient means, all the CC pipes thereon would sound, fed with wind in the common-bar windway. Some further mechanism is required to give stop selection. This device is the slider. Over the table, a veneer about $\frac{3}{16}$ in. thick is placed, usually consisting

THE WINDCHESTS

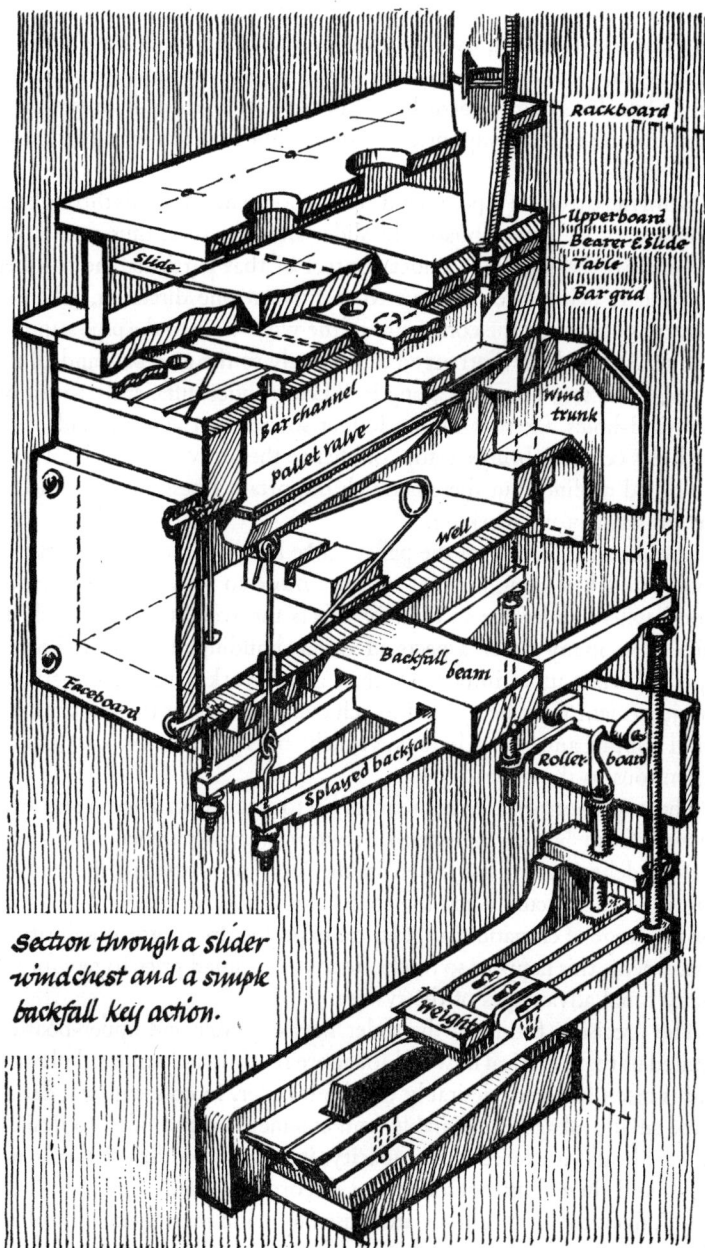

Section through a slider windchest and a simple backfall key action.

Fig. 19

of timber strips. Alternate ones are secured to the table, so that those between are free to move lengthwise. These are the 'sliders'. Above these again, there is another timber table, but not this time a continuous slab. These longitudinal boards are known as the 'upper-boards'. Upon these, the pipes stand supported in an upright position by a perforated rackboard.

From the tip of the pipe, a wind-hole is bored downwards through the three layers, the upper-board, the slider and the table; thus connecting the pipe to the windway under control of that particular note-pallet. The slider, being free to move to and fro in one direction, when so moved will destroy the continuity of the wind-hole to the pipe standing over it. As the slider is arranged transversely to the grid bars and all the pipes of one stop arranged along it, when it slides sufficiently to cut off the wind-holes, the stop can no longer sound. Drawing the slide until the holes coincide brings a stop 'on' hence the 'drawstop knob'. This is the broad outline; but there is much important finesse of detail necessary to satisfactory working.

The size and placing of the pallet-valve has an important bearing on good windchest design and at no time more so than in tracker action work, where pallet size so directly affects the weight of key touch. In this, as in many other aspects of organ-building, the know-how is equally, if not more important, than good workmanship. Experience and judgment must be applied to achieve proportions that yield ample wind supply and yet a light keytouch, over-caution on one can be calamitous to the other.

The stop-control sliders sometimes fail to slide, to stick from excessive friction from becoming nipped between warping upper-boards and the windchest table; too often in the 'on', or worse, in the half-on position. This occurs when the chests are in poor order or ill-designed for the range of climatic changes to be expected. In the great majority of instruments this happens so rarely, and is but a small price to pay for the many tonal advantages of the system.

The precision fitting of the slider between table and upper-board is limited to that practical in wood (or more recently in laminated plastics) and is often and very desirably of a high order. In conventional design some small leakage is inevitable, and channels are provided to drain it away. Should it exceed their capacity, it leaks into other channels and pipes, and these faint unbidden and discordant sounds are called 'runnings', from the fact that they are caused by wind running uncontrolled. Here again good design and the use of materials allowing more precise fitting can avoid this defect. Recent design trends are towards a resilient

THE WINDCHESTS

assembly almost eliminating leakage and excessive friction from tight fitting.

The critics of bar and slider chests refer to 'robbing' as an inherent defective characteristic. Certainly this is sometimes evident as a lack of firm in-tuneness when a chorus of many ranks stand together on one chest, say ten or more. It is often present in some otherwise admirable antique instruments. The cause is well known, and careful design can reduce it to well below the minimum tolerable to cultivated ears.

Energy is expended in causing air to flow through a valve and along a channel, and this is measurable as a gradual loss of pressure until it finally loses all on emerging from the pipe-mouth. The loss of pressure in the windchest bar channel is related to the rate of flow, so that the pressure applied at the tips of the pipes is not constant, but must vary slightly according to the number of stops supplied at any given time. A wind-hungry stop at the farthest point along the bar from the pallet-valve, can greatly affect the pressure at intermediate stops, if the channel and valve are not of sufficient and suitable proportions.

By limiting the number and character of the stops fed from one pallet-valve, this ill-effect can be avoided. The number varies as between four and nine ranks, according to scale, form and wind-pressure. The higher the wind-pressure, the less critical is the need to limit the number of stops; but other problems then arise, such as getting rid of the expanding air when the pallet-valve closes. Harmonic 4-ft. flutes and piccolos will continue to speak, to 'hang on' appreciably using expanding air alone, if the bar-channel is too large and the pressure high.

In exceptional conditions of extreme climatic dryness when the timber has not been correctly prepared, the table panel, tightly glued to the grid, will shrink until the stress can no longer be contained. Then surface cracks and long splits occur. These provide wind channels that connect the neighbouring notes. This becomes very serious if the notes sound partially, but sliders may stick. This is a sign of serious and deep-seated damage. It might be thought, and is not infrequently said, that if well-seasoned timber was used, such faults could not happen. While design and timber selection can ensure a high tolerance of climatic change, it is a myth that 'properly seasoned timber' does not shrink or swell and the resulting construction is necessarily faultless. Good timber helps, but good design is also essential.

It will be seen that there are difficulties. When the conditions are known and all practical precautions taken to minimize an excessive range of humid or dry conditions, it is possible to design bar and slider chests of great reliability and satisfying technical qualities. The Danish and Dutch organ-builders have demonstrated this. Currently some British-made slider chests are proving resistant to the exceptionally wide temperature and humidity range experienced in the very comfortably heated churches of North America. In their winter seasons timbers become not merely dry but desiccated.

The Sliderless Chests

The organ-builders of the mid-nineteenth century found that the larger and heavier pipes of the newly introduced pedal organs caused the windchest sliders to stick and to be difficult to manage. So they devised the ventil chest, in which a separate pallet-valve is provided to each pipe. Each set, or stop, had a separate section of the windchest; the pallets of like notes being connected by links, so all move as one. By controlling the wind supply to each stop windway by means of a ventil-valve operated by the drawstop knob, stop control was obtained without the use of sliders. The more generous spacing necessary with pedal organ pipes, and the less critical nature of the weight of pedal touch made this simple construction acceptable.

The sensitivity of the traditional complex joinery constructions of the slider chest, to wide changes of atmospheric humidity, and the coming of reliable pneumatic action, led to a desire to produce a chest with greater use of mechanical tools, as an assembly of repetition parts. Thus the development of the sliderless forms of manual windchest was prompted in the U.S.A. and continental Europe, but principally in Germany. They take many distinctive forms each having some special character.

The cone-valve chest

The cone-valve or kegellade chest (Fig. 20) was widely used in Germany and is still made by at least one builder in the British Isles. Each pipe has its own note valve of streamlined, self-aligning form, lifted open by external pneumatic means, usually an inflatable pneumatic motor, puffer or leather envelope, arranged upon a common pneumatic windway, so that all those connected to say, middle C, move in concert. Chests of this design must by necessity of its detail, be of considerable size and so provide spacious pipe layout. The large number of moving parts tends towards noisy working when playing but one quiet stop.

Fig. 20

The Roosevelt chest

With the use of higher pipe wind-pressures the pipe-valve opening pneumatics became incorporated inside the windchest; the most common form at first being the Roosevelt motor pallet-valve unit, named after its American originator. Stop action being by ventil-wind control, this formed a neat, quick and quiet acting windchest with short pipe windways.

The pouch-pallet chest

In the same classification came the later pouch-pallet chest (Fig. 21), widely used by the leading American builders, and at least one in England. The directness of the pipe-valve immediately under the pipe-tip, benefited reeds and the dull tones of heavier pressure voicing, but with a return to moderate and low wind-pressures and appropriate voicing techniques, these chests have little to commend them except simplicity and reliability, no mean merits of course.

The Pitman stop action

An important invention in sliderless chest design was the 'pitman' stop-action valve. A tiny light-weight moving part that is simple, silent and quick acting. When the stop is required to speak, the stop action windway or groove is at atmospheric pressure and the pitmans are held down against their seatings by wind-pressure in the note action groove. In this position reduction of pressure in this groove will allow the pipe-wind to collapse the pallet motors or pouches. The required pipes will then speak.

Should the stop-action groove then be pressure charged, the pitman valve will be impelled upwards, closing the path to the action groove or channel. Stop-action air then passes behind the valve and reinflates the pallet-valve pneumatic, cutting off the sounding note. This is the pitman stop action.

This neat mechanism overcomes a bad feature of these chests when ventil controlled, namely the straining of the pneumatic leathers by full pressure inflation when the pipe-wind is off. The leathers being much of the playing time in this condition, the pores of the fine lambskin acting as air filters become clogged hard and unsupple with dirt. This greatly shortens their useful life.

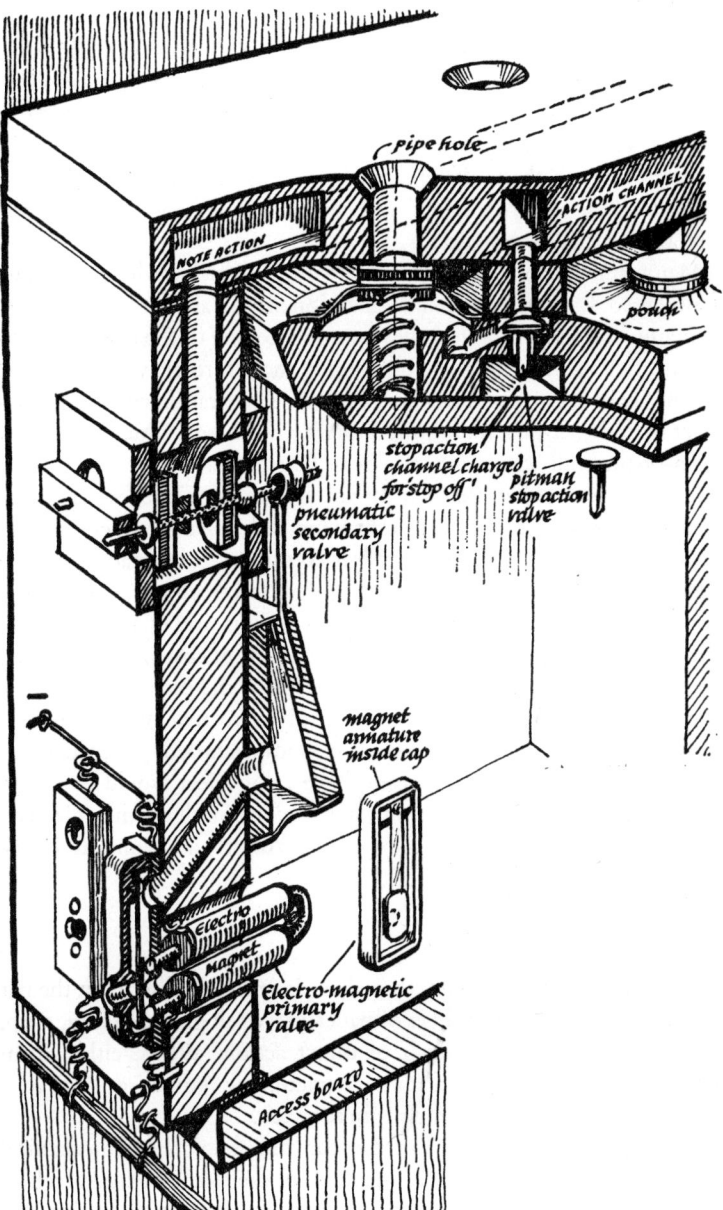

Fig. 21

Direct electric windchests

The increasing availability of precision made electro-magnetic pallet units at attractive economic prices, is producing new designs of windchests. Some are admirable, having low pressure wind supply characteristics, similar to a bar and slider chest. Some others are similar to the purse-pallet type chest, effective for reed stops but poor on critical flue stops, tending towards 'quick' speech that is not conducive to good tone or attractive intonation.

Many minor detail variations of sliderless windchests have been and are still used. Except those in unit-extension organs, and for bass off-tones, all manual or pedal sliderless chests come into one of the above classifications. Before describing and examining them further, we will review the merits of the main windchest designs. They can have a significant effect on the finer points of musical quality, when something more than a run-of-the-mill 'kist-o-whistles' is to be created.

It is a curious thing, that hardly any design of windchest, since the inception of variations from the bar and slider, has gone completely out of date, and almost every design continues to be made by some organ-builder somewhere. It might be deduced from this, that there is really little to choose between the various designs, and that conservative craftsmanship or purely material considerations of cost are the deciding factors. While in a very competitive sector of the craft this might be true, elsewhere careful consideration is given to matching the windchest to the tonal requirements and technical standards adopted.

That economic considerations do have some effect would be idle to deny. In the best work, where high standards of finish are the objective, a good windchest saves much expensive voicers' and tonal finishers' time.

The choice of chest

If tracker action must be used, then there is really no choice but the bar and slider form. Only this form of pallet-valve can give the clean, crisp, and to some, expressive touch of direct action. When, either from choice or consideration of layout, pneumatic power operation is essential, other factors become of importance.

The characteristic qualities of the bar and slider chest, mechanical touch apart, are absolute synchronization in the attack of the speech of all pipes of one note, and prompt speech from a rapidly rising but unexplosive pressure of wind in the bar-windway as the large pallet-valve opens smartly. The big windways possible and the resulting low

THE WINDCHESTS

air speeds, avoid windy or breathy speech and ensure promptness with a wind-pressure as low as 1¼ in. wg. and upwards, to any practical height. These very good and musically valuable qualities are not readily achieved *altogether* in other windchest forms.

The more difficult characteristics are the demands on craftsmanship, the lack of repetition production opportunities, requiring each chest to be expertly and individually designed, and the tendency to be sensitive to climatic conditions when these are changeable over a wide range of atmospheric humidity.

Modern examples by progressive designers are much less distressed and distorted by the extremes of well-heated churches, while they lack none of the traditional and desirable good qualities. No windchest will withstand rainwater through the roof, however well made, and those slider chests made half a century or more ago need very expert conditioning, to continue to serve in the new and drier conditions now widely experienced. Nevertheless it is still one of the best designs when quality is put foremost.

If the slider chest has so much that is good, what of the sliderless, or pallet-valve-per-pipe chest? As a class, because of repetition of a number of similar small parts, they offer possibilities of highly organized production, with the greater use of machine tools. The emphasis is on repetition precision part-making, rather than a craftsman's creation; because the former offers possibilities of lower costs. Lower cost is not to be despised, the organ is a costly instrument, and when the more economic product has the qualities desired for a particular part or section of the whole, then it should be considered. In some designs the structure is also less affected in its function by timber movements due to climatic changes.

When considering pipe speech quality characteristics, these chests belong to two classes; one of which is further subdivided (Fig. 22). They are (1) those with the pallet-valve directly below the pipe-tip; the windway being the shortest and most direct possible, and (2) those where this valve is mounted at some angle below. The windway contains one or more right-angle bends, and in consequence may be quite a number of inches long. This latter class includes two groups: (*a*) those with the pallet-valve operating pneumatically inside the pipe-wind and (*b*) those with it outside and separated from the pipe-wind.

At least one British firm, and almost all North American builders use the pouch-pallet chest, which belongs to the first-mentioned class with short windways. Most builders in England and Australia, and those not dedicated to tracker actions, use a design in the second class; mainly of

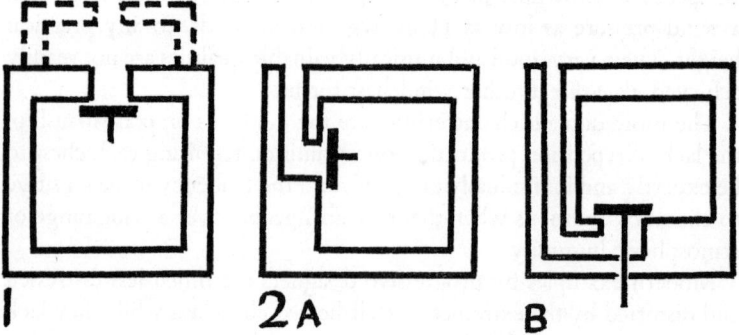

FIG. 22. Wind chests. Pallet valve positions

the edge valve type with internal pneumatics or direct electro-magnetic movements. A few (and many in continental Europe) use the bottom valve board and external pneumatic, the Kegellade chest, with its much longer pipe windway. These three forms, with their marked regional uses have distinctive qualities that affect tone, attack, choice of wind-pressure and voicing style. No one form meets all requirements with equal facility.

Let us take the last mentioned class first. The Kegellade type, because of its essential simplicity, has in the best examples the minimum of moving parts and no springs, as it relies on gravity return. The construction demands the minimum of precision-workmanship, but nevertheless, needs careful design, based upon experience to obtain to the full the several valuable good qualities. The operating pallet-valve pneumatic is outside the pipe-wind chests, and so avoids defective speech from wind-pressure disturbance by rapid movements, and importantly, permits very low pipe-wind pressures. The pneumatic can be inflated with highest wind-pressure available, to give rapid and near-simultaneous action response. These excellent features make it rather more difficult to give quiet working, especially as ventil-type stop-control must be used; which means all the pneumatics to one note must work, even when only one stop is in use.

Pouch or envelope pneumatics are most suitable, and particularly the latter, which can be made to withstand very damp air conditions. The pallet-valve is circular, and in the best examples, conical in section, to give self-centring seating and excellent streamline airflow. The loose fitting stem wire gives an immediate pressure release on the 'off'.

To some extent these good features are counterbalanced by poor accessibility for adjustment or repair. The windway is over-long with from one to three right-angle bends in it. When well designed, however, with generous dimensions, the air is delivered to the pipe-tip with a reasonably low level of turbulence as is essential to prompt firm speech attack. It is not a compact form when well made, but this is not a bad thing in most respects when space is available. In summing up, one finds the Kegellade chest is a simple form of windchest with some special advantages on low wind-pressures (when the alternative slider chests are not adopted) and when ample space in length and width can be afforded.

The very commonly used pouch-pallet valve chest of America is also made by one or two firms in England. Its manufacture is highly specialized, although in appearance, deceptively simple. The basic craftsmanship is concentrated in the thick slab 'table' which besides being perforated with the pipe wind-holes has long 'note' grooves running between them, from front to back edge, one for each note. Each groove must be airtight to its neighbour, and careful design and setting out is very necessary to prevent climatic conditions splitting the timbers and destroying this essential requirement.

The detail of these chests is very accessible and the rarely needed adjustment or repair is greatly facilitated. Good layout of pipes is possible without costly or undesirable grooving; indeed the action space often exceeds pipe space, so that the chests tend to be rather large in consequence. This matter of space, influences the design in another way; the size of the leather pouch in relation to the pallet determines the lowest wind-pressure upon which it will work with certainty, normally, this is not less than 3 in. Lower working pressure would call for very large diameter pouches. Besides demanding very large chests indeed these would involve other pneumatic complications, so that the chests are not at all suited to neo-classical low-pressure-voiced pipes.

The fact that the pallet-valve is directly beneath the pipe-tips, a little more than an inch away, is of no detriment to reeds which benefit from the sharp pressure attack characteristic. String tones on heavier winds up to 6 in. wg. do not mind, but the more delicate attack and speech of diapasons, principals and flutes on lower wind-pressure is much disturbed by the turbulent and concussive air flow in the small space a short distance below the tip. Introduction of an individual air expansion chamber of fairly critical size, minimizes this unhappy effect, but it involves complicated construction. Stop action may be either by ventil, cutting off the wind to the appropriate section of the chest, or by pitman valves as already described. The pitman control is superior, as under ventil conditions the pouches are inflated when the stop is off. This shortens the useful life of the leather and strains the glue jointing as mentioned before.

In general this is a good, reliable and durable chest, standing up to wide climatic changes when artfully made, but it is most suitable for the medium and high range of wind-pressures.

Another class, is the side-valve type, based upon Roosevelt's original design, but not necessarily using his precise form of pneumatic motor and pallet unit, although in essence they are the same system. This type is widely used, as the construction, while not as simple as the others, is of a more convenient size, having no heavy assemblies like a one-piece table. Pipe space requirements, rather than size of action parts, controls the overall dimensions of this windchest. Because the pallet-valve is not immediately below the pipe-tip and several inches of straight airway must intervene, the air supply is smoothed and less turbulent on reaching the pipe, so that when properly designed, there is an inherent beneficial expansion chamber.

Because the pipe pressure air also provides the pallet-valve opening power, there is a downward limit below which action may become uncertain. It is not quite as critical as in the pouch-pallet chest, but spatial and other limitations become difficult below $2\frac{1}{4}$ wg. pressure.

Access is good, ventil or pitman valve stop-action may be used, the latter being superior for the reason already described. The inherent large volume of air in the windchest as a whole, tends towards a steady and concussionless wind-pressure.

Clearly this class of chest, when made to obtain the advantages outlined, is a very good general purpose design, and its popularity amongst builders is well founded.

Off-note chests

The space required by the larger bass note pipes, arising from their body dimensions and the need for 'speaking room' around the sound-generating mouth, has always made their accommodation on the main windchest a matter of spatial difficulty. Their suitability as a frontal screen has lead to the common practice of setting them up apart from their upper notes. In many cases the bass pipes are best when so arranged and would be inferior if standing on the windchest, if that is not of bar and slider type.

Formerly, air was supplied from the main windchest pallet-valve via the stop-action slider and conveyed by lead-metal 'conveyances' or tubes, mitred at bends and often many feet in length. On low windpressures and with suitably voiced pipes the resulting speech is prompt and firm, free from windyness because of the absence of excessive turbulence.

In older instruments long wooden grooved boards, sometimes two or more 6 ft. to 8 ft. long, were used and with excellent results. A Father Willis pedal violone formerly conveyed 20 ft. in such a manner was later placed upon direct winded chests in a casework reconstruction. This resulted in a troublesome loss of speech attack, until the qualities of well-planned and well-made conveyancing were appreciated, in its absence.

In recent times, a handy wire-foil-and-paper flexible tube has become available, adapted from the electrical industries, and is a tempting substitute for such mitred rigid conveyancing; but it must be used in larger sizes and of sparing length as it has high resistance to air flow. Poor attack from wind starvation can all too readily result.

With the coming of tubular pneumatics and the freedom they gave to layout planning, small diameter tubular connections from the windchest upper-board and slider were substituted for conveyances. These worked a simple pneumatic-actioned bass note pipe chest; but not always with quality advantages. These chests are built like a miniature bar-chest but without sliders, having primary and main pneumatic. In some cruder low cost examples, the primary is omitted. They are quite critical to design and cannot be inexpensive, indeed attention to prompt repetitive speech in bass notes usually distinguishes between the commercial and the quality builder.

The larger pipes associated with pedal departments nearly always call for separate pallet-valves, one to each pipe (Fig. 23). The simple and safe stop-action control by means of a ventil-valve applying or cutting off wind supply is readily usable in simple circumstances. It is not therefore surprising that the earliest and crudest efforts at tubular pneumatic action were applied to pedal pipes. Today some neat combined pallet units are used by some of the more expert builders. In the larger sizes these contain exhaust pneumatic primary and secondary relay movements and generous pouch main pneumatic with a highly efficient slot-shaped pallet-valve. Repair of these is only a matter of quick removal and replacement with spare units.

The more conventional integral pneumatic forms are in essence, only variants of the basic idea of an internal pneumatic motor bellows, collapsing with the air-pressure around it and dragging a hinged

Fig. 23

pallet-valve with it. These can be either circular, square-moving, oblong, or oversize versions of Roosevelt's hinger windchest pneumatic.

Even very large pedal pipes require a smooth air flow, low in turbulence, and so the best designs have either very large pallet-valves, or the effective equivalent of an expansion chamber between pallet and pipe-tip. Pedal stops of 4-ft. pitch and upwards, can be conveniently mounted on any form of sliderless type chest. If they are independent and not 'extended', a superior synchronous attack is obtained from bar and slider chests or from the better designs of electro-magnetic pallet chests.

Besides bass notes, top notes sometimes have to be catered for separately, as when the manual compass is extended in reconstruction work. Curiously this is not easily done, and all too rarely it is well done. These tiny pipes are very critical of the steadiness of the wind supply and very audibly object to the slightest tremor. This is all too easily generated by the amount of mechanism in so small a volume of compressed air as in the usually tiny windchest. In addition to this, a long narrow wind trunk adds its own sag and surge, and a sorry whimper sounds, where there should be firm clear voice. The development of simple electro-magnetic valve units for this purpose has greatly simplified the task, but some skill is still required to apply them so that compass extension goes undetected at the keys.

Unit extension chests

In the unit organ or for the single extended rank, where one or more octave extension or unison duplexing (i.e. playing from another manual) is required, a separate pipe-valve action is necessary for every pipe. It has been done by tubular pneumatic means, but usually electro-pneumatic or more recently a combination of that and electro-magnetic is the most convenient system.

The smallest pipes or those requiring but a small volume of air can be fed directly from what is an adapted chest magnet. Larger demands involve larger magnet-valve units, or pneumatic pallet-valve units of pouch-pallet or Roosevelt pattern with a chest magnet as a primary relay. Larger volume still makes necessary a primary pneumatic relay between magnet and main pneumatic. Thus in 'extension' work there is as much action to each pipe, though a little smaller in scale, as to each note on a 'straight' organ windchest.

The actual form varies very widely, from variants of the Roosevelt, to pouch-pallet, but all are the same in working principle. The electro-magnet pipe-pallet unit, now widely available from trade part makers, greatly simplifies unit-extension chest construction within the capacity of the units available, but at the cost of much increased electrical power consumption with all its implications and complications.

As in the similarly fashioned sliderless windchest, the design problem is to obtain a concussionless wind supply and good speech attack characteristics; and the same methods are used, ample wind volume, large wind trunks and a good streamlined shape in the pipe windway.

A feature that all sliderless chests claim, is a greater stability of tuning. In most forms there is little possibility of variation in the individual wind supply to each pipe from variation in leakage losses. This is an advantage over the older forms of slider chests; when in bad condition, leakage at the slider results in pressure loss, causing individual pipes to lose pitch.

Ultra-low-wind-pressure chests

Where antique classical style tones and speech are required from the tipless pipes voiced on the flue regulation technique, on the appropriate slight wind-pressure, no other design of windchest has the same equality and firmness of wind supply to the mouth of the pipe as the bar and slider chest. No other chest assures synchronous speech or is so little embarrassed by low pressures, or so clear cut in stop action effect without wind concussion. It is not the cheapest windchest and it needs critical designing, but after more than three centuries, perhaps much longer, it is still a very good solution to the problem of windchest design. Some recent direct electric pallet chests of sophisticated design and limited size are offering a close challenge to the supremacy of the bar and slider.

Planting the stops on the chest

The planning or planting of the pipes on a windchest involves a lot of know-how, something more is called for than providing sufficient speaking room for each pipe. Surprisingly small space is required for this alone. The fact that in all 'straight' organ windchest systems, pipes of like keynote stand in line, introduces sympathetic interference between like notes of different stop ranks. In closely planted chests it is possible to tune a note by adjusting the tuning means of a neighbouring pipe. Under such conditions firm tuning in chords becomes impossible and very great skill is needed to obtain an acceptable compromise tuning. It influences windchest design in the following way.

Planting the pipes in chromatic order CC to top C in line, will pass only if all are widely spaced, especially in the lower octaves. Satisfactory examples are often 10 ft. long. It is best avoided unless ample space is available.

A better and commonly adopted arrangement, is division into C and C♯ 'sides' of alternate notes, starting with CC at one end and CC♯ at the other, or starting with the low note in the centre and falling away to top notes at each end of the chest. In this way there is a whole tone difference between neighbouring pipes in the same stop. Bass notes in the chest centre may make tuning access difficult, being now used only occasionally for display but formerly much used in swell organs. Tracker-action windchests are influenced by mechanical considerations and usually are planted chromatically from tenor C or G upwards, the lower notes being divided at either end of the chest.

So much for interference within a stop, but equally important is the avoidance of speech interference or 'sympathy' between like notes in neighbouring stops. To overcome this, stops of like pitch, of similar scale or tone family must be kept apart, interspersed with stops of at least different pitch or body length. Flute tones must be spaced apart, almost regardless of pitch. All this is of special importance to those stops commonly played together and none more so than the unison and undulating rank of a celeste. The gently undulating quality in the middle and lower octaves when accurately tuned depends, strange as it seems, on avoiding sympathetic interference that occurs when 'planted' close together.

8
Raising the Wind

THE pipe organ is a wind instrument, its powers of speech spring from a supply of air under mild compression; a requirement that varies in almost direct proportion to the volume of sound produced. This varying demand has to be met instantly, without jolt or sag in pressure, and without audible fuss. This has always resulted in some elegant examples of organ engineering.

Very early examples were simple force pumps, allied to water pump practice, but as early organ-builders were close in craftsmanship to the blacksmith, the organ bellows took on a similar form to the forge-bellows; a lung like device of leather upon a collapsible frame. Lifted open, air entered through simple automatic flap valves, then it was allowed to fall, closed by gravity acting on the weighted top, lightly compressing the contents. There were usually a pair of these bellows.

Passing through many developments, the pair of bellows evolved— one as a storage reservoir, and the other, called the feeder, to fill the reservoir. With refinements of construction, the feeders were usually set up in pairs, so that one was feeding while the other was reinflating (Fig. 24). In this form many examples still exist, although almost all are now only in stand-by use in case the supplanting rotary fan blower should be lacking its electric mains supply for the driving motor.

More elaborate forms had multiple feeders connected to a wheel and crank system, usually three, sometimes five feeders, feeding in turn and so giving a smoother supply. In the late nineteenth century, an early power source in the form of the gas engine, fed from the town gas mains was applied. Later, paraffin and petrol engines were used. As the rising bellows-reservoir filled, it cut off the unwanted power by the crude but effective device of slipping the driving belt on to a loose pulley, and back again to the driving crankshaft, when the demand again depleted the reservoir. When electric motor drive was introduced at the turn of the century, it allowed speed control and introduced a much wanted element of quietness. Many of these installations were fine pieces of engineering and of impressive appearance when at work.

Another and more elegant system peculiar to the organ parallelled

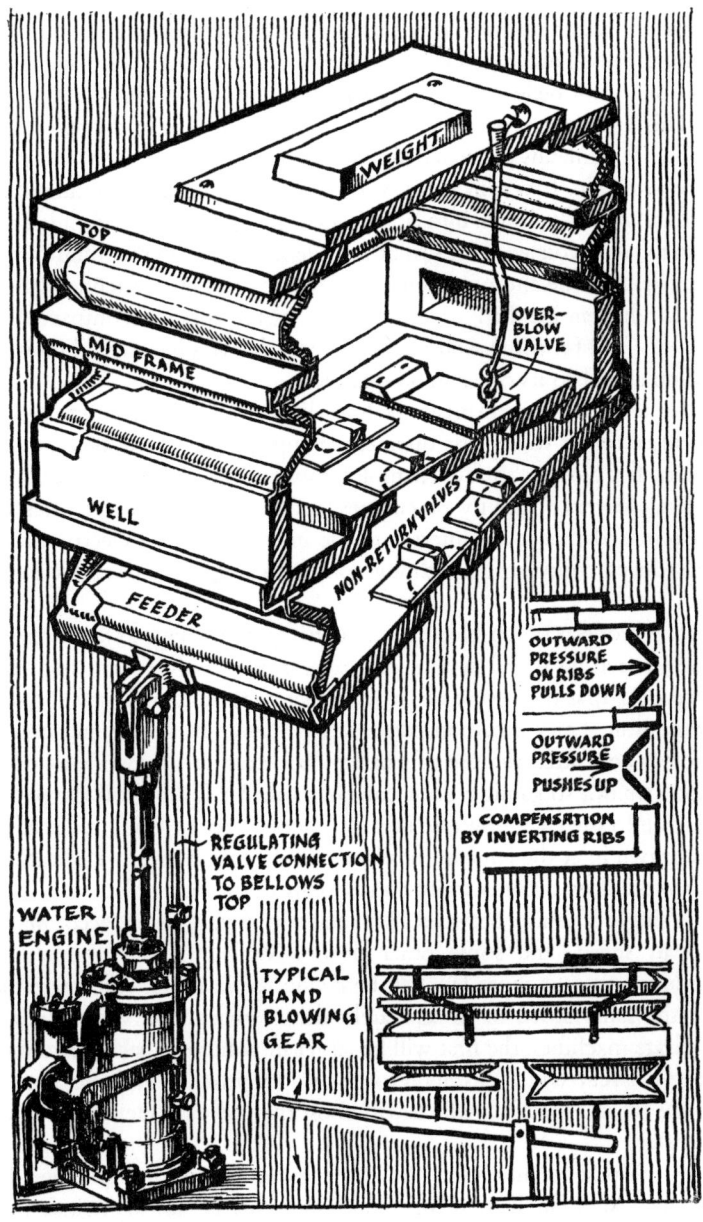

Fig. 24

this development—the application of hydraulic pressure from the domestic water mains to drive a reciprocating piston-engine of simple robust form. This was connected, in effect, to the normal blowing lever, and the rising bellows-top turned a water-tap for control.

This excellent system has almost passed out of use, the increasing domestic demands on water supplies having depressed the water pressure available. It was in many ways an ideal system. A volume of air was unhurriedly drawn into large feeders, gently compressed and passed into the reservoir without fuss or turbulence, and with the minimum of temperature rise and pulsation. After many years of unattended labour when the engine had become worn, water spray accompanied its labours, and for some well-heated organs, this was beneficial humidification added to its other good qualities.

Feeder gear was surprisingly long lived, but it was bulky and its eventual repair was costly, often exceeding the cost of the alternative, a rotary fan blower, so few examples now exist in working order.

Fan blowers driven by gas engines had a brief existence that often left an unmistakable sooty interior to the instrument. The electric motor introduced compactness, although not at first the very desirable quietness.

The modern organ blower is a centrifugal fan (Fig. 25). It is essentially a paddle-wheel within enclosing rims revolved at a high tip-speed. At first they were of large diameters turning at a low speed of revolution. Later precision construction, better balancing and quieter motors permitted the use of smaller diameters, at speeds approaching 3,000 r.p.m., so gaining great compactness. Air is flung off the paddle vanes into the enclosing case in a continuous stream, being replaced by air drawn in at the fan axis, until an equilibrium of pressure is reached. Then the flow automatically corresponds to the demands.

A single fan raises between 2½ in. and 7 in. wg. pressure, according to tip air speed, and some other details. When higher pressures are required, two or more fans can be connected in series, either together on the same shaft, or as separately driven machines. When built as separate machines, the first will be larger in volume capacity, and most of its delivery will be taken off for use at low pressure, and a part passed to the second machine which will boost the pressure. Hence the name, Booster.

In the past twenty years the efficiency and operating quietness has reached very high standards, and particularly so in British-built machines. The smaller sizes, within thick plywood sound-resisting cabinets, utilize rockwool or similar sound absorbing materials so that

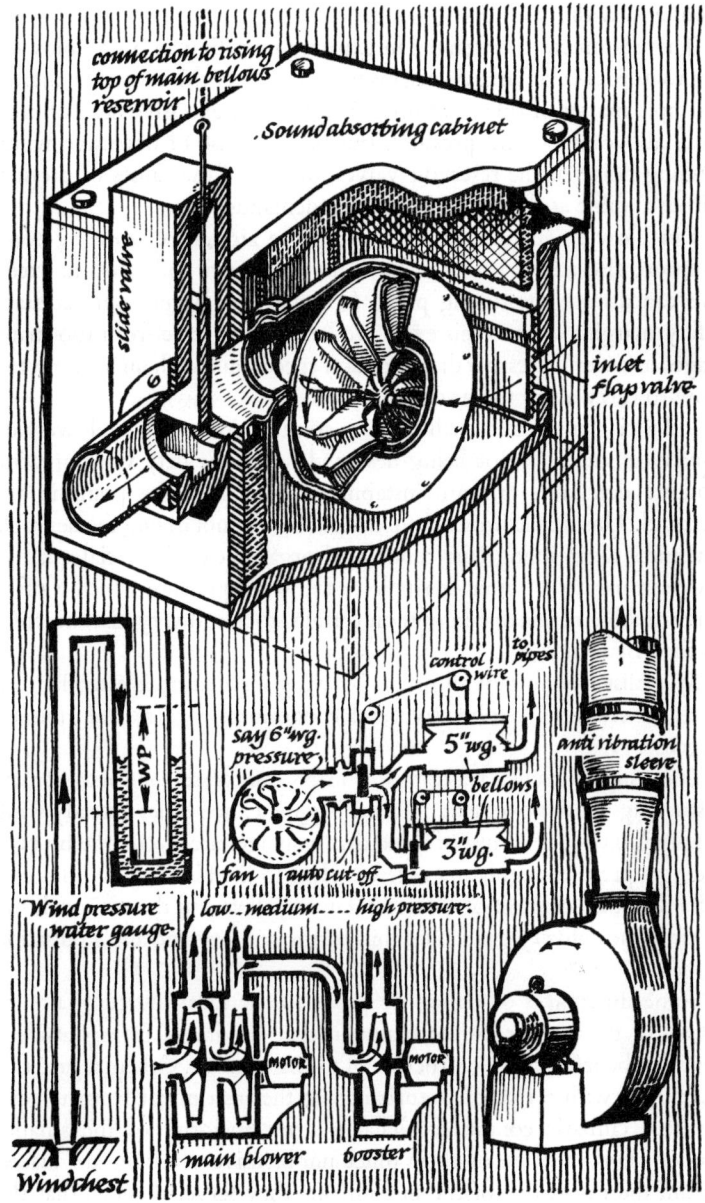

FIG. 25

they can often stand beside or within the smaller organs in open positions and without obtrusive noise.

There is much to be gained in expertly matching an organ-blowing fan to its particular task. As organs vary so widely this cannot be merely a simple matter of rule of thumb. A fan raising excessive head of pressure, above pipe-wind pressure, can be the cause of obtrusive wind-rushing noises at the reservoir valves, or one of the causes of pressure dither audible at the pipes on staccato demands.

Fan blowing, besides mildly raising the air temperature by compression, also adds frictional heat from turbulence and when in excess this can disturb the tuning pitch. In a machine larger than necessary safety margins dictate, this excessive heating can arise from too many stages in series, excessive diameter and speed, and with an air flow too slow to carry away the heat so generated.

Industrial fans of outwardly similar construction to organ blowers are usually unsuitable. Not being designed for the widely varying wind volume demands, pressure instability occurs at some point in the demand. Unsuitable impeller tip design, besides not giving the desirable quietness when idling (the centrifugal organ-blower's special quality) they can impart a flutter or ripple to the wind-pressure which is often quite audible in sustained notes on certain stops and very disconcerting to the organ tuner.

Specialist planning of an organ-blowing installation is essential if it is to be effective, unobtrusive and economical in cost and running expense.

Long supply trunks waste power in pressure losses, and may radiate disturbing wind movement noises. They may also render a steady wind supply impossible. Many of these disadvantages are overcome by providing a pressure-regulating receiver close to the blowing fan, this cuts off a direct air connection between fan impellers and the main column of air in the delivery trunk, and thus forms both a sound and a pulsation barrier.

Some differences of opinion exist as to the ideal source of the air intake to the blower. Some maintain that air drawn from outside a church is beneficial to the structure of the instrument. Others regard this as fraught with a risk of disturbance of the instrument from uncontrollable climatic conditions. That a great majority of the smaller modern fans, because of their quiet unobtrusive working are placed within the case-work of the instruments they serve, suggests that the need for the fortuitous services of occasional damp weather can safely be dispensed with in a well-built instrument. Outside air at a temperature different to that in the organ can disturb the perfection of tuning and even result in unwelcome deterioration from internal condensation. Bleeding wind trunks to drain off internal condensation is not unknown to the service man.

The compressed air of the organ, always referred to by organ-builders as the 'wind', is measured in cubic feet per minute for flow volume and inches, water gauge, for pressure. The assessment of volume usually concerns only the blower maker but as a mtter of interest the average volume required at full organ playing varies between 15 and 25 cubic feet per minute (cfm) per stop, according to wind-pressure and tonal volume demanded. Wind-pressure is measured by a very simple and reliable device, the water gauge (Fig. 25). A glass tube of any convenient diameter shaped as the letter U and half filled with clear water. One top end is open to the air and the other is connected by tube to the organ pressure to be measured. The applied pressure presses the water down one column and the displacement pushes up the water level in the other column until the weight of water in the difference between the two columns is in balance with the pressure applied. This balance of water is measured and expressed as 'inches water gauge'.

Sometimes the water used is from any source on hand and at least one village organ was finally voiced on 3 in. of water and one tadpole!

Organ wind-pressures range commonly between $2\frac{1}{4}$ and 10 inches, exceptionally down to $1\frac{1}{2}$ in. and up to 15 in. and more rarely up to 20 in. Flue-pipe wind-pressures range from $1\frac{3}{4}$ in. to 7 in., and commonly are between $2\frac{1}{4}$ in. and $4\frac{1}{2}$ in. wg. Powerful and/or very smooth reed tones demand up to 15 in. wg. Pneumatic mechanisms, deriving their power from the pressure and volume used, are clumsy at pressures below $3\frac{1}{2}$ in. Usually the highest available in an instrument is used for power purposes such as slider draw-stop actions, electro-pneumatic swell louvre mechanisms and the like. As $3\frac{1}{2}$ in. wg. wind pressure for example, approximates to 2 oz. per square inch, in engineering terms the pressures are very small indeed.

The wind-pressure supplied by the blower is not constant, varying slightly with the changing demand in terms of volume, so to apply a steady wind-pressure to the pipes some means of pressure regulation must be provided (Fig. 26). The familiar bellows, with concertina-like folding ribs of wood and leather, when inflated, supports the floating top panel and any weight or spring tension as well. The amount of this imparts the 'wind-pressure'. When air is added or released the floating top rises or falls. This movement is used to close or open a valve or gate arranged to cut off supply when almost fully inflated, or progressively

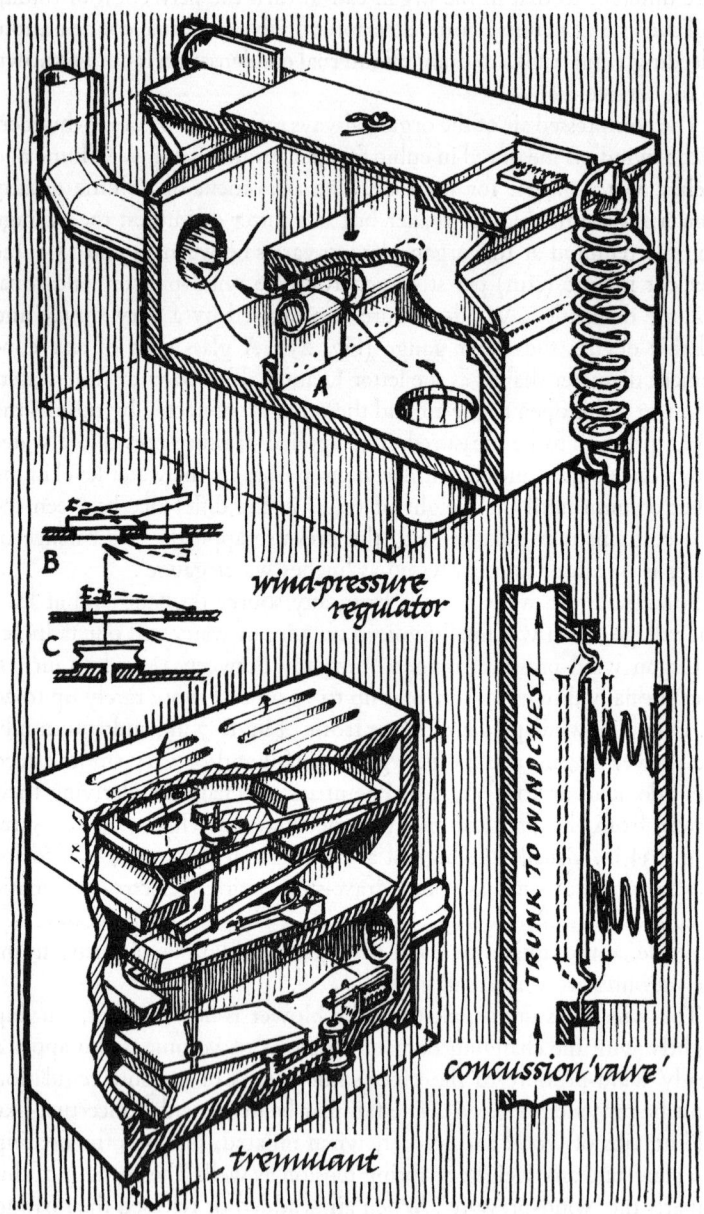

Fig. 26

open it when the volume contained is reduced by demand. In the range of movement between a full reservoir and valve closed, to the valve fully open and regulator almost empty, the riser of the regulator must impart an unvarying pressure. When weight loaded the ordinary single pair of folding ribs will only do this for a small part of the 'rise' as the total movement is called, giving a heavier pressure when almost empty. This is due to air-pressure on the inside of the folded ribs. When the ribs are almost closed they present a smaller area to support the load of weights, hence a higher pressure. Conversely, when almost fully extended, the larger area results in a fall of pressure. In old instruments and in some today, this varying of the air-pressure by the folding action of the ribs is overcome by adding a further set of ribs, but inverted. These ribs fold outward instead of inward and so are mutually compensating (Fig. 24).

In old hand-blown and also hydraulic-blown instruments these 'double-rise' bellows-reservoirs were made of considerable area, often almost the whole floor area of the organ. This was necessary for air storage, but it also imparted a valuable cushioning to the wind against concussive effects in staccato playing. With modern fan blowing, storage is rarely needed and such clumsy receivers are unnecessary. The anti-concussion precautions are then taken care of by large volume in trunks and windchests and nicely graduated control valves. In recent times designers are attempting blowing fans delivering variable volumes at constant pressure, for greater compactness and economy by elimination of the regulator in very small instruments.

The 'Concussion bellows' is a small lightly constructed air reservoir, having spring tensioning only, designed for low inertia and low momentum. It is a device to eliminate unsteady wind supply, cushioning the supply by instantly meeting momentary demands, and absorbing surges caused by abrupt cessation of demand.

The choice of spring or dead weight to impart pressure to the air in the bellows or regulator is not one of mere convenience. A hundred pounds of dead weight or of spring tension, imparts identical wind-pressure, but dead weight has inertia against quick movement and the momentum of the mass retards prompt stopping. These are negligible factors with springs. Loaded with weight alone, there will be momentary hesitation and then surging, producing wavering speech from the resulting unsteady wind-pressure.

Springs alone give very prompt movement, so prompt that a rippling vibration may be excited in the reservoir top, which is audible as a flutter in the pipe speech. This can be damped out by substituting a proportion of dead weight, and by providing ample volume in air chambers and wind trunks.

Springs of normally useful shapes and dimensions give varying tension, decreasing steadily as the spring extension decreases. This weakening pull would result in a weaker wind-pressure as the regulator-reservoir closes, unless this characteristic is matched to compensating variations in the regulator-reservoir response to tension. Fortunately the single-ribbed regulator has the required compensation characteristic, when the shape and size of the regulator has been expertly computed. Spring tension alone on double-rise bellows is likely to be unsatisfactory in this respect as there is no compensating characteristic for the spring tension loss. Hence double-rise regulators can only be dead-weighted and must in consequence be much larger to ensure slow movement and avoid pressure surges.

Wind Trunks

Successful design for the desirable steady wind supply involves consideration of many factors. These vary significantly because of the dimensional differences in each instrument. Nevertheless, there is one underlying principle that must be observed. Air flow in trunks, regulator top movement and regulator-valve movement must all be contrived to be as slow as is practically possible. This is achieved by means of larger diameter and easier turns in the wind trunks, adequate area of regulator top, and generous volume in the windchest. This needs space and costs money, but when well done, provision of a tremulant becomes nearly impossible by the normal simple means of jerking the wind supply.

Regulator valves

The regulator control valve has many forms, from the simple 'chopper' slide-valve widely used on fractional-horsepower blowers where the pressure is low and volume moderate, to the refined roller-blind type, rapid and precise in movement.

The crudest and earliest valve design is the 'pallet and sticker' with its air-pressure resistance to opening, causing abrupt movement and jarring the wind supply. This leads naturally to counterbalanced forms such as the 'monkey-tail' and the compensated pallet types. Some blowing engineers with their all-metal approach, contributed the disc or 'butterfly' pattern tap-like valve inside the main wind trunk.

All these simple and durable forms serve well when the difference between the supply and regulated pressures is small, say about two inches maximum. The placing of the main or first control valve as near to the fan as possible is a useful contribution to a quiet supply, especially if the valve is of rigid construction to resist vibration.

In large instruments, greater wind volumes must be controlled and larger pressure differences are often unavoidable. For this the neat and effective 'roller-blind' design, having very low operating resistance and weight, was widely developed so that it may be geared up in a simple way to give rapid movement. This meets large demands with the minimum of hesitation and wind-pressure sag.

Some tiny pressure drop is unavoidable in any organ wind system, for without it there would be no flow or movement to work the regulator valve whatever its form. Good design has to ensure that this is well within the limits that the organ pipe and the critical ear will tolerate. On the very low wind-pressures and when the antique system of flue regulation voicing is used, the tolerable margin becomes very small indeed and then very good design becomes absolutely essential.

The wind trunks whether between blower and regulators or to windchests cannot be too big in cross section. Generally, the rule is that a larger size means steadier wind supply. Trunks to windchests must be kept to a minimum length as the ill effects of length, dither and sagging pressure, cannot in practice be fully compensated for by a larger cross section. A true story. Two practical organ-builders were in the unusual position of consultant and builder. Mr. S. thinking to challenge the knowledge of Mr. I., the consultant, asked 'How big would you have the swell soundboard trunk?' Mr. I. parried with, 'How much space have you Mr. S.' The perfect reply.

Normally the vibrato of the organ is produced by a tremulant (or tremolo) a device that applies a periodic concussive shock to the wind system, causing sufficient wind-pressure variation, swinging either side of the normal to produce a just audible amplitude and pitch change in the sounds of pipes supplied from the disturbed source. Mostly this is done by gusts of air regularly released by automatic pneumatic means. The rate of these pulses is below that of unsteady wind which is damped out in good design, and in this way the wind has a tremolo-causing shake impressed upon it. The tremulant is an assembly of inherently unstable pneumatic parts. Air inflates a bellows-motor which, as it rises, closes the inlet valve abruptly and at the same time opens a ventilating hole on the bellows-motor top causing the inflating pressure to fail. The top then falls back, reopening the inlet valve and the cycle starts again.

An electronically excited equivalent has the same effect and within certain limits can be remotely regulated. In recent times electro-mechanical means have been devised, a slow speed electro-motor turns an eccentrically weighted flywheel revolving at the desired tremolo rate and is mounted upon the wind regulator to be trembled.

In the 'Universal Windchest' designs, notably that by Austin and more recently by Hill, in which the windchest is not only combined with the regulator but is big enough to contain the organ-fitter regulating the action, the absence of wind trunks and the great volume, results in a wind supply so free from concussions that a tremolo by normal pneumatic means is impossible. A fan or paddle-wheel wafting pulses of air at the pipe-tops is used to produce an acceptable vibrato. There is a trend towards general adoption of the fan tremulant in this country.

We are not here concerned with artistry or otherwise in the use of the organ vibrato, but we would venture the view that most tremulants are allowed to lapse into poor adjustment and so become unworthy of serious use. Were a more critical standard of performance demanded, it would produce an artistic device, deserving in turn, greater practice and acceptable use.

Electric action current supply

All electric and electro-pneumatic actions need a reliable source of electrical power. The domestic electrical supply mains are at a pressure too high to use directly, it would require costly standards of insulation to be safe and besides the simple quiet working contacts and magnets generally used would be unsuitable. An electrical pressure between 8 and 15 volts is usual in organ actions.

Primary sources, such as dry batteries, wet cells and later accumulators were in common use up to about 1920. In his sales promotion demonstrations the late Robert Hope-Jones, who did so much to set the pattern of successful electric organ-action design, claimed and demonstrated that on his system a large four-manual instrument needed only the energy in a tiny 4½-volt pocket torch dry battery.

The cinema theatre organ of 1925-35 gave a great boost to electrical organ actions and to the development of the blower-motor-driven low-voltage generator. Many similar installations still serve well. They generated voltages, according to organ make, between 8 volts and 15 volts D.C. usually adjusted by speed change through variation in belt pulley diameter. The better installations had generators with compound field windings giving a high degree of automatic voltage regulation over the wide range of current demands that arise during playing. These vary from ·2 amperes with one stop and one note, to 50 or more amperes at full organ playing on a large instrument. In this respect the generator is still the ideal organ-action power source, but today organ-action current generators are rarely used in new installations other than the largest, being supplanted by the static mains-transformer unit incorporating selenium or germanium rectifiers. These combine great reliability with quietness in working and are undemanding of maintenance attention. One such instrument gives a smoothed D.C. output of ·2 to 30 amperes at 15 volts fairly closely regulated and in addition a 9 volt 50 cycle A.C. outlet for auxiliary uses such as signal lights, etc.

Organ humidifiers

Until about 1930, instruments were made for and became conditioned to the atmospheric conditions in churches with no more than a rudimentary system of space heating often resulting in winter temperatures barely reaching 58° F. Modern church heating systems reflect the rising standards of comfort demanded in homes and public buildings so that churches heated to 66° F. or more are not uncommon. However well seasoned the original timbers in the organ construction may be, such temperatures produce further shrinkage and internal stress because the higher temperature reduces the relative humidity (RH) of the air around and in it. This drier air in turn absorbs moisture from the timbers until a new equilibirum is reached. When moisture is withdrawn from any timber, no matter what its age, some shrinkage occurs. Most of the older windchests are so constructed that any substantial change from the long established mean condition results in severe distortion and failure to function correctly. Repair is both uncertain and costly. Some systems of heating, because of their extreme rapidity of heating, accentuate this desiccation effect.

Sometimes when an organ has excessive leakages caused by dry heating, pails or small pans of water are hopefully placed inside the instrument to moisten the air and restore normal dimensions. This is rarely effective, since evaporation is too slow because the surface area is small and the air stagnant. Effectiveness can be judged by how much topping up water is needed, it is usually remarkably little and at long intervals, so that very large water areas are needed for such means to have useful effect.

The air supply to the organ offers a useful channel for air conditioning should that become necessary, as is increasingly the case.

By providing a *cold* evaporating source of water vapour and pumping it into the organ wind system at very low wind-pressure, timber humidity can be restored to original or safe levels and distortion corrected. Experience shows that by a process of diffusion, in time, moisture reaches all the vulnerable parts. Such a system must be largely self-regulating. In severe cases moist air is also ducted in tiny amounts in and around the organ structure to recondition external surfaces by producing a blanket of air of controlled humidity over the organ parts. Clearly this is economically more practical than attempting total air conditioning of the entire volume of the building.

The organ-builder can do much by careful design and accumulated know-how to guard against the ill effects of excessive dry heating (or over-humid conditions) when building new instruments. It is not his fault that instruments forty or more years old suffer costly damage under these new and trying conditions. The old and matured timbers must and will shrink or swell in an endeavour to be in equilibrium with new atmospheric conditions and no amount of skill or responsibility can guard against ill effects if this movement is considerable and reaches rupture point. Consultation between organ-builder and heating engineer when a system is being modernized is a wise precaution. He can advise precautions that may save great expense by avoiding desiccation damage. Authoritative technical references are available to him from professional sources.

9
The Swellbox

PLACE a substantial cabinet around the pipes of a manual division, arrange a set of louvres in one side, designed to open or close at will, and you have a 'swellbox' giving a *crescendo* or *diminuendo* effect to any sounds produced within it (Fig. 27).

Compared with other musical instruments, this sort of *crescendo* control is a crude device, but undeniably it has value in traditional church service music and in precise inter-manual tone balance control.

It seems almost certain that the idea first came to light in Spain sometime in the seventeenth century, when sliding sashes were used. A swell 'front' of this form is preserved, but out of use, in Wymondham Abbey, Norfolk. Only later was the pivoted louvre adopted. An extremely early example of the latter in England, was in the one manual by Samuel Green dated 1790 and now (1963) in the Private Chapel, Buckingham Palace.

The introduction of the swellbox had a deep influence on the tonal development of the organ, making acceptable the newly developed coarse-toned gambas and keen viole tones, the early coarse reed tones became tolerable in chorus, leading to the great improvement that they were later to get at the hands of Willis, Hill and others. In other countries the effect was not dissimilar, although strong national schools of design developed rather differently to our own, where the swell reed chorus developed to a perfection not attained anywhere else.

When sound is reflected from a wall surface, some component parts of that sound are absorbed in some degree and so withheld. This absorption is rarely uniform in effect throughout the musical frequency range, but usually highly selective so that the reflected sound is robbed of some of its power and the tone-colour smudged. This fact is important in relation to swellbox design, its thickness and the material used therein.

Some twentieth-century swellboxes have comprised the entire organ chamber with louvres in a tone opening, the walls being of some rigid and heavy building material. This arrangement will give a very wide range of *dimuendo* and *crescendo*, but the pipe speech must be forced and

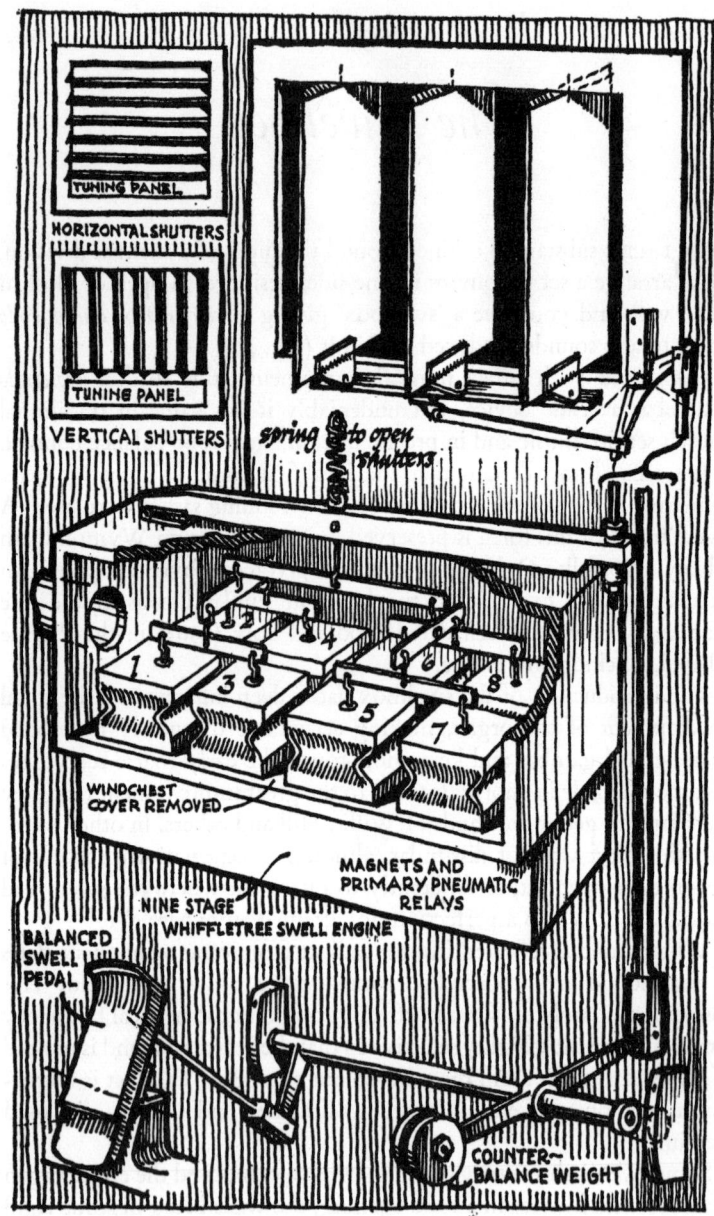

Fig. 27

the *pianissimo* will be muffled, thin and lacking in tonal warmth and roundness. The great weight and rigidity of construction tends to hold back all frequencies almost equally, more especially those of lower frequency. As the ear is less sensitive to bass at low levels of power, this robs the tone of warmth and textural softness. In the more conventional construction of about 2 in. solid timber, fitting fairly closely around the pipes, some part of the lower frequency component of the sounds will leak through and the *crescendo* is achieved when the opening louvres let out added brightness, an effect akin to *crescendo* effects in almost all other musical instruments except the electronic organ. The latter mostly have an astonishing dynamic crescendo range but imparting only bigness or littleness, and seem musically cold in consequence.

An interior surface that readily absorbs the higher frequency sounds, even only partially, can clearly destroy swell organ tone-colours and also make the 'swelling' less effective. A composite construction incorporating within stiff hard surface panels a non-conductor layer, can have good effect by ensuring tonal contrast between sound leaking through the walls of the closed box and that coming through the open louvres. A layer of loose sawdust and wood shavings is sometimes used for this purpose, but many modern alternatives are now available.

There seems little technical support for the advocacy of large and spacious swellboxes apart from lofty height, for it is a common observation that tightly enclosing boxes of minimal dimensions are outstandingly effective in dynamic range and tonal qualities.

The old Hill bonneted or cottage-roofed swellboxes are good examples of this. The main objection to large swellboxes is the large sound leakage area offered and the need for much heavier construction to reduce it to reasonable proportions. Also the proportionally large louvre frame has a much higher leakage area with consequent loss of 'shut-down'. Deep swellboxes tend to smother and modify the tone of the rearward ranks. To some extent extra height and a sloping top will help to minimize this, but a shallow box of double width or double height is much to be preferred.

A well-designed swellbox takes into account good and easy tuning access combined with desirable compactness. Taking a shutter out and reaching in to tune is all very well in tiny instruments but pivot centres wear and become loose in the handling, and slack and noisy in wearing.

The best plan, when space allows, is an internal tuning passage-way but not so generous that the swellbox is acoustically weakened by excessive sizes. The old style swellboxes with basses in the middle and trebles at each end tuned from end doors has much to recommend it but fine tuning from bottom to top really requires the tuner inside the swellbox within easy reach of all pipes, leaving the shutters intact. North American organ-builders are consistently good in this respect, the ease and convenience of the tuner is often elaborately cared for by internal steps, ladders and footholds bringing every pipe within easy reach. As tuning costs increase, these time-savers will merit more attention here.

The louvres or shutters are usually made of solid timber, often laminated to ensure stability of shape, with the edges felted and bevelled or double bevelled to give a good sound-tight enclosure. Box-like framed and panelled shutters are fancied by some, but lightness of weight and easier movement seem to be their only certain virtues. Some also use a feltless sound-trapping shutter edge; physicists argue for and against, and it is not demonstrably consistently superior. Avoidance of excessive clearance at shutter ends is important as this can represent a considerable leakage path destroying the crescendo range.

How many swellbox shutters should there be? There is no exact way of ascertaining this but certainly too large is better than too small. There is no way to compensate fully by louder voicing the smothering effect on the open tone when the louvre area is too small. General observation suggests that 20 per cent of the swellbox wall area is a fair minimum. The maximum really depends upon the organ-builders' skill in designing and making a warp-free *wide* shutter, that is not also too heavy to swing easily and accurately by normal balanced swell pedal means. Clearly a few wide shutters closing tightly will close more effectively and open more clearly than an equal area of numerous narrow louvres, with the possibility of up to 100 per cent more edge leakage. A larger area of wide shutters could be upwards of 30 per cent of the wall area with every advantage.

The foregoing raises comparison with those swellboxes that are organ chambers with louvred openings, wherein the shutter area is usually much less than given above. Observation of the more extreme examples shows pipework necessarily voiced more loudly and coarsely, while the large volume and greater wall area produces a blurred attack and outline. This is curiously often more evident in recorded performance than in direct listening.

It is now a common practice when restoring an instrument to specify that the interior of the swellbox should be finished in a light-coloured enamel paint. While it might be difficult to be sure that one could detect a difference between before and after, there is a sound reason for adopting this finish. Certainly the light colour makes the most of the normally limited illumination available to the organ-tuner and should lessen the accidental disturbance of pipes. Also by smoothing what may be a rough or pitted surface, it does reduce its ability to absorb sound, increasing its reflectivity at the brighter end of the musical scale.

Sometimes the layout suggests that besides shutters in the front, more on one end would be advantageous. Besides making a tight closure more uncertain, such a plan exposes one half of the pipes to extra expression, a crude and clumsy device unless pipes are arranged in strict chromatic order, and most voicers and tuners dislike this for very good reasons.

Vertical or horizontal shutters? Because shutters do not usually move through more than 45° when fully open, there is a slight directional bias. Apart from avoiding horizontal shutters opening upwards because they usually tend in time to deposit dust on the first inside stop, which is calamitous if a reed, the choice is entirely a matter of the best direction to suit the organ layout. Shutters in swellbox tops have the dirt-deposit objection although a lightweight close-meshed screen between shutters and pipes can take care of this in the exceptional case where a marked advantage could result from this arrangement.

It should now be clear that a swellbox is not just a piece of carpentry but something that when well designed to match the organ layout, and competently made, is complementary to the musical artistry of the voicer in creating the more romantic organ tone-colours.

Operating mechanism

The means of operating the swellbox louvres is best by a system of rigidly connected mechanical traces to a pedal shoe having a rocking action, 'a balanced swell pedal' in organ parlance. The mechanical traces should be so made as to have very little loose action or lost motion. Sensitive expressive control is only possible when a smooth, positive motion is imparted to the shutters. For this reason systems using strained wires or long torsion rods (trundles) are never satisfactory as they introduce whip and springiness.

A steady rate of opening cannot produce a regularly increasing crescendo of sound, because each added like amount of movement, is a decreasing proportion of the whole. In good examples the shutters are made to move more slowly in relation to the pedal when just opening and more rapidly when almost open. An artful use of cams in the connections achieves this.

With the increased degree of console detachment allowed by the use of electric key actions, occasions arise when a path for a direct mechanical connection is difficult or impossible. Length is no real difficulty since 100-ft. runs exist, giving every satisfaction. The alternative is an electro-pneumatic swell expression action, referred to as a 'swell engine' or 'swell motor'. Mostly, these machines move the louvres in a number of steps and not in a smooth progression. This is achieved by either a concertina device or the 'Whiffletree' gear. The number of steps is optional and in practice varies widely from as few as five positions, which cannot give fine graduation, to seventeen positions in more elaborate examples. In practice six seems the practical minimum and thirteen a good almost stepless control. Whatever the number of steps there must be a slight hesitation and a lack of sensitivity compared with direct mechanical control.

One system, the Willis 'infinite-graduation' swell expression action, attempts a really elegant solution of power-operated remote swellbox control. This system is really stepless, and has remarkable qualities once the radically different pedal control technique has been mastered. Outwardly the pedal is like the common balanced shoe form but is sprung to a midway position and does not therefore represent the louvre position. Moving the pedal slightly towards the normal open position sets mechanism in motion that very slowly opens the swellbox, continuing until it is fully open, or until the pedal is released to spring back to the midway position. A slight movement towards the normal closed position produces slow closing. The extent that the pedal is moved against its spring determines the speed of opening but not its extent. Very considerable power is available under sensitive control so that either extremely slow or crash movements can be made. An indicator is necessary to remind the player of the position of the louvres.

In a more rarely used system of electro-pneumatic remote control, the louvres are not ganged up to move as one but instead have individual actions, sometimes two stage. Each shutter opens in turn, and represents a step in the swell pedal movement. Towards the full open position several may move together, the order and degree being adjusted in each installation to match the acoustic considerations. Clearly there should be some ten or more shutters if reasonably unobtrusive steps are to be possible and this limits its wider application.

Modern telemotor controls as developed for aircraft and similar applications would seem to be applicable, but they have access to power supplies on a scale not applicable to organs and usually do not meet the need of quiet unobtrusive operation. In the forms achieved so far that are practical in an organ, an inherent response lag makes them inferior to well-designed, well-engineered direct mechanical actions. Contemporary organ designers have turned against totally enclosed organs and where real effort is made to obtain a complimentary acoustic condition there are good and sound arguments to support their idealistic views. However, in large, galleried, non-reverberant buildings with the organ unavoidably buried in a chamber, the acoustic help to unenclosed pipework is negligible, and here the added expressiveness or volume-control can be made much of by enterprising performers.

Should a choir organ division be enclosed? This is quite a different consideration. With the trend of design away from quasi-swell or quasi-solo voices and towards a balanced yet colourful chorus related in power and of contrasting pitches to the great, there is good argument for a gentle speech in favourable open position. Nevertheless, there are some convincing examples of placing at least the softest flue voices and half-length reed tones under expression so that all schools of the organ literature are to be catered for.

10

The Console

THERE cannot be many other artistic activities where, as in playing the organ, almost all the senses and every limb of the body are in continuous active, and highly co-ordinated use. It is not therefore so remarkable that the place for these artistic exercises, the organ console, has been a point of continuous design development, from the rudimentary fist-keys of the 'organ-thumper', to the sumptuously designed and finished 'control-desks' of the four- or even five-manual mammoths that occasionally emerge, the pride of their makers and owners.

The manual keyboards

They are the very centre of the organ console whether it be but one or five 'rows'. A dissertation upon the merits and origins of multiple keyboards is outside our scope; the purpose and simplicity or otherwise of music to be performed, the depth of the purse and the ego of the player all come into the facts surrounding the choice, of more than two manuals. More than four manuals of keys is rare nowadays, many former cathedral five-rows have been cut down in rebuilding, and the majority of new consoles built in recent years are of three-manual form, closely followed by the two-manual, in standard, utility, and miniature classes.

Manual key compass

After some early uncertainty in pre-pedal organ days, this settled at CC in the bass. In an upwards direction examples of 54 (CC–F), 56 (CC–G) are becoming rare as rebuilding usually includes compass extension to the widely accepted standard of CC–C 61 notes. However, the top A 58-note compass was frequently made as late as forty years ago, and is again turning up in economically designed small instruments today. Except for some organ music of French origin and a few contemporary composers, it meets almost all requirements. Compass extensions are

THE CONSOLE 97

costly and in church work rarely justified unless they are added to compasses shorter than 56 notes, or where solo concert performances are envisaged which must cover the whole literature.

In some large instruments, and especially so in North America in the past half-century, the windchests and stops have their compass continued upwards for the benefit of the octave-coupler. This is sometimes to E (65 notes), more often to G (68 notes), and just occasionally to C (73 notes). With the trend to question the artistry, if not the musical utility of octave-couplers, this upward extension is only justified in special cases and these are usually the more romantic solo tones which can thereby be exploited.

Weight of touch

With the coming of pneumatic power-assisted actions the considerable effort necessary to depress the keys of a large instrument could be reduced to comfortable values. Tensions as high as twelve ounces per key could be brought down to four ounces or less. The need to have deep key movement to obtain a mechanical advantage also passed, so that what was often almost half an inch became a bare three eighths. These changes greatly reduced the fatigue of playing a recital or service on coupled manuals.

The general passing into disuse of direct mechanical (tracker) action changed the 'touch' from a characteristic crisp top-resistance to a 'soft' effortless touch. In poor examples, there is a marked increase in tension as the key is depressed; a spongy touch, lacking in precision and definition of movement. In well-designed examples, incorporating essentially, long-levered keys and generous-proportioned springs, a clean firm touch is obtained. This is essential for precise fingerwork.

Attempts to simulate the definition of movement of tracker-action keys, has produced results better called 'top resistance' rather than 'tracker touch'. In these the initial weight is usually a full four ounces decreasing as the key is depressed to about one and a half ounces, simulating more nearly a pianoforte touch than that of the desired tracker action, nevertheless the good examples, those on long-levered keys, are a significant contribution to clean fingering and are part of refined console design.

What is usually called 'false touch', a depression of the key a short distance before any action movement is initiated, is a very desirable feature. It is a means of safety clearance against accidental key movement, especially where there is pneumatic transmission. Where there is electric action, some false touch is inherent and its nice adjustment is an important factor in combining good attack and clean repetition.

The use of the more costly ivory to cover the keys is to be preferred to the various synthetics or plastic coverings available, because of the uniformity of surface 'slip' irrespective of dry or moist conditions. Most substitutes tend to become 'grippy' to moist hands.

Key dimensions

The length of the ivories and their relation, manual to manual, is probably the most widely used and longest established of the many advocated standard dimensions. Five-and-a-half-inch-long ivories arranged to overhang the lower manual 1½ in. at a vertical distance between 2½ in. and 2¾ in. are generally adopted. But in recent times this has been challenged by world renowned players who maintain that the resulting 4 in. from manual to manual is too close, giving insufficient clearance when playing repeated octave spans on the black keys, as called for in some French music. Some builders now make this clearance 4¼ in. and in consequence reduce the overhang to 1¼ in.

Curiously, the actual manual key scale or note to note centring, varies slightly from builder to builder, usually in pursuit of some compromise that overcomes the narrower clearance between F♯, G♯, and A♯, as compared with C♯–D♯ which results from a strict mathematical division of the octave.

In keyboards of three or more manuals, it has become the practice of some firms progressively to incline up and away, the great, swell and solo keys. This is a matter of a few degrees only but has the effect of bringing the more distant rows nearer the player and at a more convenient angle in moving from one to the other.

In some four-manual designs the lower manual slopes down and away very slightly. It is very comfortable but it must be carefully planned in angle and in height in relation to the player and pedal board.

Pedal keyboards

Although starting very much later than the manuals, the pedal board has developed rapidly to a convenient and precise means of control. In the British Isles and North America one sees it in its most sophisticated form. Not all players in all countries see advantage in both radiation and concavity in the arrangement of the pedal keys (Fig. 28).

There remain in England a few flat and straight sets, usually of short

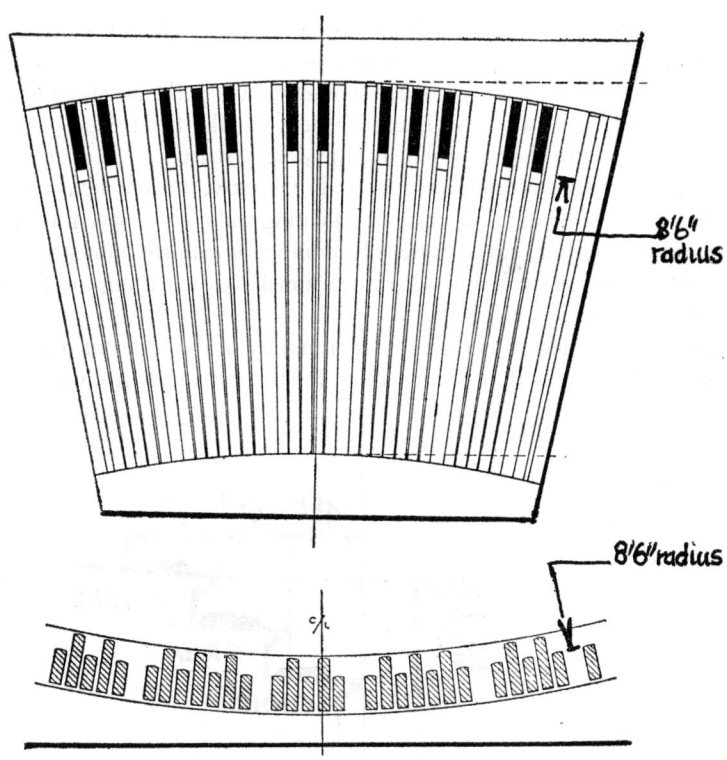

FIG. 28. Radiating and concave pedal board

compass. Rather more examples are of the straight concave pattern but the great majority are both radiating and concave. These vary in the depth of concavity from the old shallow 'R.C.O.' pattern of 1904 having a 12 ft. 6 in. radius, to the modern and fairly generally accepted 8 ft. 6 in. radius. The splay or radiation of the keys has remained with infrequent exceptions at about 8 ft. 6 in. radius.

While these basic dimensions are now widely adhered to, other and in some respects, equally important details vary in a most unfortunate way for the visiting organist. The commonest fault is in sideways relation with the manuals, CC (No. 13) pedal key being under manual Middle C (No. 25) a relic of when it was comfortable to have only 27 or 30 pedal keys placed centrally under 56- or 58-note manuals. This is as much as two pedal semitones too far to the right, when as is usual today, the 32-note pedal board is placed logically and conveniently central under 61 manual keys. This is most conveniently expressed as DD pedal under mid. D manual, 'D under D'. It places the player always in the same relative position, whether manual compass be 56, 58 or 61, and pedal keys 30 or the modern 32 notes.

There is also the relationship in the other direction, the distance under the manual, from a plumb line dropped from the front edge of the lowest manual to the tip of the pedal middle D sharp key (Fig. 29). In old instruments this often measures only from two to five inches. For comfortable playing, a full compass radiating and concave pedal board needs to be eight inches or more. The number of manuals influence this position, as the player's limited arm reach makes closer sitting to a four-manual keyboard a necessity.

In England these dimensions are commonly of the order of 6 in. to 8 in. for two manuals, 8½ in. to 10 in. for three manuals and 9½ in. to

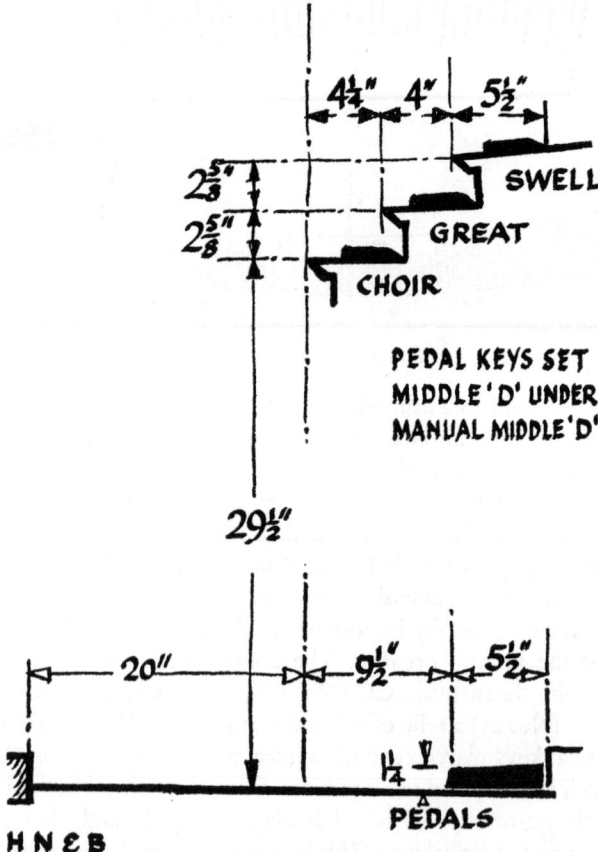

FIG. 29. Console standard basic dimensions

11 in. for four or more rows of keys. Standardization has been and still is being attempted by the Incorporated Society of Organ Builders. A survey shows the foregoing range of figures are still to be encountered in new work. The Royal Canadian College of Organists (R.C.C.O.) has attempted to bring up to date the American Guild of Organists (A.G.O.) recommendations of the 30's, without being dimensionally too precise. Their recommendations in the main differ little from common British practice except in one significant feature, the height of manual keys above the pedals which is about 1 in. to 1½ in. lower at 29½ in. Observation suggests that this stems from a different pedalling technique involving a much firmer seat on the organ bench, which is therefore set lower and nearer the pedal keys. British organists who have tried consoles built to these dimensions find them very accessible and comfortable and in this our Canadian cousins may have done us a good service.

Other pedal design-points are width of keys, depth of touch, height and length of sharp key and key spacing. Keys wider than ⅞ in. look well but reduce safe clearance between naturals. Thinner keys look poor, but are easier to play cleanly. Touch depth needs only to be sufficient to give definition of movement and ½ in. at sharp key-tip is generally accepted as good practice. Related to this is the amount of depression of the sharp key-stalk below the naturals. If this is insufficient, accidental sharp key depression results; ¾ in. is a minimum and allows a little for ntural key wear. Key spacing in the best examples is generally accepted as 2½ in. between the naturals or two sharp keys at the sharp front line, although one well-known builder narrows this between E and F, and B and C, to 2⅜ in. Sharp keys must be long enough to allow passing one shoe over or under the other when on a sharp key, also to clear swell pedals and like projections, and so they are usually between 5 in. and 5½ in.

The height of the sharp key-tip above the natural seems more important than any recommendations have realized. Tests have shown that high sharps need, for comfort and convenience, to be farther away under manuals, and thereby uncomfortably extending the leg reach to the pedal-board extremes. What is required is an upward projection in excess of the ½ in. touch depression, to give clean playing, a wear and tear allowance, and passing clearance. This needs to be ⅝ in. and with ½ in. touch gives a sharp key height of 1 in. to 1¼ in. More can be an embarrassment.

A top resistance pedal-key touch has no appeal, but the normal spring touch should nevertheless be clean and free from sponginess. The pedal movement should have very definite up and down positions and be weighted to between 3 lb. and 4 lb. at the playing point. Sufficient buffing to ensure reasonable quietness in rapid playing is desirable, and this is helped by avoiding thin and drumming platform floors under the console.

Stop-control systems

These fall into three basic classes with a number of distinct sub-classes. Stop-knobs, stop-keys or tablets, and luminous controls cover those most usually encountered. The traditional stop-knob has many adherents, who claim ease of identification and quick reading of position (Plate 10). There is also some psychological satisfaction in its positive and substantial movement. The pedal trombone somehow has a grander authority drawn by knob than when flicked on by stop-key. The 2½-in. or more 'draw' of old mechanical stop-knob action has shrunk to something around three-quarters of an inch in modern consoles; just enough to ensure clear indicating position. The best examples move on or off with a slight snap action. The knob size too has shrunk from almost 2 in. in diameter to 1 in. or slightly over, allowing closer spacing and group handling. Stop-knobs are usually set in panels arranged at an angle of between 30° and 60° to the keyboards, most are at about 45°. On larger multi-manual consoles sharper angles can give a better reach. Some recent examples have the jambs as faceted arcs so that all the draw-knobs seem to face the player. Whether this really gives better comprehension of indication and easier movement is very dependent upon careful positioning and design.

The stop-keys or tablets

This group includes many variants but has now settled down to two, the stop-tongue or stop-key, and the stop-tablet or rocking tablet. The stop-key (Plate 10a) is usually an ivory or composition tongue, projecting at a low angle from a facia at which point it is hinged, with a vertical movement at its tip of about ¼ in. It is very conveniently moved up or down (for 'on') by fingertip movement reached from the manual beneath them. The form was developed sixty or more years ago and had its heyday in the theatre organs. Now in a dignified form it continues in church organ use, particularly for two-manual detached consoles, where it has a useful compactness of dimension, and in particular low height. There is also another compelling advantage, that of lower cost, although with electro-magnetic action improvements this is tending to diminish.

A unique arrangement of stop-keys was that used by Rothwell in which miniature stop-keys are arranged along the facia under the front edge of the keyboard, that is between swell and great keys in a two-manual. So close, that thumb movements from the swell and finger movements from the great can control stop registration. In a medium to large scheme the unavoidably wide spread of controls diminishes the inherent convenience, which probably accounts for its lack of wider adoption.

The horseshoe layout of stop-keys, so highly developed in the theatre organ, is desirable in its lesser form of a gentle curve, to assist easy viewing and identification when there are thirty or more stop-controls. The exaggerated display form is unnecessary.

The rocking-tablet form (Fig. 30) is the one in which an ivory or composition substitute tablet, is hinged horizontally about its middle and is set nearly vertically in the console facia. Depressing the lower half brings the stop on and remains so as an indicator. Various makes differ slightly in detail, the most effective have in addition a small *vertical* displacement that assists in the rapid reading of the registered combination. Rocking tablets are very satisfactory and convenient

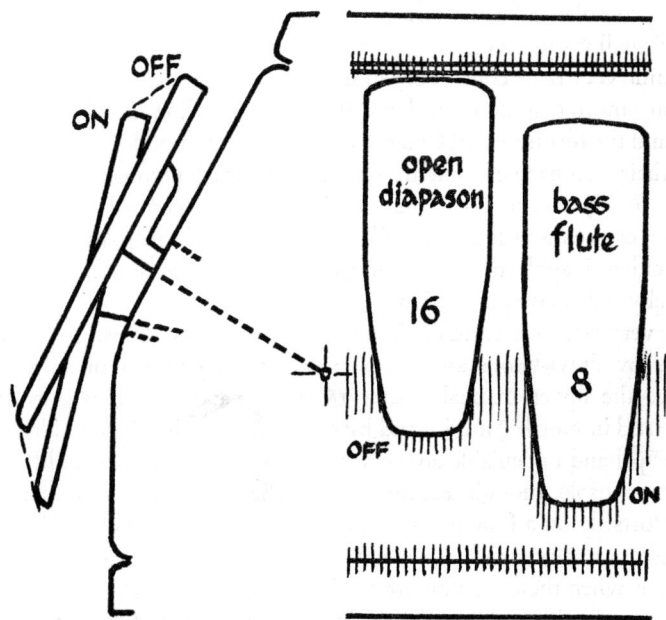

FIG. 30. Stop or Rocking Tablet stop controls

when arranged in a straight row; perhaps not so readily moved by fingertip control as stop-keys, but they can give a clearer indication of position when in considerable numbers (Plate 15).

Stop-key or tablets arranged on angle jambs seem to have little to commend them except cheapness and possible avoidance of a high music desk. They cannot be found almost blind like a stop-knob, and quick comprehension depends very much on good lighting. It is a hybrid form, of debatable value.

Another form related to rocking-tablet movements was the N. & B., circa 1910–20, double miniature-knob system. The upper was really a push button which pushed out the lower miniature knob and indicated that the stop is on. A similar pushing action to the lower knob cancelled the stop. The lower miniature knob could also be used as a plain draw-knob. Blind players found them more manageable than stop-keys or rocking tablets.

Three-manual stop-key consoles (Plate 13) while having the inherent compactness of the style are not easy to lay out in a logical and consistent manner. When they are of over forty controls, they tend to fall far short of the quick comprehension, the convenience of registration and the dignity of the traditional stop-knob pattern. Fewer stop-key or tablet consoles are made now than formerly and those are mainly for very small instruments.

Some very large concert organ stop-key consoles have been designed having more than 200 stop-keys, the Dome Pavilion, Brighton (Plate 14) and the former Regal Cinema Concert Organ, London, are justified by their compactness and mobility. The casual performer on them tends to rely very much on the combination piston controls. The simple layout conventions such as usually assist one to find a stop-knob quickly are either inapplicable or insufficient to give a logical layout, and thereby quick comprehension.

A very practical combination of the two basic systems, is speaking stops by draw-knobs and couplers by rocking tablets or stop-keys above the upper manual (Plates 18, 19, 20 and 23). This is widely practised in North America and by some United Kingdom builders. Its principal and undeniable advantage is in reducing the bulk and height of the console, though tending to push the music desk up rather uncomfortably on a four-manual console. Some designers claim that the couplers are more readily reached, but this is subject to some qualification, as when these are numerous, there is some difficulty in quick and accurate identification despite distinctive colouring and careful grouping.

Luminous indicator stop-control systems

These have made but a limited showing and only two forms have been in continued production. One form uses a rocking tablet, sprung to a midway position and has a small indicator lamp that lights up when the stop is 'on'. Normal rocking-tablet hand movements are used, a touch at the top or bottom tip brings the indicator light on or off respectively, but does not leave the tablet displaced as in the ordinary form. The simplicity of the latter is to some extent offset by the complexity in the keying mechanism that precludes any economic advantages. St. Martin's-in-the-Fields in London has such a console, by Rutt.

A more original form had its origins in cash-register key design. It consists of large translucent studs carrying engraved titles and arranged much as cash register keys are on an inclined and angled jamb. Pressing the face with a push-button action operates an electrical on-or-off mechanism which puts the stop 'on' and lights up the translucent face to indicate this, a second touch reverses the action. This was developed by Estey in the United States. At home, Compton applied the same movement to large stop-knob-size buttons set in normally placed stop jambs. A notable example is the B.B.C. Langham Place Concert Hall Organ. Double-touch can be applied. Pressing deeper against added spring resistance can be made to produce cancelling or suitable pedal bass or similar registrational aids. The system has been quite highly developed, usefully breaking away from conventions while aiming at great registrational ease. The system does, however, require the player to develop a new fingertip technique, and changes cannot be made blindly as an unnecessary touch of confirmation has the opposite effect to that desired, as it causes cancellation.

The trend of taste and design is set solidly towards a rationalized stop-knob form (Plates 16, 17, 21 and 22). Aided by the constantly improving electro-mechanical design behind the stop-knob, this will allow smaller knobs at closer spacing and more convenient location.

The accessory controls

These cover registrational aids and control of expression.

Expression or 'swell' pedals for operating the swellbox louvres are universally of the balanced or centrally-hinged form in new work (Plate 25). A few old-style lever pedals still survive, usually with a hitch-down or latch device to hold in the full open position. While the possibility of leaving the swell louvres in any desired degree of openness is a useful feature, it is most probable that the real attraction of the 'balanced swell pedal' is its convenient central position. This has become standardized by the general practice of placing the 'swell' expression pedal between pedal keys No. 16 (D♯) and No. 19 (F♯) with choir and or solo pedals to left and stop-*crescendos* (where fitted) to the right. This is based on the natural forward swing of the right foot quickly finding the most used swell pedal.

Where the connections to the organ must be electrical, it is possible to have a switching system connecting all or any particular swellbox to any pedal of a multi-pedal array. This has been done in a number of large concert organs.

The crescendo pedal sometimes called Stop or Register Crescendo, is more widely used in North America and Germany than in the United Kingdom. In English-speaking countries it takes the same outward form as the swell expression pedal and like it, the closed or off position is when the heel is fully depressed. Progressive movement by toe pressure brings on stops in a predetermined and fixed order, usually starting with the P.P. on each manual, introducing appropriate intermanual couplers as next stage and thereafter building up to a comprehensive full organ. Usually the simple means used precludes elimination of string tones and cloying flutes as the build up proceeds, and so some players regard them as inartistic devices. However, if a little more thought was given to the design and use, the solo tone elements eliminated and a true organ tone dynamic build-up obtained, it could be used for many purposes in place of manual thumb pistons, and these would then be available as special-purpose combinations.

Combination mechanisms

In early organs the obvious convenience of a group control of stops was achieved by cutting off the wind supply to the group by means of a convenient foot pedal as may be seen in many French organs. This is the Ventil System, a simple device needing no elaborate mechanism, but of limited application. Out of it undoubtedly arose the idea of operating the sliders in a number of predetermined groups via mechanical connections from the 'combination pedals', using for power the weight a player could apply with one foot when seated at the console. On small instruments such a device added a valuable control for simple service playing changes, for instance between the playing-over and the beginning of a hymn accompaniment. On a single manual instrument two such pedals are very useful and worth the small cost.

THE CONSOLE

When pneumatic power superseded the mechanical means for putting stops on or off, the effort needed to operate combination pedals became so much less, that working them by pneumatic power became practicable. The light touch controls then possible, brought into being the thumb piston, those small press-buttons between the keyboards. Nevertheless, for many years the pedal controls retained their blacksmithy look of robust wrought ironwork, and some players have a preference for the deliberate movement involved in using them.

The basic principle of combination movements was a moving member engaging with studs on the appropriate drawstop-rods. Two such members moving in opposite directions produced both 'on' and cancelling movements. Quite soon, inventive minds found ways of altering the position of the engaging studs by remote control, making combinations 'adjustable at the console'. The cost, however, was not low and the action tended to be bulky. It became the custom to set up the limited number of combination devices, in a progressive tonal build-up that often remained unchanged over long periods.

North American players used to exploiting the tonal resources of larger instruments more actively and with their taste for greater variety of tone-colour, require all combination controls to be instantly adjustable, leaving building-up combinations to the stop-*crescendo* pedal.

Where tubular pneumatics were formerly used the combination mechanism was substantially the same in principle on either drawstop-knobs or stop-key, or tablets. They were often very bulky and were thus inconvenient for the detached console. Electro-pneumatic or electro-magnetic mechanism has greatly reduced the bulk of the action to more manageable proportions and present-day detached consoles are marvels of compactness. With electric combination action, depressing a manual or toe combination piston makes either a number of electrical contacts, or a single contact working a multiple contact relay, which closes one circuit for each stop-control to be moved. The electrical charge is then directed via a switching device of one sort or another to either the 'on' or 'off' magnet windings of the knob or stop-key.

This switching device can be one of several basic forms: (*a*) the very elementary provision of two terminal pins labelled 'on' or 'off', to either of which the charged wire is soldered (*b*) a simple wire spring contact manually set on one or other of two busbars (*c*) a miniature two-way switch, mounted so as to be accessible to the player (this is better) (*d*) electro-magnetically operated switches for remote control, giving instant adjustment on the 'capture' system (Plate 26). In (*d*), a desired combination is drawn and then 'captured' by the setter mechanism, which is set into action by first pressing a 'setter' piston and then the piston upon which the desired combination is to be set or captured.

Electrical capture-piston adjustment actions fall into two classes: those in which the charge from a relay is switched to 'on' or 'off' through a remote-controlled switch, and those (Plate 26) in which the relay contact is electro-mechanically switched, giving greater compactness and important self-cleaning qualities.

Stop-keys or tablets are now mostly electro-magnetically moved, there being two magnets, one for off and another for on. Stop-knobs have either a double solenoid movement, or when compressed air is used, two electro-pneumatic valves.

The longer travel of the stop-knob, usually just under one inch, is not easily matched to the characteristic of simple electro-magnets, so it is usual to use solenoids which have a longer pull and are suited to the space available.

Electrical efficiency calls for close fitting and a rather light touch so that metallic rattles cannot be entirely eliminated. Improved designs, however, are incorporating new materials and new features including electro-magnetic holding in 'on' or 'off' position.

Electro-pneumatic working is still preferred by some designers as it allows a firmer and more definite hand action of the draw-knob as there can be ample power to overcome it. Even this can now be electro-magnetically simulated given a sufficiently ample power supply.

Some eccentric variations of thumb-piston forms have been used but the simple push button form now finds general acceptance. Mostly they are circular ranging in diameter from $\frac{1}{2}$ in. to $\frac{7}{8}$ in diameter, and usually engraved with an identifying number or inscription. One firm has devised a simple solid ivory cube, a dice-like form which has found many friends after they have overcome the shock of the unconventional shape.

In recent years more attention has been paid to careful positioning of thumb-pistons and a fairly general degree of standardization is coming about, placing No. 1 piston under middle C (Key No. 25) and subsequent numbers at about two key spaces apart towards the treble end. The Royal Canadian College of Organists has proposed that No. 1 should be under Tenor G (Key No. 20) and this is supported by the contention that this places six or eight pistons and one or more on-or-off coupler-control pistons about the epi-centre of the hands and readily within thumb-reach in normal playing. The position of the general cancel piston and the capture-setter button have become standardized, the former at extreme treble end and the other at the bass end of the lowest manual.

Good practice dictates that the numbered piston under each manual should be in line vertically as this assists quick location, particularly those of the choir which may be out of sight.

Reversible or on-or-off pistons, either thumb or toe, are usually intended to give quick changes of pedal or manual couplers, sometimes tremulants, major reed-stop or a *tutti* (full organ). Much ingenuity has been exercised in devising neat mechanisms for this purpose, indeed a book could be written about the many ingenious designs devised for this one piece of organ action.

Sometimes double-touch thumb-pistons are specified. These have two stages of movement—the first up to a firm spring stop, the second requiring thereafter about twice the pressure to overcome it. This gives a second position or touch, which can be made to do a number of useful ancillary control movements. Most often this is used to give a suitable pedal combination to the first-touch manual selection. Perhaps it is the neat and deliberate technique necessary to avoid accidental working that has not endeared it to many players.

In designing an organ console, and almost every organ specification has some individual speciality or peculiarity that deserves thought as to its best control, certain rules must be observed, besides the generally accepted positions for individual manual controls. Easily the most important is that a system of control should not require the player to remember that at times the stop-knobs do not tell at a glance the true stop registration on each manual. *Crescendo* pedals are objectionable on this score and also, but to a lesser extent, the Continental 'Free combination' system. Relevant couplers, those augmenting the division in particular, are best grouped with the stop-knobs, to ensure quick comprehension at a glance. The use of separate rocking tablets for couplers is open to criticism for this reason, and can only be justified when the console height must be kept low (Plate 18).

Where a stop-jamb indication cannot be made very clearly, as for instance where the *crescendo* pedal or a 'full organ' piston is 'on', an arresting luminous indicator should be provided. Many tuners can tell of urgent journeys merely to find a *crescendo*-pedal just engaged. Special couplers such as great reeds on choir, should not only be placed conveniently to hand, but also where they can be quickly and accurately read in conjunction with the relevant manual stops.

In this matter of quick comprehension of the state of registration, the use of colour contrast is of great importance. Red and black engraving is a useful difference. The introduction of other colours is rarely successful in the prevailing lighting, as the alternatives, blue, brown or green are of low contrast to an ivory surface and therefore not easy to read. These considerations of colour contrast also come into the woodwork finishes; however fresh and attractive bleached or limed oak may seem, there is a loss of definition by contrast, and this explains the popular but funereal black stop-jamb panels so often adopted. A dull finished dark oak or walnut jamb is just as effective and less harsh in contrasting appearance.

What does the future hold in organ console design? The long life expectation built into most organ parts tends to preclude bold experimental changes. Small improvements here and there can point to a trend in design. One that can be noted is the shrinking bulk of the detached console, brought about by the difficulty of finding a suitable position in the average congested chancel. In turn this has encouraged development and improvement in the electro-magnetic mechanism which has inherent compactness, and with its wider use, cost reductions can be expected. This lighter mechanism, less rigid in structure, may yet produce something better than the doubtful advantages attributed to the adjustable, or rise-and-fall stool. Instead we may yet have stop-jambs adjustable to our reach, and in place of the rise-and-fall bench, a rise-and-fall pedal board, which a moment's reflection will confirm as being a logical way of meeting the wide variation in bodily dimensions amongst players. It may also be the answer to the difficulty of getting builders to adopt common fundamental dimensions.

Most console designers wonder why they go to the considerable trouble of making lockable enclosing doors or covers when they see how often they are not used. Elimination of enclosing covers can materially reduce console bulk and make a useful cost saving. Security can be had by an automobile style lockswitch to the blower starter. Anyway daylight keeps the keys and knobs whiter, if they are of ivory, as in the best work.

Some design points still defy general solution, notably music desk details and lighting. Should desks be solid panels or open framework to see through? The use of laminated glass has possibilities, being transparent (when clean!) and yet providing a solid ground when making pencil annotations. At present the available transparent plastics are insufficiently scratch-proof and their marked electrostatic properties attract excessive amounts of dust. Perhaps the most useful thing to say about music desks is that for service playing they cannot be too big (Plate 27).

There is a trend in design towards reducing detached console costs for the smaller, simpler instrument in which full scale 'magnificence' is a high overhead on otherwise economical designs. This is being achieved by simpler lines in cabinet work and internal layout (Plate 11) while still respecting basic dimensions. This is an interesting manifestation of contemporary industrial design in organ-building.

11
The Stops

(a) Flue pipes

The stops of the organ may be divided into two classes, the reed stops and the flue stops. As flue stops are the most numerous we will discuss these first. A flue pipe is what the ordinary lay person thinks of as an organ pipe. It consists of a long tube known as the 'body' which is supported by a generally shorter conical section known as the 'foot'. Where these two portions adjoin, there is an opening in the front of the pipe, the 'mouth', and inside, there is a partition called the 'languid' which separates the body from the foot, with the exception of a small slit from which the wind issues. This is the 'flue', from which this type of pipe is named.

A full scientific explanation of the principles of operation of flue pipes would be out of place here, and indeed, the facts are not entirely out of the realm of controversy. A brief description will however be necessary. Air supplied by the bellows is let into the foot of the pipe by the 'chest' or 'soundboard' on which the pipe stands, the tip of the pipe, which has a hole in it, being shaped to fit in the countersunk hole on the top of the chest. This air emerges from the foot at the flue, whence it is blown upward across the mouth and into the upper lip. The air passes alternately on either side of the lip giving rise to a vibration known as the edge tone. The natural pitch of the edge tone depends on the speed of the air flow and on the distance between the flue and the upper lip of the pipe (known as the 'cut-up'). It is normally much higher than the actual speaking note of the pipe. The edge tone vibration is closely coupled to the air in the body of the pipe which has a natural resonant frequency. As the amount of air in the body is many times greater than that vibrating in the mouth, it is the natural resonance of the former which, to a large extent, determines the pitch of the resulting note. The air in the body merely acts as a resonator and amplifier—the original energy comes from the edge tone. The recorder, and to a slightly lesser extent, the orchestral flute, work in much the same way.

The range of fundamental pitches generated by organ pipes ranges from about 16 beats per second, which is the C below bottom A on the

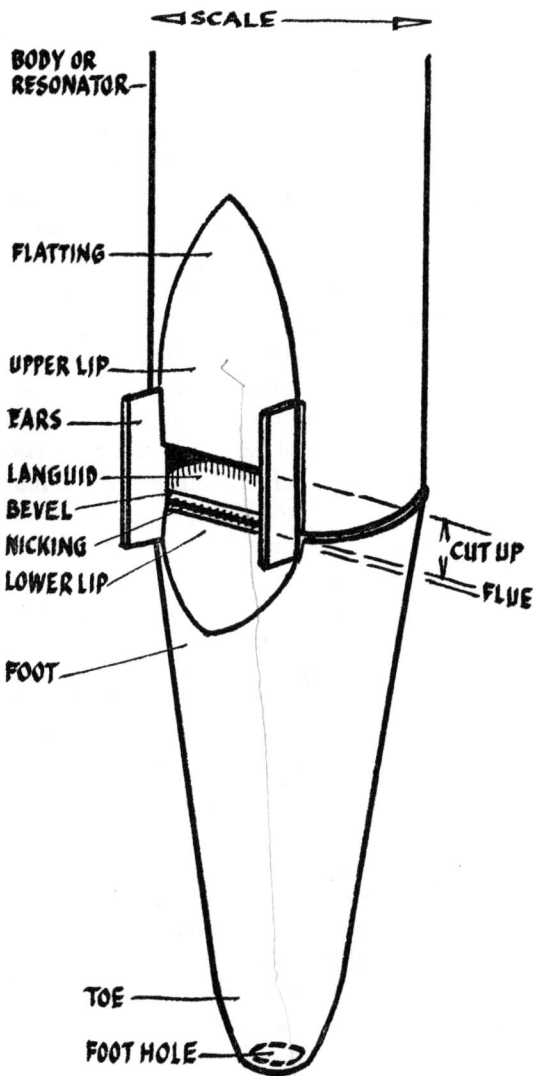

FIG. 31. The parts of the flue pipe

piano and as low or lower than most people hear as a musical note, up to approximately 8,000 cycles per second which is about as high a note as the average radio will produce. The length of the body of the pipe varies inversely with the pitch, from about 32 ft. for the lowest notes to ¾ in. for the highest. The foot of the pipe, however, has no influence on the pitch, almost its only function being to hold the rest of the pipe up. Its length varies from about 7 in. for the highest notes (the minimum required for the pipes to stand easily in their racks and about 90 per cent of the total length) up to some 2 or 3 ft. for the largest (which is only about 10 per cent of the total length, and the minimum required for the air to lose its turbulence after leaving the chest). This great length of the bass pipes, is one of the major difficulties in fitting organs into restricted locations. Fortunately, stopped pipes need have only half the body length of open pipes, but use of these implies acceptance of limitations in both tone quality and power. The 'Haskell' pipe which is an ingenious method of getting 'open' tone from a pipe of stopped length, still has a limited power and frequently suffers from slow speech. Coupled with the complications of its manufacture, this has prevented its wide acceptance.

The tone quality of a musical sound is governed by the strength and nature of the overtones, both harmonic and enharmonic, which accompany the fundamental. The air in the body of the pipe can only vibrate in a harmonic way, but mild enharmonic sounds may be generated at the mouth. The most important factor controlling the tone quality of an organ pipe is its 'scale', or diameter of the body. This is because the higher resonant frequencies of a pipe are not quite in tune with the harmonics of the fundamental pitch, and since the air can only vibrate in a harmonic manner these out of tune resonances are not excited. For a given pitch, the greater the diameter of the pipe, the more pronounced the effect, and the flutier the resulting tone.

It might be imagined that, this being so, the proportion of diameter to length should remain the same throughout the compass of a given stop. On the other hand, some of the very earliest organs apparently had all the pipes of the same diameter. In fact, experience has shown the ideal to lie between these two, the diameter of the pipe being halved when the length of pipe has been reduced to rather less than half. The proportions of the pipes, therefore, get slowly more 'tubby' as one ascends the scale. The reason for this lies at least partly in the varying sensitivity of the ear to different pitches. In the middle of the nineteenth century Töpfer proposed that pipe scales should be made to a definite geometric progression, instead of to haphazard empirical scales as

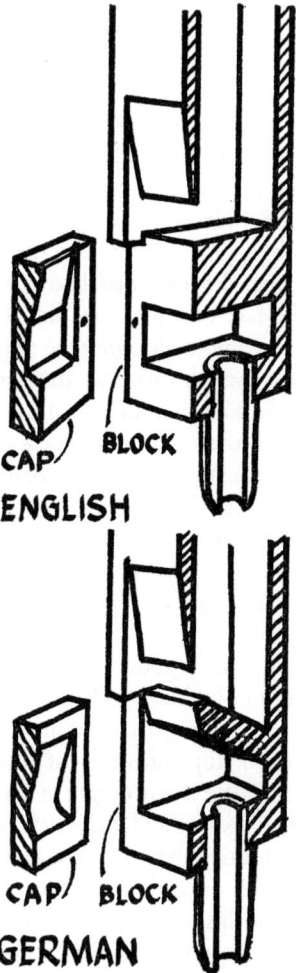

FIG. 31a

hitherto, and quoted some rather doubtful pseudo-scientific reasoning in favour of all stops halving on the seventeenth note. In Germany and America, Töpfer's progressions have been widely adopted, but in England, whilst using his progressions for ease in specifying and setting out scales, most organ-builders vary the progressions in different octaves and between different stops. These may vary between halving on the twentieth note for strings, or even slower for flutes, 'to halving on the fifteenth note for 16-ft. diapason basses, but each organ-builder has his own individul rules and is generally reluctant to disclose them.

We have seen that variations in scale produce differences in tone quality, and this is of course one of the major differences between different stops. In this connection it is well to remember that, within limits, the scale and the power of the stop are interchangeable; for instance a soft dulciana has approximately (though not exactly) the same tone quality as a Schultze open diapason, but at a much lower power level, and with a pipe barely half the diameter. It will be appreciated, however, that the tonal match in this instance is not exact, and this underlines the fact that there are limits to the variations to scales which can be used without changing the tone. In fact, as a general rule it could be said that, though variations in the scale of top notes and high-pitched stops produce changes in tone quality rather than power, minor changes of scale in the 16- and 8-ft. octave produce changes in power rather than tone quality. The best organ-builders use this to compensate for differences in the acoustics of different buildings. One example is a modern church with large areas of glass and possibly a suspended ceiling, causing a low reverberation period in the bass and demanding correspondingly increased scales in the bass to compensate.

Despite what has been written above, it is regrettably true, however, that in the past many organ-builders, not of the first rate, have used the same scales for all their organs, regardless of the size and acoustics of the church, differently named stops on different manuals also frequently being of identical scales. There is one organ, in a noted school of music, where the great open diapason and the swell Salicional [*sic*] are of exactly the same scale and treatment! This was, I believe, not uncommon in the products of this organ-builder, now happily defunct.

It may be of interest at this point to give some idea of the different scales used by organ-builders for different stops, for buildings with average acoustical qualities.

The smallest scale commonly met with is about $\frac{7}{8}$ in. at 2 ft. C (Middle C of an 8-ft. stop), this, or even smaller scales being used for really keen strings, particularly those of the 1900–30 era. Such stops generally bear the name of 'viole, or viole d'orchestre', softer versions being echo viole or viole sourdine. The milder strings of the 1865–90 period generally named viola da gamba have returned to favour in recent years with a scale of $1\frac{1}{4}$ in. at 2 ft. C. Their softer versions, staple fare of the English swell for many years, the Salicionals, Angelicas, etc., generally measure about $1\frac{3}{16}$ in. at 2 ft. C. The dulcian however

Plate 1. One manual organ in Carisbrooke Castle Museum. Built in the Netherlands in 1602, it is surely the ultimate in enrichment, even the pipes, all of wood are richly carved from the solid.

Photo Crown copyright

Plate 2. (*Top left*) Cambridge, Pembroke College Chapel. The projecting "chair" organ case is English form of the continental Rückpositif.

Plate 3. (*Top right*) Germany, St. Lamberti, Gladbeck (Johannes Klais). A modern example of the "werkprinzip" or spatial disposition of the diversions. Centre forward is the Rückpositif with behind and above the player the Brüstwerk (swell) topped by the Oberwerk (great), and flanked by the pedal in two towers.

Plate 4. (*Left*) Portugal, Braga Cathedral. One half of the towering two Rocco organ cases featuring the traditional Iberian projecting Trompet.

Plate 5. (*Below*) Craftsman's pride. Snetzler signed all his works but hid inside the windchest.

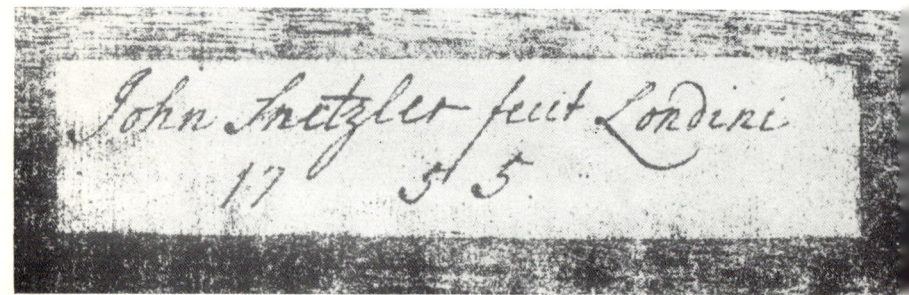

Plate 6. (*Left*) London, The Hyde Park (Mormon) Chapel. A small concert-organ arranged in the open display manner, great organ to left, pedal to right and pedal reed and swell at back. (Hill Norman & Beard.)

F. Watson

Plate 7. (*Below*) Organ pipes in their ranks. *Left to right,* tapered gemshorns, stoppered flutes, open spotted metal principals, ear-tuned chimney flutes and diapasons.

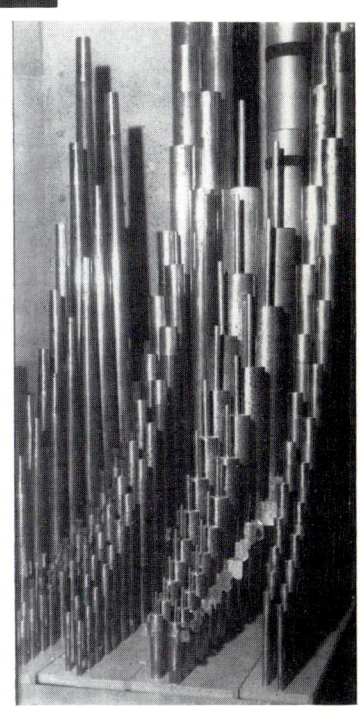

Plate 8. (*Above*) An organ of 1602 now in Carisbrooke Castle Museum. A rear view with the ornate case removed revealing the simple essentials of organ construction. Below the bench of the sturdy frame is the wind system, a double ribbed diagonal feeder, worked from the foot pedal, surmounted by a similarly ribbed and hinged bellows or reservoir, here shown closed and empty. On its top is a simple over-blow valve, tripped by the projecting arm striking the bench overhead. The hollowed wood trunk conducts the air to the windchest of the soundboard. The device on the moulded bracket at its top is the tremulant. The windchest pallet valves are under the keys and out of sight. The stop-knobs can be seen at the ends of the pipe chest. The first row of pipes, with very short turned and hollowed resonators, is the regal, a softly buzzing reed stop; next are two flutes, the upper notes of walnut hollowed out and fancifully turned and carved. The stopper handles are shaped and cut to represent thistle heads.

Photo Crown copyright

Plate 9. A modern functional tone-cabinet cased gallery organ. Heptonstall Church. (H. N. & B.)

Plate 9a. Tone cabinet casework, part of the acoustic design of a five rank chorus one manual. (H. N. & B.)

Plate 10. A typical arrangement of draw stop knobs, keyboards and combination thumb pistons.

Plate 10a. An alternative stop control system, stop keys arranged above the manuals.

Plates 11 & 11a. An ultra compact two manual stop-key console design achieved by slide-in keys and a drop-hood cover. (H. N. & B.)

Plate 12. Two manual stop-key console for a larger instrument and cased for a prominent position. (H. N. & B.)

Plate 13. Three manual stop-key console with all controls concentrated in an arc close to the manuals. (H. N. & B.)

Plate 14. A concert organ four manual stop-key console, mobile and relatively compact. A showman's console. (Dome Pavilion, Brighton — H. N. & B.)

Plate 15. Two manual stop-tablet console, with combination setting switches in side drawers. (H. N. & B.)
F. Watson

Plate 16. Two manual plain stop-knob console of contemporary compact design. (H. N. & B.)
F. *Watson*

Plate 17. Three manual stop-knob console. An essentially plain British design in a Canadian Cathedral. (Kingston, Ont. – H. N. & B.)

Plate 18. Three manual stop-knob console. Coupler controls by stop keys achieves low height. (H. N. & B.)

Plate 19. Three manual stop-knob console. Wider stop jambs and stop-keys for couplers gives lowest practical height. (Ottawa, Ont. St. Matthews – H. N. & B.)

Plate 20. Stop-knob console designed to Canadian requirements, the height is minimised by stop tablet coupler controls. The facetted jambs present each column of knobs in the same aspect to the player. The clock is an aid to radio broadcasting. (A. Q. St. Lambert, United Ch. – H. N. & B.)

M. Mornay

Plate 21. "As beautiful as a field of daisies", comment by proud foreman on its arrival at Norwich Cathedral. (H. N. & B.)

Plate 22. (*Above*) Four manual massiveness – Marlborough College Chapel. (H. N. & B.)

Plate 23. (*Left*) A four manual designed to be low enough to see over. (Winnipeg, Man. St. Lukes – H. N. & B.)

Plate 24. (*Below*) The rare four manual stop-knob console clearly displaying progressively inclined keyboards. (Moosejaw, Sask, St. Andrews – H. N. & B.)

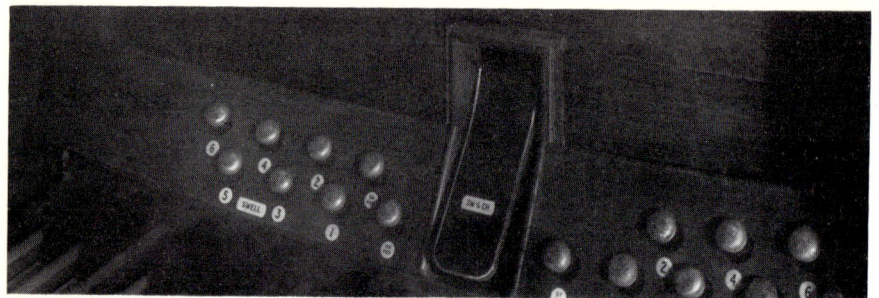

Plate 25. Foot controls: pedal keys, toe combination pistons and swell expression pedal.

Plate 26. This precision engineered relay can instantly memorise six thumb piston combinations of 15 stops, on the combination capture systems. (H. N. & B.)

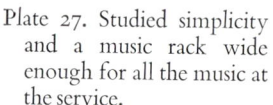

Plate 27. Studied simplicity and a music rack wide enough for all the music at the service.

Plate 28. Flue pipes in their varied shapes, lengths and sizes, showing ear-tuning, stopper tuning and sleeve or slide tuners.

Plate 29. A reed voicer's workshop

Plate 30. The mounted cornet, a short compass 3 rank mixture stop set up clear above the other stops. (Cambridge, St. Mary the Great – H. N. & B.)

Norman S. Hall

Plate 31. An early example of the revised use of Trompette-en-chamade. (Dunster Church – H. N. & B.)

Plate 32. (*Left*) Holbrook Royal Naval School, Suffolk. Probably the largest organ grille in the U.K. (H. N. & B.)

Plate 33. (*Below*) Bass pipes with elegantly proportioned foot lengths for a simple functional screen, aided by some "overlength" on those of smaller diameter. (Griffnock Church – H. N. & B.)

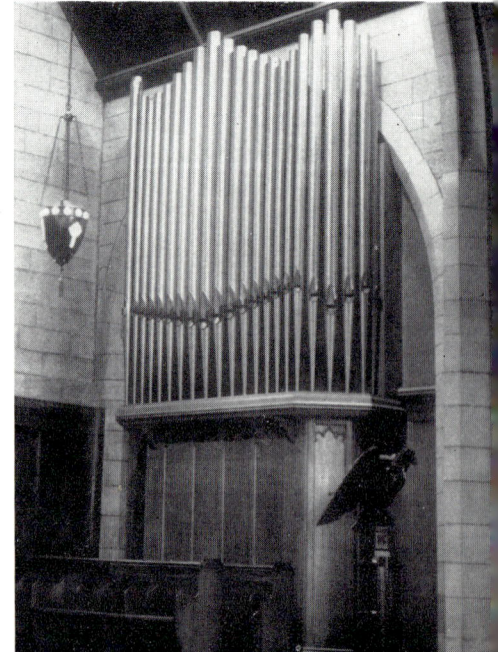

Plate 34. Open display of pipework relying on natural size and length progressions, and contrasts in pipe shapes and materials to form an interesting composition. (Hyde Park Mormon Chapel – H. N. & B.)

Plate 35. A notable 19th century monumental composition of mighty bass pipes (32 ft.) and open display through arched openings. (London, Royal Albert Hall – Willis.)

Plate 36. 17th century British classical which in its original shallow form incorporated tone-cabinet effects. (Cambridge, St. Mary the Great; Father Smith; recast and restored – H. N. & B.)

Plate 37. (*Above*) A free-standing antiphonal organ designed to lead large diocesan gatherings (Bradford Cathedral – Sir Edward Maufe.)

Plate 38. (*Right*) A modern Cathedral organ case in 17th century style. This case owes much to the carefully proportioned foot lengths and the scale of the superb enrichment. (Norwich Cathedral – S. Dykes Bower.)

Plate 39. The two manual "werkprinzip" clearly stated. (Doetinchem, Holland.)

Plate 40. Natural length bass pipes and en-chamade trumpets composed as a case by openly expressing the necessary stay framing. Viewed through the ancient screen there seems a conflict of verticals. (Dunster Church – Norman.)

Plate 41. (*Below*) Small organs can look well. A lively scaled-down Netherlands style of tone cabinet case. (The Denham – NP Mander.)

Plate 42. (*Below*) Tone cabinet design as an integral part of the acoustic design of a five stop chorus organ. (The Quintet – Norman.)

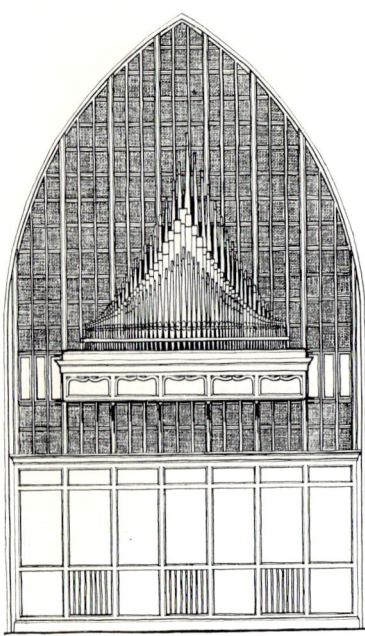 

Plate 43. A combination of projecting unenclosed pipework and large free area grille on a west gallery. (Trinity College School Chapel Port Hope, Ont. – H. N. & B.)

Plate 44. Getting the great organ out of the confining arch was the reason for this bracketed treatment in oak and polished tin. (P. Q., St. Lambert, St. Barnabas Church – Norman.)
Fred Knapton

Plates 45 & 46. Careful control of functional detail and the rigid elimination of all "casework" in an organ that may be viewed from all four sides. (Heptonstall Parish Church – McGuire & Murray and H. N. & B).

THE STOPS 117

is on much the same scale as the viola da gamba ($1\frac{5}{16}$ in. at 2 ft. C is commonly used) the main difference being in power and treatment. $1\frac{1}{2}$ in. or just over is a scale seldom used successfully for manual stops, though it is common for pedal violones, and the smallest diapasons, named violin diapason and geigen diapason are generally about $1\frac{5}{8}$ in. or a little more. $1\frac{3}{4}$ in. to 2 in. is the normal scale for diapason work though in large buildings $2\frac{1}{8}$ in. has been used with success, and this was the usual scale too, of the leathered open diapason of the 1900–30 era. Schultze and his followers used scales of $2\frac{1}{4}$ in. and upwards with success but these are seldom found today. The classical block flute scales around $2\frac{1}{2}$ in. and the largest stop of all is the nachthorn, up to $2\frac{3}{4}$ in. at the 2 ft. C.

The relative scaling of the different elements of the diapason chorus is, and always has been, a matter of some controversy, as it depends to some extent on the power relationship expected of the different pitches—a critical factor in the tonal composition of the *tutti* and one always susceptible to variations in the climate of musical opinion. In the era of suppressed upperwork the scales were naturally smaller, the fifteenth sometimes as much as eight or ten notes smaller than the 8 ft. diapason. In Schultze's work, as also in that of 'Father' Smith, the scales were much the same for all the diapason stops of whatever pitch. Some today would make the higher-pitched stops of larger scale than the unison, it being argued that in an 8-ft.-based chorus for instance the 4-ft. stop should be larger than the 8 ft., just as the 8 ft. is commonly larger than the 16 ft. in a 16-ft.-based chorus. There is indeed some truth in this, but logic by itself is no reliable guide, and one must constantly check the practical results of different scales, as measured in the light of current and probable future musical requirements. Different acoustical conditions in different buildings play their part too, a non-reverberant building calling for upperwork which is soft and fluty, and a reverberant one calling for the reverse.

The tone of the stop is affected not only by the scale of the pipe but also by the shape, the stops mentioned above all having plain parallel bodies of ordinary length. Some pipes, however, are made of double length for their pitch, a hole drilled at the mid-point of the side of the pipe making the pipe speak an octave above its normal pitch. The flute tone which results is reminiscent of the orchestral flute and the stop is generally labelled 'harmonic flute' or 'flauto traverso'. Particularly in 4-ft. pitch this stop found great favour in the latter decades of the nineteenth century as the normal 4-ft. flute on the great organ. Although an excellent solo stop, preferably in 8-ft. pitch, the hard and nearly pure tone of the harmonic flute blends badly in combination with diapason tone, and it is now less frequently made than in the past. A stopped harmonic pipe, of one and a half times the length of a normal open pipe, has also been used, the stop being named 'Zauberflöte'. The most common type of pipe after the normal open pipe is the stopped pipe. In this, alternate harmonics are suppressed giving a characteristic tone, and the pipe body is only half the normal length, hence its popularity for bass notes. This saving in height is of course the origin of the old stopped bass to soft-string stops, together with the fact that the technique of voicing basses to small-scale stops was only developed about eighty years ago. However the break in tone quality so frequently found in the old type of stopped bass is quite unnecessary, a stopped bass voiced on Quintaten lines can make the break between open and stopped pipes well-nigh undetectable.

The elimination of alternate harmonics in the stopped pipe, and the difficulty of voicing it with a low cut-up has resulted in most stopped stops being of a more or less fluty quality. Curiously the most fluty generally found is the smallest scale. The Lieblich Gedeckt, or in 16-ft. pitch, lieblich bourdon, is the commonest flute stop found on English organs built in the last 100 years, though paradoxically its origins lie in Germany and it was not known here before 1850. It is particularly popular for pedal organ 16-ft. stops because of its short length, small size and not least, relatively low cost. The normal scale for a Lieblich Gedeckt is about 2 in. at 4 ft. C, somewhat larger on the pedal. The 8-ft. and 16-ft. octaves, at least, are generally made of wood, as, until the introduction of zinc, it was not possible to make these pipes satisfactorily in metal, since the force of the stopper would split the soft pipe-metal.

The other common stopped stop is the stopped diapason, so called because, if of metal, the pipes in scale and mouth treatment approximately correspond to open diapason pipes cut in half and stoppered! The scale of this stop is accordingly about 3 in., or a little less, at the 4 ft. C for a metal pipe. Stopped diapasons, particularly in the eighteenth century, were, however, more usually made in wood throughout. Later nineteenth-century examples were generally cut-up fairly high to yield a fairly pure flute tone; but before that, and again more recently, the cut-up is kept quite low giving a characteristic tone which has a considerable range of harmonics.

The Quintaten is a much less common stop, still nominally a flute, but actually with a harmonic range comparable to a diapason or even a mild string. The scale is of a medium scale midway between stopped diapason and lieblich bedeckts, the tone quality being derived from its very low cut-up and the difficulty in voicing it accounting for its relative rarity. It is said that Father Smith intended to put one in his organ for St. Paul's but that it was one of the stops crowded out by Sir Christopher Wren's too-small case. Were it not for this misfortune it might have become a common English stop. In 16-ft. pitch it makes an excellent sub-unison stop for the great chorus, giving gravity without weight, and its highly coloured tone can be of great value as a solo stop at 8-ft. pitch. It can be made of wood and a mild wooden Quintaten in 4-ft. pitch was not an uncommon stop in eighteenth-century organs under the name of nason flute. It has always been common in Germany, but the small scale used there gives the stop an acidity which has never found favour in England.

One of the most common modifications to the stoppered pipe consists of adding a small open chimney to the pipe, either by soldering a metal chimney on top of a solid-top metal pipe, or by drilling a hole in the stopper of a stoppered-pipe, which has the same effect. This treatment adds a trace of the harmonics of the open pipe plus a little tang of its own, frequently being applied to stopped diapasons, and less often to Lieblich Gedeckts as well. A fairly full and fluty version of the stopped diapason so treated is commonly called chimney flute or rohr flute. The chimney treatment seldom extends below 4 ft. C as the chimney would have to be unreasonably long or the pipe would be put off speech.

The Koppelflöte, and its smaller-scaled brother the Spillflöte, is an interesting hybrid between open and stopped pipes, the tone quality resembling a chimney flute in the bass and a gemshorn in the treble. The body of the pipe is mainly cylindrical, surmounted by a cone with a relatively small hole in the top. Valuable as a fairly pure solo flute it is also an excellent blending stop with diapason tone, unlike many open flutes, and thus useful in the chorus as well. The trouble and expense of making, accounts for the relative rarity of this stop.

The Gemshorn is yet another variant on basic organ-pipe shape, frequently indicated by the German prefix Spitz-. This is a stop with a conical or tapered body, the top of the pipe being a smaller diameter than at the mouth. As it is a little more trouble to make than a parallel pipe one frequently finds a so-called gemshorn which is just a principal with a slot in the top to make it sound 'horny'. The true tapered stop, however, has a distinctive and unmistakable tone which is very attractive. Some of the earliest strings were constructed on the gemshorn principle, William Hill's viola da gambas having in addition a bell or flare on top of the pipe—hence the name 'Bell-Gamba'. The Spitzgamba is the only string considered respectable in continental neo-Baroque circles. The Spitzprincipal is the normal Gemshorn form, common in 4-ft. pitch on nineteenth-century English swell organs. The Spitzflute (or more accurately Spitzflöte) is a large-scale open flute, the taper giving it blending qualities that would otherwise be lacking. This tone can be particularly useful in $2\frac{2}{3}$-ft. pitch. The converse of the Gemshorn, the Dolce or outward flared pipe, has a hard horny tone which has made it little more than a curiosity.

Having considered the scale and the shape of the pipe, the next important factor which needs to be specified by the organ designer is the width of the mouth. The latter is measured as a fraction of the circumference of the pipe and varies between a sixth and a fourth or even wider. In general, the wider the mouth the more powerful and less refined is the tone of the pipe and vice-versa. Thus a powerful Shultze-type diapason frequently has a two-sevenths or 'three and a half' mouth, and for diapasons anything less than a two-ninths or 'four and a half' mouth is too anaemic. Dulcianas and mild strings are generally made with a fifth mouth, and nachthorns from which a relatively gentle tone is required, despite the large scale, have a sixth mouth.

Since the vibrations are air vibrations rather than the vibrations of solid parts characteristic of stringed instruments, one might expect that the organ pipe material will have little effect upon the tone. However, an experienced organ-builder knows that this is very far from being the case, and that although one cannot radically change the tone of a pipe by a change of material, the effect is not inconsiderable. Except for pipe constructed of very thick material producing a hard 'dead' quality, the vibrations of the body caused by variations in the pressure inside, react on the tone, causing a diminution of some harmonics and reinforcement of others.

The great majority of organ pipes are constructed of a tin-lead alloy, known to organ-builders simply as 'metal', which is easily worked, almost corrosion-proof, and can be readily cut and manipulated by the voicer. This alloy is made up into flat sheets of different thicknesses by a casting-cum-extrusion process which has remained unchanged for centuries. In this, a rectangular wooden box filled with molten metal travels the length of a level 'casting table', the rear edge of the box being raised slightly to leave a narrow slot between it and the 'table', the dimensions of which govern the thickness of the metal sheet obtained. The sheets are then cut out to the patterns of the individual pipes according to the scale selected and the pipes formed by beating the metal round wooden mandels, the seam and all other joints being soldered. As solder is itself a tin-lead alloy this amounts almost to a welded joint. The feet of the pipes are of course made separately and joined to the bodies after the languid has been inserted. Not unnaturally the quality or otherwise of the workmanship, particularly of the mouth parts, will have a definite effect on the finished results. Whereas a bad voicer can easily spoil a good pipe, a good voicer can seldom overcome the handicap of a bad pipe, or indeed one specified with the wrong quality or thickness of metal.

These two important factors, the thickness of the metal and the proportions of tin in the alloy go hand in hand. If one wishes for a bright tone one uses a relatively thin metal, with more tin in it, if one wishes for a dull, bland tone one uses a thicker metal with less tin. If the pipes are to be voiced very loudly, as for Edwardian-style open diapasons and in the theatre organ stops, thick metal is also needed, as a thin pipe will vibrate so as to kill the tone. An alloy with much tin in it is said to be 'rich'. Since tin is at present twelve times the price of lead this seems highly appropriate. A thin pipe of 'poor' metal is not commonly found as it would be so easily damaged, an increase of tin making the pipe much stiffer, and conversely a thick pipe of 'rich' metal would be expensive and wasteful. In England the most commonly used alloy is 'plain metal' about 20 per cent tin, and is used for most flutes and many diapason stops also. The other alloy frequently met is 'spotted metal' containing 40–50 per cent tin, which has a distinctive appearance of bright irregularly shaped spots. This effect, which is quite unmistakable, goes right through the thickness of the metal and is entirely natural. Despite its expense this metal is normally used in good-class work for string stops and frequently for some diapason stops also, particularly for the treble pipes where its added strength is an additional asset. Spotted metal is also used occasionally for front pipes owing to its decorative properties. On the continent even higher proportions of tin are regularly in use, 70 per cent tin being usual, but this alloy is rarely used in England as the very bright tone obtained is really only suitable for very reverberant buildings, which are less common here than in Europe. Although 'tin metal' looks superficially rather like 'plain metal', it is much whiter in colour than the blue-grey tint of common plain metal.

Large pipes of plain metal tend, as age softens the metal, to collapse under their own weight. The front pipes of old Samuel Green organs are particularly notorious in this respect. The only way to overcome this is to use high proportions of tin but this costs a lot of money and since about 1870 most pipes more than 4 ft in length have been made of cold rolled zinc. This has a hard brighter sound than 'metal', but this is reduced by the lips and other mouth parts made of 'metal', which are let into the zinc so that they can be cut and manipulated by the voicer. The zinc pipe is lighter and stronger than the equivalent 'metal' pipe. It is also much more resistant to bruising. In America soft baked zinc is frequently used for ease in manufacturing the pipes, but has a poor reputation in so far as its tonal qualities are concerned. Copper has also been used for bass pipes mostly on the Continent, partly on the ground of its striking appearance as front pipes, and partly as a 'half-way house' between the admittedly thin tone of zinc basses and the fabulous cost of solid tin ones.

Pipes made of wood, have been in use for a long time. In old organs, because of the tenderness and cost of large 'metal' pipes wood pipes were used for nearly all the basses, and of course the power and weight of the English 'pedal open' would be quite out of the question with any reasonably constructed 'metal' or zinc pipe. Wood pipes were invariably used for the basses to all the stopped ranks since, until the invention of the canister-topped pipes (made of zinc), the construction of large stoppered metal pipes was impractical.

In spite of their being more trouble to make than metal ones, wood is also used for treble pipes, where a mellow sound is required, as in orchestral flutes such as the Wald Flute and Hohl Flute. The stopped diapason is also frequently made of wood, and if the material is carefully graded to thickness and quality, a characteristic attack and tone quality can be obtained which differs appreciably from that of a metal pipe. In a wood pipe the mouth is always as wide as the width of the pipe, the effect of varying mouth widths being obtained by varying the proportion of width to depth of the pipe. Thus a deep pipe has a relatively narrow mouth relative to the cross-sectional area of the body, and the effect of a very wide mouth is obtained with a triangular pipe. Most wood pipes are made of spruce, the smaller ones requiring particularly high-grade timber. Sometimes small wood pipes are made of mahogany, or with an oak front, though this has little audible effect. Some old builders however have used oak for wood basses, giving a slightly brighter tone than spruce.

(b) Flue-pipe Voicing

Although the pipes have been made with considerable precision as to scale, thickness and mouth, they have as yet only hesitant and uncultured speech, if any at all. Imparting musical speech is the step known as voicing.

A voicer has many adjustments open to him that will make or mar the finished results according to intentions or taste in these matters. The most important is the 'cut-up' that is the height of the upper lip from the lower lip. The less this is, the lower the height or cut-up, the edgier is the sound produced. The higher it is, the more hollow the sound. This must be qualified in that a lower cut-up is needed on soft voices such as the dulciana and quite a bit more for loudly voiced stops. To a limited extent, a voicer can make up for errors or deficiencies in scaling, by applying slightly higher cut-up when underscaled, but the similarity between small-scale cut-up high and a large scale with a low mouth is only superficial. The latter has a deliberate and interesting sound, well suited to unenclosed divisions, whereas the high-cut smaller scale will have a harder, ringing sound, with more carrying power, more suited to enclosed departments, and if used in the open is inherently more tiring to the ear than the speech of larger scales.

Many voicers measure the cut-up as a proportion of the mouth width. This method compounds inaccuracies of scale, or mouth width, which may occur in making the pipe. Accuracy in cutting-up is an important factor in securing regularity of quality throughout a stop. If mouth height is measured from a carefully prepared scale, not only is accuracy more easily achieved, the voicer can also vary the relative extent of cut-up in the different parts of the compass by varying his progression, or rate of change.

The 'cut-ups' commonly used vary surprisingly little. Dulcianas and gambas are cut up from $\frac{3}{16}$ in. to $\frac{1}{4}$ in. at 2 ft. C, depending upon the power required; diapason chorus stops and stopped diapasons $\frac{3}{8}$ in. to $\frac{1}{2}$ in. and lieblich gedeckts about $\frac{5}{8}$ in. Cutting-up is done with a sharp, short and thick-bladed knife that cuts the soft metal with ease.

In general, the higher the cut-up the more wind the pipe requires to give the same volume of sound, and this brings us to the somewhat vexed question of wind-pressures. From the aspect of tone production it is the pressure in the pipe-foot that is significant, not the pressure in the windchest. With conventionally voiced pipes, which are regulated by adjustment of the foot tip-hole, these two are not the same. For a given tone and power and therefore pipe-foot pressure, the soundboard pressure may vary widely, provided it is above the required foot pressure. In practice, chamber organs excepted, the minimum will vary from just under 3 in. wg. for favourably placed unenclosed departments, up to 4 in. wg. or more for small-scaled enclosed pipework.

The upper practical limit is set by the 'windy' noises made when a high pressure is reduced by a very small tip-hole. It is difficult to get prompt speech with very high pressures, as the wind takes time to fill the foot of the pipe through the necessarily small tip-hole. The upper limit is around 6 in. or 7 in. wg., but 4½ in. wg. is quite sufficient for all the flue pipes in a properly sited organ.

The next factor in voicing is 'nicking', which is the series of light nicks in the edge of languid and the lower lip. This nicking has the effect of reducing the amplitude of the 'edge-tones' which it will be recalled, is the oscillation at the mouth of the pipe and the fundamental basis of tonal generation. In practical terms this has two results. Firstly because the basic source of energy is reduced, the pipe tends to speak less rapidly if nicked, and when it does speak will sound very nearly its correct note when sustained. When the pipe is not nicked the energy in the edge tone, which, acoustically uncoupled to the resonance of the pipe, is relatively high-pitched, can cause a transient 'spit' or 'chiff' before the pipe settles down to its correct note.

Secondly, light nicking reduces the high-pitched and in part non-harmonic edge tones heard when at close quarters with the pipes. Heavy nicking goes further and considerably curtails some of the upper harmonics in the sound generated. The more powerfully blown a pipe is the more nicking is required to produce acceptable musical results.

Where pipes need to be only moderately blown, they may be voiced on the *flue regulation* system. In the conventional system of voicing already described, the air supply is regulated by making a more or less large hole in the tip of the pipe-foot, using a sharp pointed knife or a swaging tool in the form of a cone, a knocking-up cup. The flue of windway at the mouth is left fairly wide, its adjustment not being particularly critical. In the flue regulation method, the pipe-foot tip is left wide open resulting in the pipe-foot pressure being very near that of the windchest, which in turn is kept low, not above 2¾ in. wg. The power of the pipe speech is then regulated by critical adjustment of the lower lip, widening or narrowing the flue or windway. The range is quite small. The narrower flue restricts the amount of air blowing across the mouth, this making the 'edge tone' more amenable to control by the pipe and producing to a limited extent the effect of light nicking. In a pipe so voiced, nicking may not be required, particularly if the pipes are to go into a reverberant building, where a proper amount of 'spit' in the speech of the pipes will assist in giving clarity to polyphonic music.

It cannot be overemphasized that either *the absence or the use of nicking is not a virtue in itself but a means to an end.* It is in fact quite common for the top octave or so of a fifteenth to be voiced without nicking.

The thickness of the lip is also a factor that has a bearing on the finished tone quality. A lip bevelled to a thin edge gives a slightly edgier sound than one cut squarely with a knife. The effect is somewhat similar to reducing the nicking slightly except that it seems to affect the steady tone more than the initial speech. A finely bevelled top lip is essential for good string stops, but most flutes are cut square. Square-cut lips are also generally used when voicing with flue regulation and minimum nicking as they reduce some of the inharmonic 'windy' noises in the tone. The leathered lip, which is a normal lip artificially thickened by a covering inside and out of thin leather, was much used by voicers in the Edwardian period. It drastically reduced the higher harmonics of the pipe and is now thought by musicians to have been a mistake.

In stops with a very high cut-up, such as Lieblich Gedeckts and Bourdons, the top lip is frequently arched, that is the cut-up is greater in the centre of the mouth than at the sides. The purpose of this is to permit the mouth to be high in the centre where the air is flowing most rapidly across the mouth in order to get as pure a fundamental as possible, whilst not having it so high at the sides, where the air flow is less rapid, as to cause unsteadiness in the note.

The next important adjustment in voicing is concerned with the position of the languid. With properly made wood pipes this is automatically correct, but with metal pipes the height of the bottom surface of the languid relative to the lower lip can be varied. This will make a considerable difference to the speech and tone of a pipe. The adjustment is also affected by the position of the top lip of the pipe. If this is slightly pushed into the pipe it has the same effect as having the languid too high. In this latter case the pipe will be 'slow' on speech, or may not speak at all, as the air flow from the flue will miss the top lip of the pipe. This can be demonstrated by blowing hard at the mouth of such a pipe, when on the voicing machine, as this will almost always cause the pipe to speak, for a moment anyway. A 'voicing machine' incidentally is the name given to a specially constructed small organ in which the pipes are stood whilst being voiced so that their speech and tone can be readily adjusted.

The height of the languid is normally adjusted by tapping it up or down with a long piece of stiff wire pushed down the pipe (for the smaller pipes) or with a special tool held in the mouth (for the larger pipes). If it is tapped too low the pipe will be 'quick' on speech and the pipe will have a hard uninteresting tone. If the 'quickness' is more extreme the pipe will 'bubble' or even fly up to the octave. This appears to be due to a closer coupling of the edge tone to the pipe resonator when the air flow is diverted more into the pipe. In general, flutes are voiced fairly 'quick', but with diapasons and dulcianas an old voicer's maxim, somewhat Irish is: 'Make them as slow as you can without them actually being slow.' Pipes voiced with little nicking and flue regulated should, however, be voiced slightly quick, otherwise the initial 'spit' or 'chiff' becomes too long drawn out.

The final position of the languid to get the best speech does depend to some extent on the type of chest on which the pipe is to stand. Where a slider chest is used the languid can be higher than with those sliderless chests in which the pallet is directly under the pipe. Sliderless chests with 'expansion chambers' have the same effect as slider chests providing these are large enough (not less than 6 cu. ins. at 4 ft. C). A further effect of sliderless chests without expansion chambers is to make lightly nicked pipes 'chiff' more violently in much the same way as they do when the key is hit rapidly on a tracker instrument.

Being made of a lead-based alloy, the languids of the pipes tend to sink over the years, making the pipes gradually more and more quick, and conscientious restoration work has to include the resetting of the speech of old pipes. Dulcianas always seem to be particularly in need of attention after sixty years or so.

With narrow-scaled string pipes, particularly in the bass, it will be found that there is no position of the languid in which, unaided, the pipe will speak promptly without flying up to the octave. This precluded the voicing of such stops until about eighty years ago, and accounts for so many mild string-toned stops which stop at tenor C in early nineteenth-century instruments. However, this has been overcome by the invention of what is variously known as the 'bar', 'roller' or 'beard', which is generally a piece of wood, probably round in section and pinned between the ears of the pipe. When critically adjusted this restores the tone to the fundamental whilst permitting prompt speech.

With the other adjustments now made, there remains only the relatively simple matter of tuning. A voicer knows from experience how long the pipe needs to be, but in any case it can be fairly accurately calculated for open pipes from the formula: half the theoretical wavelength, less one and a half times the diameter of the pipe. For stopped pipes it depends rather more on the cut-up, but is never longer than one quarter the wavelength.

The method of tuning normally adopted today for open pipes is to fit the pipe with a tinned steel slide. This grips the top of the pipe with its own springiness and can be moved up or down with a sharp tap to make fine adjustment of the length of the pipe. The old method of 'coning in' the tops of the pipes with a specially shaped 'tuning cone' is now seldom used in new instruments because of the damage done to the pipes over a period of years in hitting them with the 'tuning cone'. Pipes tuned with tuning slides are, however, not quite as stable in tuning as cone-tuned pipes. Eventually the slides go rusty, but this affects their appearance more than their utility, and in any event they are relatively inexpensive to replace.

Methods of tuning stopped pipes are more diverse. Wooden pipes normally contain a wooden stopper with a handle, and in England stopped metal pipes are generally fitted with a cork stopper (not always with handles) in a similar manner. However, these stoppers swell and shrink with the atmosphere whilst the metal pipe does not, so that this method is not entirely satisfactory, and some builders, especially in North America, make use of metal 'canisters' which fit over the top of the pipe and are sealed with felt. Another method is to fix the top of the pipe, and tune by means of long flexible ears at the mouth. This latter method gives very stable tuning, but is a little extra trouble in the initial voicing and cutting to length. It is not new, having been used by Snetzler 200 years ago.

We have seen the processes which make up the important art of voicing. Basically the art is in the voicing of the first pipe—the decision as to the desired tone and power of a given stop. The craftsmanship comes in making all the other pipes match the original conception without perceptible break or variation. The final picture is not complete until all pipes are in the finished instrument and regulated individually to suit the acoustics of the building. This requires much time and patience and costs money, but only then does the instrument acquire musical personality.

(c) Reed pipes and their voicing

The reed stops are less numerous than flue stops, and are often omitted entirely in the smallest instruments. Nevertheless, as stops capable of very interesting tone-colours and also of considerable power they merit an important part of our attention. They are more complex in their construction, and are more trouble both to make and to voice, than flue pipes.

In the bottom of the reed pipe (known as the 'boot') is a brass tongue, the 'reed', which beats against the open side of a brass tube known as the 'shallot'. The tongue, which is removable, is held in position by a little wooden wedge. This fits with the shallot in the bottom of a lead casting called the block which rests on and in the removable body of the boot of the pipe (known as the socket). The vibrating length of the tongue can be varied by means of a specially shaped wire which holds the tongue against the shallot, the other ending projecting up through a hole in the block. This is known as the tuning spring. From the top of the block projects the resonator, or tube. This is connected to the inside of the shallot by the hole in the block. The resonator can be of many different shapes, but in the majority of reeds it is conical.

The reed pipe, scientifically speaking, is a coupled system like the flue pipe. The source of tone is the reed tongue vibrating on the shallot, and the air pulses so generated are modified by the resonator to the required tone quality. The reed is a much more powerful tone generator than the edge tone at the mouth of a flue pipe, and for this reason reed stops tend in general to be louder than flue stops. The reed is also less controlled by the resonator than the edge tone of a flue pipe and the pipe can be tuned both by altering the reed and by altering the resonator, unlike the flue pipe which can generally only be tuned by altering the resonator.

The shape of the resonator determines the broad tonal quality of the stop. A plain inverted conical resonator is used for trumpets and for other stops with a tone quality related to orchestral brass, such as horn, tromba, tuba, etc. Such a resonator gives a full series of harmonics without any selective bias, and as stated above, is the one most commonly employed. As with flue pipes the resonators may be made double length or 'harmonic'. This is commonly done with some of the upper notes, especially if the pressure is at all high, in order to secure extra power and tuning stability. Unlike flue pipes however, one can also have fractional length resonators, and this is sometimes used in the bass, on low wind-pressures, to restrain the power of the stop and give prompt speech. Thus on this basis a 16-ft. bass may have pipes only 8 ft. long, and this is possible because the reed determines the fundamental pitch rather than the resonator.

Another shape of resonator, used for stops of the oboe family, is a fairly narrow inverted conical tube surmounted by a 'bell' or cone of large diameter. These stops are sometimes 'capped' or fitted with a cover over the top, which acts as a type of mute, reducing the power. Lift-up or half-caps are, however, more common. Stops of this family are the oboe, generally voiced with a more horn-like quality than its

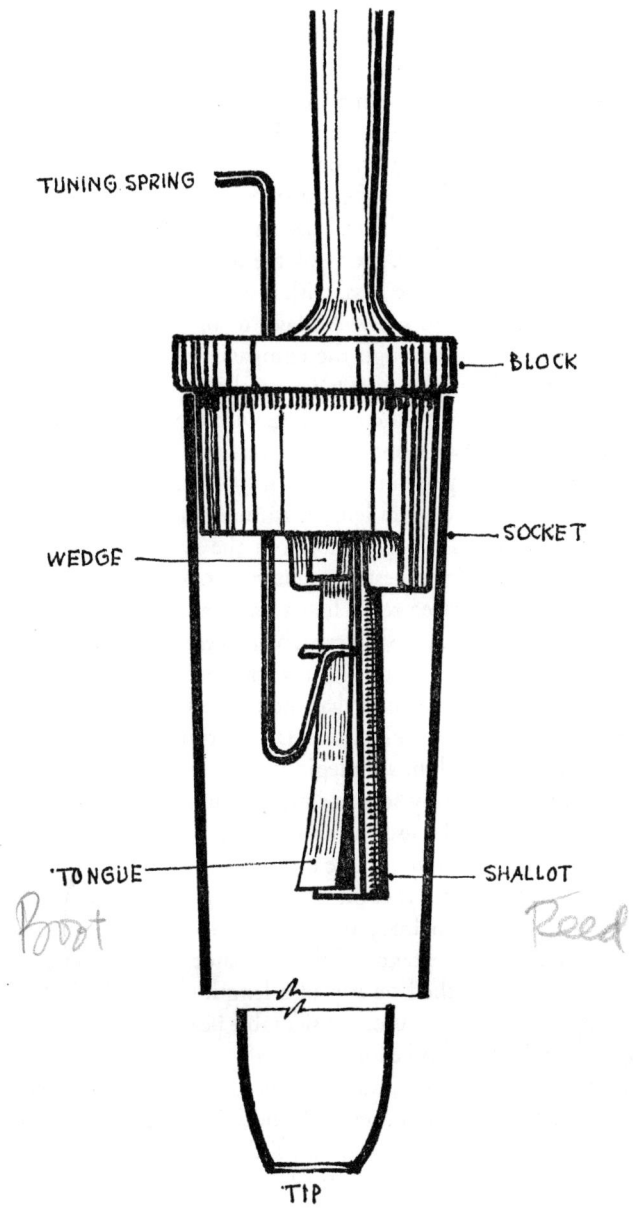

Fig. 32. The parts of a reed pipe

orchestral counterpart, and the so-called 'orchestral oboe' a romantic stop generally voiced as thin and acid in tone as possible. Another romantic stop of somewhat similar quality is known as the 'cor anglais'. It is generally constructed with a 'double bell' consisting of an inverted cone on top of the usual 'bell', and voiced somewhat less thin than the orchestral oboe. The Shalmey or Oboe-Shalmey is the neo-classical form of the oboe and named after the oboe's predecessor as an orchestral instrument. As with its orchestral namesake, it is voiced as a thin echo trumpet with oboe colour. Stops of the oboe family are generally of bassoon construction in the bass, with resonators of trumpet shape, but smaller scale. 16-ft. stops known as fagotto or bassoon often carry this construction right up through the compass.

Stops of the clarinet family have parallel resonators (except for a short portion at the bottom connecting with the boot) and correspond in harmonic content to stopped flue pipes, that is, only the odd numbered harmonics are prominent. Like stopped flue pipes, the pipes are only about half the nominal length. Romantically voiced clarinets are generally capped, and when enclosed in the swellbox can be a fairly close imitation of their orchestral counterparts. Some clarinet stops have also been made with free reeds like a harmonium instead of the conventional beating reed. The lower two octaves are a remarkable, if lifeless imitation of the orchestral instrument, but the treble notes are so lacking in attack and character that the stop is little more than a curiosity. The classical form of the clarinet is the Krummhorn or Crumbhorn or Cremorne—the spellings are legion! Here the stop is of smaller scale and voiced more brightly so that in this form it can combine with the flue chorus as well as be used as a solo stop.

A stop not fitting into the above three categories is the Rohr Shalmey. In length and appearance it comes in the clarinet family, but its sound is similar to the Oboe-Shalmey though slightly more coloured and less trumpet-like. The appearance of the resonator is best described as like a small cocoa tin perched on top of a length of gas pipe! Despite the comic appearance its tone is of considerable beauty and interest and it is a stop which deserves to become more popular.

The last category of reed stops is a broad group of stops with very short resonators only a fraction of the nominal length. Such resonators modify the tone of the reed relatively little and do not amplify it much either. The resulting tone is relatively soft and of a rasping character which is somewhat of an acquired taste, being frequently regarded by laymen as rather comic. It does, however, blend well with fluework, when in tune.

Because the resonators of these fractional-length reed-stops exert relatively little influence over the reed, they have to be made with what would otherwise appear to be exaggerated shapes in order to make any worthwhile alteration to the tone. The possible shapes for the resonators are accordingly very many. They may, however, be very roughly grouped into three types: vox humanas and bär-pfeife, rankets and sorduns, and regals. The vox humana type are made with resonators either of truncated clarinet form fitted with caps or half-cap, or with a 'double bell' type of resonator. The former is almost invariably used for the romantic form of the stop. Vox humana resonators normally have a proper ratio to the natural full length. Frequently the ratio changes from bass to treble in one or more breaks. Thus the resonators may be one-eighth length in the bases and finish up half-length in the treble, the appearance of the stop somewhat resembling a mixture! The Bär-pfeife, literally Bear-pipe, is a larger scale version of the vox humana, the larger scale giving it a deeper growl, presumably sounding more like a bear than a human! It is not used in romantic instruments.

The Ranketts and Sorduns, named after obsolete orchestral instruments, have resonators consisting of a tube leading up into the top of a metal or wooden box, the top of which is closed, but the bottom of which is open to atmosphere either by some form of inverted flap or by a series of small holes drilled around the lower edge of the box. The effect of such a resonator, scientifically speaking, is rather akin to that of the silencer of an automobile. In a very small space it tends to cut the higher harmonics drastically but to affect the fundamental rather less. The final effect from a pipe with a resonator no more than about twelve inches long at 16 ft. C is of a very soft deep growl.

The regals are reed-stops made with no resonator at all, or only a very short one. The short resonator may be a plain cone (Trumpetenregal), or it may be one of a range of shapes, some very bizarre, which quite defy classification. The tonal effect is of a soft bright buzz.

A type of pipe which mechanically can be considered a reed is the diaphone. This was invented about the turn of the century by Robert Hope-Jones, but is no longer made. It consists of a circular padded valve on the end of a spring which vibrates over a hole connected with the resonator, which may be either full-length or fractional length. The pipes were used for the low notes of 16 ft. flue stops. The tone resembles that of a full-toned 16 ft. metal open diapason, but with considerable weight and power and a more prompt speech than large flue pipes can attain. They were extensively used in theatre organs for those reasons, but their essential reed nature precluded a good match with a flue-pipe treble.

The adjustment and regulation, particularly of the upper notes, is not easy, and those without experience are well advised not to try.

Reed-stops are made, in general, of the same materials as flue stops. The blocks are normally cast of almost pure lead and the sockets and resonators of organ metal of various grades. The quality of metal used is, however, rather more a consequence of mechanical factors than tonal ones. With a pipe which is larger at the top than the bottom, too little tin can cause early collapse. This applies with additional force to reeds *'en chamade'*. Ordinary lead-tin metal is unsuitable for 16 ft. basses purely on these mechanical grounds and the basses of trombones were formerly almost always made of wood. At the present time they are usually made of zinc, or copper. Zinc is satisfactory on mechanical and economic grounds but its hardness is undesirable on tonal grounds. This can, however, be minimized by using an adequate thickness and certain modifications to the boot. Copper is used in continental Europe. Copper-plated zinc has been used, but to the writer this seems quite pointless.

The tongues and shallots are normally made of brass, though other materials have been experimented with, and hardwood shallots are not uncommon for the bottom octaves of 16-ft. and 32-ft. stops. The tuning spring can be made of steel, but is best made of phosphor-bronze, which does not corrode.

The scales of reed-stops vary more between organ-builders than do the scales of flue stops but some general ideas can be given. Reed scales are of slower progression than flue-pipe scales, giving proportionately larger trebles. A common progression for trumpets is a scale halving on the 44th note, and stops of the clarinet family are generally made to a slower scale still, it being not uncommon for the entire top octave to be the same diameter! It is usual, however, for the basses to be made to a somewhat more rapid progression than the treble.

An average trumpet will scale $3\frac{1}{2}$ in.–4 in. at 8 ft. C, and horns and Cornopeans $4\frac{1}{2}$ in.–5 in. Trombas are also about the latter scale, as are most tubas, the difference being in the voicing treatment. Echo trumpets and fagottos fall in the range $2\frac{3}{4}$ in.–$3\frac{1}{4}$ in. and the bassoon bass of an oboe generally scales about $2\frac{1}{2}$ in., Clarinets less than 100 years old are nearly always made $1\frac{1}{2}$ in. at 8 ft. C, but older clarinets and krummhorns are generally smaller.

An important factor in the design of a reed stop is the choice of shallot. These are a number of different types. The simplest to describe is the plain 'open' shallot, of approximately the same diameter throughout its length, with a square end and with an opening running the full length of one side. A modification of this is the 'French' shallot with a domed end instead of a square one. Stops so fitted are often given French names viz.: Trompette 8 ft., Clairon 4 ft. The latter is not a spelling mistake for Clarion! The precise effect of the domed end, if any, is a matter about which reed voicers disagree. An 'open' shallot fitted with a bevelled end instead of a square one is known as a 'beak' shallot. It was frequently used until 100 years ago, and is again finding favour. The effect is to add an increased 'rasp' or 'edge' to the tone.

None of the shallots described above gives a smooth tone and for more romantic reeds this is achieved by using what is known as a 'closed' shallot. These are made tapering, the smaller end being inserted in the block. The opening is restricted to the larger end of the shallot and is of an elongated triangular shape. The shorter the 'V' of the triangle, the softer and smoother the tone, the pulses of air generated by the reed being very much less violent, and therefore less rich in harmonics than with an 'open' shallot. If an even greater degree of smoothness is required, as with stops imitative of the French horn, then a 'filled' shallot is used in which the triangular opening is moved somewhat towards the block, the end of the opening being filled with an extra piece of brass. 'Closed' shallots need to be of larger scale and need higher wind-pressures, to get the same power as an open shallot. Except for orchestral oboes, the use of 'closed' shallots was almost universal in England from about 1860 to 1950.

Having decided on the type of shallot, one must decide the scale required. This is largely a matter of experience as to what is suitable for a given pipe scale and pressure. However, in general it can be said that the smaller the shallot the softer the stop, all other things being equal. The shallot scale has also to be considered in relation to the scale of the inside of the tip of the pipe. The inside of the shallot should be no larger than the inside of the tip and is commonly a half to three-quarters of the tip size.

The actual voicing of reed pipes consists of the manufacture and curving of the reed tongue, its assembly with the shallot and other parts in the block, and the regulation of the finished pipes. It is probably the most specialized art in the whole of organ-building, and demands in particular a very high degree of manual skill in order to make the parts to the precise accuracy required by relatively simple hand processes.

Almost everything about the actual reed tongue is a matter of individual preference among reed voicers, within certain wide limits of practicability. The brass from which the tongue is cut must be of the

K

correct grade. In the past, fairly soft brass was used with, it is said, some tonal advantage. However, over the years the curve or 'set' of a reed tongue gradually deteriorates as a result of movement of the tuning spring over it, and this deterioration is accelerated if the brass is too soft. It is usual nowadays to use 'half-hard' brass. The thickness of the tongue is especially a matter of personal method and choice. The higher the pressure the thicker the tongue needs to be, and naturally the tongues are very much thinner for top notes than for basses.

After the tongue has been cut out its surfaces must be polished on fine flour paper, and it is then ready for curving. It must of course be completely flat with no kinks or bends in it. The curving of the tongue is the core of the reed voicer's art. The tongue is clamped at the tail-end to a specially flat hardwood or composition block and burnished with a two-handled steel burnisher until the tongue has taken up the desired curve. This must be done so that the curve is even, without kinks or flats, otherwise the tongue will strike the shallot instead of rolling down over the opening, and cause a metallic 'rattle'. Furthermore the curve must be correctly distributed over the length of the tongue in relation to the tone quality desired, and this must be maintained evenly from one note to the next. If the total curvature is too great in relation to the wind-pressure, the pipe will fail to speak or speak only slowly. If on the other hand there is too little, a thin note will be obtained which is inclined to 'fly' up to the octave. The adjustment is in fact a little like the adjustment of the languid of a flue pipe. Bass tongues of 16 ft. and 32 ft. can be curved with finger and thumb, though the special curving machines used by the leading voicers are vastly preferable. These machines are very individual in design, no two looking even remotely alike, but all sharing the common characteristic of having apparently been designed by the late Heath Robinson of delightful memory.

The tongues of the bass notes are by far the most difficult to do. Not only is there less margin between quick and slow, but no matter how accurately they are curved, they always tend to generate a certain amount of unwanted metallic noise. One way of overcoming this, popular until recently, was to cover the shallot with very thin leather. This has two grave disadvantages, one that it spoils the tone, and two that by its softness it permits the tuning spring to distort the tongue over a period of time, thus making the tone still worse. Other possible methods are the use of wood blocks, wood shallots or wood boots.

There is a tendency, more marked as the wind-pressure is increased, for the bass notes of reed-stops to be unduly loud in relation to the treble, and this is a common characteristic of old French reed-stops in particular. Attempting to regulate such pipes to a lower power causes them to 'fly' to their octave. Such an increase in the power in the bass, is desirable of course for French music which takes this feature into account and even exploits it. It is, however, an embarrassment for music of the romantic era. The normal way in which this power can be curbed is to fit a weight on the end of the tongue. This shortens the vibrating length for a given pitch and so softens the note and at the same time gives it a smoother tone. The form of the weight or load is individual almost to each reed voicer, but it is generally either hard felt, or hard felt and lead, fixed to the tongue with thermoplastic 'Chatterton' compound, or a brass weight screwed to the tongue. Obviously the degree of 'loading' which is used is a matter of musical preference about which there can be many opinions. Unloaded basses have a very distinctive tone in which the upper harmonics are modulated or 'chopped up' by the fundamental note, which gives freshness and clarity to music written with this type of tone in mind. Loaded basses have a smoother sound in which the upper harmonics are not only reduced but are also more nearly continuous, not being 'chopped up' by the fundamental note. Bassoons, contra-oboes and other soft 16-ft. reeds of full or half-length are only possible if the tongues of the basses are loaded.

The tone of a reed-stop is very much affected by its regulation. This is adjusted by varying the relative tuning of the tongue and the resonator. As we have said, the tuning of the pipe is controlled both by the tongue and by the resonator. A given pipe is first made flat to the correct note by tapping upwards the tuning spring (which controls the vibrating length of the tongue). It is then sharpened again until the note is in tune, by opening the tuner at the top of the pipe. The resulting note will be louder, brighter and more 'free' than before. The converse operation will produce a note which is smoother, softer and more 'close'. There are thus two important points: firstly, that the regulation of a reed is inherently bound up with its tuning, and secondly, that the character and tone of a reed stop can be widely varied by its initial regulation. It is an important corollary of this that the reed voicer must always have a good idea of the power required of a given stop. This is because subsequent alteration in the organ, either much louder or softer, will alter the tonal quality.

In the early years of this century, when 'smooth' reeds were considered musically desirable, this was achieved by regulating the pipes to a 'close' tone, and using relatively heavy pressure and larger scales in order to obtain the necessary power. Large scales and heavy pressure are not interchangeable, but their effect is broadly similar, and the two were normally used together. The pressure however has the greater influence, and wherever the expenditure could possibly be justified, the reed-stops were placed on a separate soundboard. This had its own wind supply so that heavy pressure could be used independently of the pressure for the flue pipes. Tracker action was thus ruled out for such instruments. For maximum power with smoothness, such as an Arthur Harrison Tuba, very high pressures are required, 20 inches being not uncommon in large buildings. The smoothest reed stop of all is the relatively rare imitative French Horn, in which the pipes are voiced so 'close' that despite pressure of at least 6 inches, the power is little more than that of a flue stop.

Where brighter-toned non-imitative reed-stops are required, the pipes must be voiced and regulated to a much more 'free' tone and the wind-pressure kept low in order to avoid excessive power. Such reeds have good blending properties, both with each other and with flue stops, and a greater suitability for music of the so-called 'baroque' period. The lower practical pressures are governed with low-pitched stops, by the difficulty of voicing 16-ft. and 32-ft. bass pipes without excessive mechanical 'rattle'. This is due to the practical difficulty of correctly curving the tongues to the very slight curvature required. Undoubtedly very low-pressure bass pipes are one of the hardest tests for a reed voicer's technical skill. In the writer's opinion pressures much below 3 in. are undesirable for 16-ft. reed-stops, and a similar limit of about $2\frac{1}{4}$ in. applies to 8-ft. reed-stops. In general, however, for practical reasons of economy and mechanical simplicity, the reed-stops are voiced on the same wind-pressure as the flue-stops on the same manual. This may, of course, call for some small degree of compromise, not too low if a 16-ft. reed is involved, but not too high or the fluework may be spoiled.

Some very low-pressure reed-stops also suffer from practical difficulties at the other end of the compass, in the matter of tuning stability. Dust is the enemy of the organ reed. In small quantities it upsets the tuning of treble pipes, and particles large enough to be seen with the eye cause rattles in the bass notes and can put a treble note right off speech. This is particularly noticeable with light-pressure reeds as there is less force of wind to blow the dust from the tongue, and the thinner and lighter tongue is more susceptible to interference. Thus in general, light-pressure reeds do not stand in tune as well as heavy-pressure ones. Two classes of stops which appear to resist this failing are Rohr Shalmeys, which have no funnel-shaped portion of the resonator to direct the dust down towards the tongue, and Spanish Trumpets, whose position projecting horizontally from the casework protects the tongue from dust.

There are, of course, a number of ways in which the effect of dust can be reduced, though not eliminated. It is standard practice in England to make a two-cut mitre, known as a 'hood', in the top of all reed-stops not enclosed in a swellbox. Another method is to fit the top of the pipe with a fine muslin cap.

The tuning stability of reed-stops is a matter of major concern to the player. Now, with flue stops the pitch of any pipe is determined almost entirely by the resonant frequency of the air column in the pipe body, which is in turn dependent on the speed of sound in air. This varies with the temperature, and the pitch alters correspondingly, becoming sharper with increasing temperature. Middle C of a 4-ft. flue stop will vary in pitch, relative to a tuning fork, by about one beat for every two degrees Fahrenheit.

With reed-stops, however, the pitch is only partially determined by the resonance of the air column in the resonator, the reed tongue itself also exerting control. As the reed tongue is relatively little affected by temperature, the net effect on the tuning of the whole pipe is a compromise, the average trumpet-type of reed pipe sharpening with increasing temperature only about one-third to one-half as much as a flue pipe. Reed-stops are heavily outnumbered by flue stops in most organs so their tuning tends to be judged in relation to the flue stops. Hence it is the reeds that appear to be out of tune in extremes of temperature, whereas in fact it is the flue stops whose pitch has varied the most.

It must be admitted, however, that this is not the full story. Because the tongue is more predominant in fractional-length reeds, the tuning of clarinets varies less with temperatue than that of trumpets and oboes, and the tuning of vox humanas and stops of the rankett and regal classes still less so. This means that not all reed-stops stay in tune with each other under changes of temperature. Nor is this all, because even within a given stop the tongue is more predominant in the trebles and the resonator relatively more so in the basses, so that a stop may well not remain in tune within itself under extreme temperature changes. Harmonic trebles, by increasing the control of the resonator help to improve the balance and thus tend to stay in tune better, all else being equal. The same argument applies in reverse to half-length basses.

Obviously the magnitude of these tuning problems depends to some extent on the environment of the organ. Buildings equipped with thermostatically controlled winter heating present some action problems in relation to the drying out of the timbers of old organs, but they are certainly of great benefit to the tuning of clarinets, vox humanas etc., which are then found to be quite stable in tuning, contrary to their reputation. Conversely an organ-builder is unwise to specify fractional length reeds in remote churches with little or no winter heating as these stops will be almost unusable half the year. Indeed it may be wiser in such circumstances to avoid reed-stops altogether.

It is hoped that what has been said above will give the reader some knowledge of the intricacies which form the controversial art of reed voicing. Reed voicing is a more empirical art than flue voicing, as the scientific facts behind it are at present much less clear. Consequently many differing opinions are sincerely held by practising voicers, and it is hoped that what is written here may not seem to have been unduly biased in any one direction.

Almost daily new experience and renewed understanding is being gained in the *disciplines* essential to the design and layout of good tracker action for organs under modern conditions. With this there is coming a new appreciation of the musical potentials inherent when they are strictly observed; clear phrasing, synchronous intonation of the notes of several stops together particularly in the bars octaves, and the new opportunities this accuracy offers to interpretive techniques. We have not yet seen the end of tracker action for modern organs.

12

Glossary of Stop Names

THE stops are grouped according to structure and scale, as these factors have most influence on the basic tone-colour. Subtle differences arise from type and thickness of metal or wood used, and in the size and shape of the mouth, the point where the speech is generated. The range of these controls and their effect is set out in each group. In this way much more comparative detail is possible than in the usual brief glossary which seeks to associate the visual shape with the audible impression.

The stops listed are those most likely to be encountered in the British organ. The prefixes 'double', 'contra', 'octave' are omitted unless in practice they also indicate a tonal shade other than that normal to the unison pitch. Similarly 'Echo' 'Magna' 'Gross' and 'Orchestral' are assumed to indicate only a relative power level. Obsolete and eccentric shapes and scales are not included in our survey.

The flue pipe groups are:

1. Diapason or Principal
2. Dulciana and Salicional
3. Mild string stops
4. Orchestral string stops
5. Inverted conical open pipes.
6. Mixtures
7. Open metal flutes
8. Open wood flutes
9. Harmonic flutes
10. Tapered pipes
11. Stopped pipes, wide scale
12. Stopped pipes, narrow scale
13. Pierced stoppered pipes
14. Mutation stops

DIAPASON OR PRINCIPAL

GROUP I

Open Diapason	Octave	Superoctave
Principal	Prinzipal	Fifteenth
English Diapason	Diapason Cantabile	Octavin
Violin Diapason	Horn Diapason	
Geigen Diapason	Geigen Principal	Geigen octave
Contra Bass	Major Bass	

(See Fig. 33.)

The characteristic foundation tone peculiar to the organ. It has a comprehensive range of upper partials present, at an even or slightly diminishing level of power, giving neither flute nor vivid solo tone-colour. This lack of emphasis on any harmonic, gives a satisfying fullness, a singing tone that is present throughout the compass from 16 ft. to 2 ft. and possessing the clarity required for contrapuntal music. It is the basic sound in all mixtures. Ranging from the unassertive *English Diapason* of modest power and mild flutyness, through traditional *Diapason*, to the less fundamental and louder *Principal*, it covers all the pitches of the classical chorus.

Emphasis of the upper harmonics, usually by lengthening and 'slotting', a tentative approach to gamba tone yields the *Geigen Principal* tone family. This treatment extended gives *Violin Diapason* with a trace of string tone. Increase the scale along with higher wind-pressure, coupled with increased cut-up and power, and we have the Edwardian *Large Open Diapason*. Sometimes this has the top lip leather covered and in

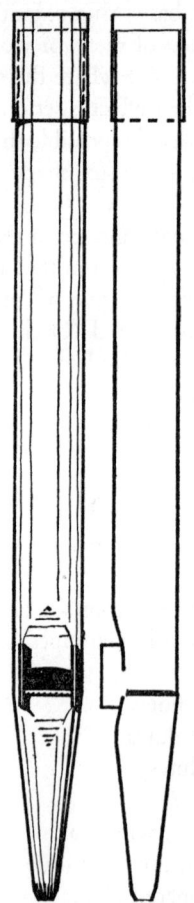

FIG. 33. Diapason. Group I

GROUP I

extreme examples this leads to the *Diapason Phonon* of impressive power and an impenetrable texture.

Pedal Open Diapasons of wood are not diapasons; lacking sufficient harmonic development they are properly regarded and classified as wide-scale open flutes.

Shape: Open flue pipe with cylindrical body
Scale: Historically the 'narrow scale' of the 'werk' principle, it is nevertheless medium between narrow-scaled string-toned stops and large-scaled flute stops. Schultze used a scale as large as 2¼ in. at mid. C 8 ft. Scales as small as 1½ in. have been used in small organs. The norm is 1¾ in.–2 in. with a mouth width of one-fourth to two-ninths of the circumference, although as wide as two-sevenths has been used.
Material:
Most commonly 'plain metal' (20–30 per cent tin). Large-scale romantic unison diapasons were often made of very thick metal with a rough cast surface to further stiffen the pipe. A medium thickness is normal and leading builders use spotted metal (50 per cent tin) for the treble pipes. European continental builders sometimes use a 70 per cent tin alloy, this is rare in Britain.
   Plain metal 8-ft. bass octaves were universal up to about 1870. Since then, except for the occasional spotted metal 'front', they are generally made of hard rolled zinc, which must be of adequate thickness. 16-ft. basses are mostly of zinc, but may also be of wood as *Contra Bass*. Successful wooden 8-ft. basses can be encountered and copper can be used as in continental examples, also highly polished tin when in casework display.
Voicing: Mouth height or cut-up is usually ⅜ in. to ½ in. at 2-ft. pipe, but leathered Edwardian unison diapasons were cut higher than this. The top lip is normally bevelled, except when voiced on the flue regulation system. 'Quick' speech spoils the characteristic tone. Pipes of the 16-ft. octave are generally voiced with bars between the ears (bearded) to give prompt speech.
Musical Use: An organ normally contains more stops of diapason tone than any other, and the provision of a chorus of stops of this type in different pitches is generally considered the first essential of tonal design. Nevertheless in very small instruments the 8-ft. principal is not an essential if the 8-ft. flute is correctly designed.

DULCIANA AND SALICIONAL

GROUP 2

Dulciana	Dulcet	Dulcetina
Aeoline		
Salicional	Salicet	Salicetina
Echo Diapason		
Celeste	Voix Celeste	
Vox Angelica	Unda Maris	

(See Fig. 34)

A group of medium-narrow scaled pipes, distinguished for gentle speech and soft silvery singing tones. The basic sound is *Echo Diapason* or *Dulciana*. Similar scaling but with a 'slotted' top to the body and sometimes a bearded mouth yields *Salicional* which is slightly stringy and may be regarded as an Echo Geigen.

The *Aeoline* is slightly less than average scale and the quietest and keenest though not quite an echo viol.

The silvery tone and modest power of this group is sympathetic to use in combination with a similar rank tuned slightly sharp. This is the *Celeste* effect, a slow undulation of the pitch. When of dulciana pipes it is called *Unda Maris* or *Vox Angelica*. With the brighter toned salicionals it becomes *Voix Celestes* or *Vox Celeste*.

The dulciana was one of the earliest narrow-scaled stops, and is generally believed to have been invented by Snetzler.

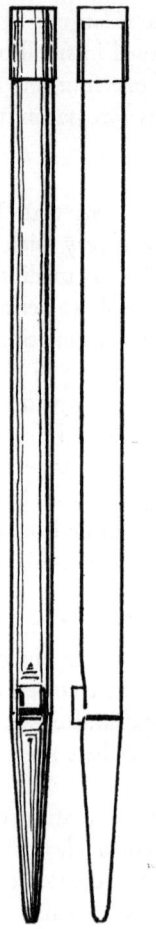

FIG. 34. Dulciana. Group 2

Shape: Open flue pipe with cylindrical body.

GLOSSARY OF STOP NAMES 143

GROUP 2

Scale: Normally around ten notes smaller than the diapason, middle C dulciana is commonly $1\frac{5}{16}$ in. Salicionals run two notes smaller and Aeolines two or more smaller still. Mouths of one fifth circumference are usual.

Material: Most commonly 'plain' metal (20–30 per cent tin) but are better if made of spotted metal (50 per cent tin) and kept quite thin. Except when in frontal displays in spotted metal basses are usually of zinc as invariably are the 16-ft. octaves.

Voicing: The cut-up of the mouth at mid. C 8 ft. is normally $\frac{1}{4}$ in. for dulcianas and a little less for Aeolines. Nicking must be fine, not deep, and the upper lip bevelled. The adjustment of the speech of dulcianas is particularly critical, if the speech is at all 'quick' the tone is spoiled and loses its freshness. 8-ft. basses are normally voiced with bars though they may be omitted when used as front pipes.

Salicionals and Aeolines are often bearded, except in the two top octaves where they are also voiced with a slot at the top of the body, whereas the dulciana has a plain top. Where space is at a premium the 16-ft. and 8-ft. octaves may be of stoppered Quintadena pipes of metal or wood. When 16-ft. octaves are so treated the break can be scarcely noticeable. Celeste tuned ranks should properly be regulated softer and blander toned than the in-tune rank.

Tone: The dulciana has a tone similar to the diapason but softer. It is very sweet and restful in character. The Salicional though similar is harder and brighter while the Aeoline is softer and bright.

Musical Use: These are the softest organ voices and are intended purely for soft accompaniment. Dulcianas are normally in 8-ft. pitch on choir manuals or on the great in two manual instruments. The sub-octave pitch finds use on great and pedal. It is a rare stop outside English speaking countries.

The harder tone of the Salicional suits swellbox expression and forms a staple constituent of many British swell organs.

MILD STRING STOPS

GROUP 3

Viola		
Viola da Gamba		Gambette
Violone	Violoncello	Cello
Fugara		
Keraulophon		(See Fig. 35.)

GROUP 3

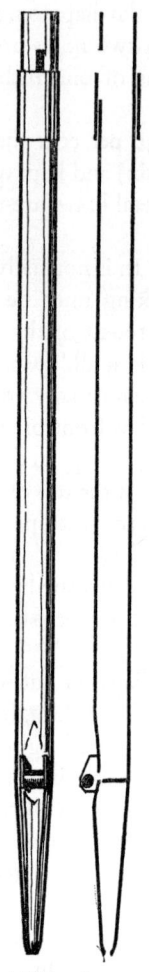

These are physically similar to the dulciana group, being of medium narrow scale, but differing radically in power and in having slotted over-length resonators, narrow mouths and in being voiced with roller bridges or beards. The resulting tone content is fairly low in fundamental and reminiscent of the viola and violoncello instruments.

With the *Viola da Gamba* as the basic sound, the louder and fuller toned *Violoncello* comes from a small increase of scale. In sub-octave pitch this becomes *Violone*, although when used as a pedal stop the scale is normally further increased, to emphasize the fundamental and become less orchestrally imitative.

When this tone group is used in 4-ft. pitch at normal manual chorus power the name *Fugara* is appropriate.

The *Keraulophone* is a nearly obsolete nineteenth-century English stop, and an early attempt at string voicing before the use of beards had been invented. A horn-like tone quality is achieved by the presence of a circular hole about one diameter down from the top of the body.

FIG. 35. Mild strings. Group 3

The tone though not soft, is relatively unassertive. It never extends below 4 ft. C.

Shape: Open flue pipe with cylindrical body, slotted at the top in extended length.

Scale: Manual stops usually about $1\frac{5}{16}$ in. at mid. C 8 ft. Pedal stops two or three notes larger. Mouths two-ninths or one-fifth circumference are usual.

GROUP 3

Material: Preferably spotted metal (50 per cent tin) but plain metal is also used. It should be fairly thin. The bass pipes may be spotted metal also but are usually of zinc. Wooden 16-ft. and 8-ft. bass pipes were introduced by Schulze and are not uncommon, though seldom made today.

Voicing: The mouth cut-up is similar to dulcianas at about ¼ in. at the 2-ft. long pipe, or rather higher for pedal stops. The pipes are, however, voiced more powerfully than Group 2, and the use of bars (or beards) is essential to obtain prompt speech. The top lip should be bevelled. Medium to fine nicking is used.

Tone: In this group it is not too dissimilar to that of the open diapasons save that the fundamental is attenuated and the higher harmonics are more prominent.

Musical use: Stops of this type react well to expressive control and are frequently found in swell organs, where a viola da gamba 8 ft. is useful as the main 8-ft. stop in medium-size instruments. It is also found in Victorian choir organs. The Pedal Violone is of use where medium power with adequate definition within itself, is required. Stops above 4-ft. pitch in this group are very rarely made.

ORCHESTRAL STRING TONES

GROUP 4

Viol	Viole	Violina
Violin		
Viole d'orchestre		
Viol Sourdine		
Viole d'amour	Viola d' Amore	
Viole Celeste		
(German) Gamba		

(See Fig. 36.)

This group comprises those stops having open parallel resonators of the narrowest scale in common use. The small diameter diminishes the ground tone so that these stops tend to lack warmth. Narrow mouths voiced with beards, coupled with slotted overlength assures a keen and deliberately imitative tone simulating orchestral stringed instruments. The *Viole d'orchestre* is the representative tone but examples range from rich orchestral lushness to an edgy grating sound, depending very much upon the voicer's skill and critical ear.

GROUP 4

At its softest is the *Viola d' Amore*, a little less restrained but still delicate sounding is the *Viole Sourdine* or muted viol which latter name perhaps fairly describes the sound.

Larger dimensions within the range give a loud but still keen tone with marked orchestral colouring. This is the so-called *German Gamba*.

The use as an off-tuned rank to producing rapid pitch undulations enhances the softer imitative tones and is appropriately called *Viole Celestes*. As the tone is already sharp-sounding it is usual to counter this by tuning the beating rank a shade flat.

Shape: Open flue pipe with cylindrical body, slotted at the top.

Scale: Very narrow, usually less than 1 in. at 2-ft. length pipe, Mouths are one-fifth circumference or narrower.

Material: Spotted metal (50 per cent tin) or tin metal (70 per cent pure) is essential. Bass pipes are invariably of zinc and sometimes the 4-ft. octave also.

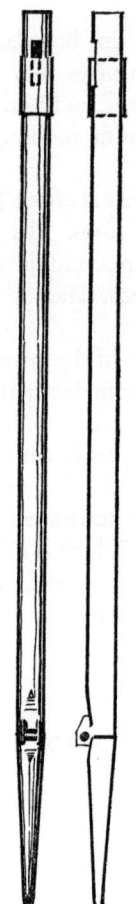

FIG. 36. Orchestral strings. Group 4

Voicing: The mouth cut-up at mid. C 8 ft. is $\frac{3}{16}$ in.–$\frac{1}{4}$ in. depending upon the loudness required. The nicking must be very fine and the upper lip shaved to a sharp edge. The bar (beard) must be of large diameter. Its position is very critical. The slot at the top is usually kept narrow, either one-fifth or one-sixth of the diameter. Voicing of these stops is difficult and tedious. They go off speech very easily.

Tone: Very prominent upper harmonics and an attenuated fundamental. Sometimes described as scratchy, the tone is edgy and restless.

GLOSSARY OF STOP NAMES

GROUP 4

Musical use: As solo stops in 8-ft. pitch in romantic style organs. Enclosure and expression are essential. These stops are becoming obsolete in all but the largest instruments.

INVERTED CONICAL OPEN PIPES

GROUP 5

1. Bell Diapason   Flute à pavillon
2. Bell Gamba   Glockengamba   Cone Gamba
3. Dolce   Dolcan

(See Fig. 37.)

In scale, character and use, these sounds are near relatives of the dulciana family, their inverted conical form imparting a plaintive sweetness.

The amount of inverted taper is usually small. When 3 : 4, that is one-third larger at the top and with a very narrow mouth cut low, the quiet nasal sweetness of the *Dolce* emerges. Increase the upward flare to 2:3, provide a slightly wider mouth and the plaintive singing accompanying *Dolcan* is produced. These delicate sounds are easily destroyed by poor acoustic layout, swellboxes, high wind-pressure or mistakenly attempting to cut up the mouth to voice as a flute. The result then is not worth the costly construction.

Of hybrid construction is the *Bell Diapason*, a parallel body of diapason scale surmounted by a flare of 'Pavillon'. Belled in organ-builders' terms, voiced on flute lines it produces an |unassertive cross between diapason organ tone and un-imitative flute.

Of very similar construction though smaller in scale is the *Bell Gamba*.

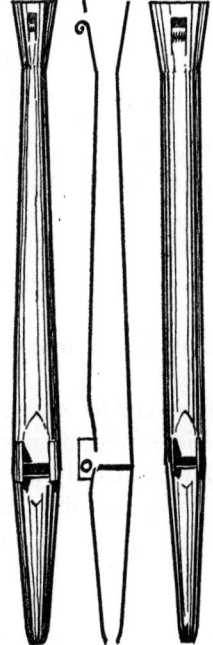

FIG. 37. Belled open pipes Group 5

GROUP 5

Many of these stops, however, have a tapering body as well similar to the *Cone Gamba*, tapering to one-third diameter at the junction with the flared top. Voiced on gamba lines it has a mildly imitative string tone evocative of the viola in an unassertive mood. A pleasant romantic sound but hardly worth the complex construction.

Shape: (a) Parallel body surmounted by an inverted conical flair or 'bell'. (Bell Diapason.)
(b) Tapered body with a bell as above. (Bell Gamba.)
(c) The entire body of inverted conical form. (Dolce.)

Scale: (a) Similar to an open diapason with the addition of the 'bell', flaring to about $1\frac{1}{2}$ diameters. Two-ninth mouths are usual.
(b) At middle C 8 ft. $1\frac{3}{16}$ in. at the mouth and top of bell, and $\frac{7}{16}$ in. at the joint with the flair. Two-ninth mouth.
(c) Scale at mouth $1\frac{1}{8}$ in. at 2-ft. pipe flaring to $1\frac{5}{8}$ in. at top. A narrow ($\frac{1}{5}$th) mouth is usual.

Material: Normally plain metal (20–30 per cent tin) of medium light weight.

Voicing: (a) Treatment as for a small open diapason. Tuning is either by flexible ears shading the mouth or by a rotating cam-lift sleeve at the flare.
(b) Flexible ear tuning. Cut-up about $\frac{5}{16}$ in. at 2 ft. C. This stop never extends below tenor C, the bass being either plain cylindrical or stopped pipes.
(c) Similar to that for a dulciana.

Tone: (a) More flute-like than ordinary diapason, the bell giving a 'horny' quality.
(b) A mild viola da gamba with a slight 'horny' tone imparted by the 'bell'.
(c) Similar to the dulciana but hollow and less sweet.

Musical Use: (A & C). These were curiosities of nineteenth-century design and are now almost obsolete. (B) Was an early attempt at string tone, prior to the invention of the 'bar' by William Hill.

MIXTURES

GROUP 6

Mixture	Quint Mixture	Full Mixture	Grave Mixture
Quartane	Rauschquinte	Sesquialtera	Sext Tertian

GROUP 6

| Furniture | Fourniture | Plein Jeu | Harmonics |
| Sharp Mixture | Scharf | Acuta | Cymbel |

Whatever the name, the purpose of a mixture is the same. The highest pitched ranks of the diapason or principal-toned choruses of the organ are grouped under a single stop-control. Unlike most other stops, a mixture always has two or more ranks of pipes, the actual number being indicated on the stop-knob, usually in Roman numerals. In large instruments there may be more than one mixture in a chorus.

There are a number of reasons for grouping the ranks under a single control instead of each forming a separate stop. While the inconvenience and mechanical complication of the latter is one aspect, much more important is the control of balance between pitches and the means to that end. If each rank was separately controlled, the addition of each succeeding pitch to those already drawn would add less and less as each stop were added, until the addition of the last rank would be scarcely audible.

Alternatively each rank would have to be louder as the pitch ascends resulting in a top-heavy 'plein-jeu'.

For normal registration three or more ranks should come on together with about the same audible addition as in adding single stops at lower pitches. Adding a mixture to 'great to fifteenth' should make about the same addition proportionately as adding fifteenth to 'great to principal' or in adding principal to diapason.

Why do we have breaks in mixture ranks? Firstly and most obviously the top notes of an unbroken mixture rank would degenerate into inaudible squeaks by the time top notes were reached.

Secondly because the function of mixtures is to add brilliance and power. In the bass it adds brilliance by continuing upwards the harmonic series of the fundamental pitch, giving a sense of power, and in the trebles it adds power by reinforcing the principal, twelfth and fifteenth, again giving emphasis to the highest audible pitches with resulting brilliance.

It is important that this 'breaking back' should be carried out inconspicuously—many mixture stops fail on this test. Too often the entire mixture breaks back one octave, e.g., 15:19:22 become 8:12:15. This makes a break unavoidably obtrusive. To overcome this, and for some other reasons, the voicer arranges them to break more gradually, e.g., from 15:19:22 to 12:15:19 and then to 8:12:15, up to the top note.

The pitch combination or composition of a mixture is important in determining the tone-colour to be achieved. This is generally expressed as the notes sounding at bottom C. Obviously the higher the pitches the brighter the mixture, but the intervals in the chord sounding under one key is also important.

The more complex the harmonic series used, the reedier is the tone, particularly if the flat 21st, the seventh harmonic or septieme is included. This is a possible advantage in a reedless chorus, but generally it clashes if used in conjunction with free-toned reeds. This is largely because mixture ranks must have their intervals tuned perfectly if the full chorus effect is to be obtained. Tempered intervals make nonsense of the resultant tones in these high pitches. 'Borrowed' interval mixtures with their tempered intervals sound 'gritty' for this reason, whereas a correctly tuned mixture has a buoyant brilliance. Organ-builders try to ameliorate the conflict between perfect and tempered intervals by reducing the power of the tierces and quints relative to the unisons but this is at the expense of tone-colour and dramatic impact. The solution is to restrict tierces to mutation ranks and to cornets not intended for chordal music. Fortunately tempered fifths are not far from perfect and so quint mixtures can be used in chords without disturbance by clashing intervals.

Now that the proper complement of mixtures is recognized as a necessary part of the tonal design of an organ, save the very smallest, a proper understanding of the different types can help avoid misuse and disappointment.

Often the stop is just called *Mixture* without qualification, usually it is straightforward upward continuation of the diapason chorus when of III ranks commonly the composition is:

CC to B	15	19	22	(2 ft. $1\frac{1}{3}$ ft. 1 ft.)
Mid C to Mid B	12	15	19	($2\frac{2}{3}$ ft. 2 ft. $1\frac{1}{3}$ ft.)
Treble C to top	8	12	15	(4 ft. $2\frac{2}{3}$ ft. 2 ft.)

This is a *Quint Mixture* in that it has only quints and unisons and avoids other intervals.

A *Grave Mixture* is one of relatively low pitch, frequently of only two ranks, just twelfth and fifteenth, in which case no breaks are necessary or needed.

Two-rank mixtures are commonly named according to the interval between the ranks, thus the *Quartane* or *Rauschquinte* has an interval of a fourth between ranks with the composition in the bass of either 19:22 ($1\frac{1}{3}$ ft. and 1 ft.) or 12:15 ($2\frac{2}{3}$ ft. and 2 ft.).

GLOSSARY OF STOP NAMES

GROUP 6

A *Full Mixture* is one of three or more ranks of relatively low pitch:

(block)	12	15	19	22
(1st break)	8	12	15	19
(2nd break)	5	8	12	15

the quint in the second break is an harmonic of the sub-fundamental or 16-ft. pitch, to give weight to the treble.

When correctly composed, the *Sesquialtera* is a two-rank with the composition of 12:17, an interval of a sixth between them. Despite the diapason tone of the pipes of which it is formed, the prominent tierce or seventeenth renders the tone more useful as an ingredient of a solo tone rather than a chorus component.

Many eighteenth- and nineteenth-century English organs, however, contain a so-called *Sequialtera III*, generally of 17 19 22 form in the bass, voiced as a straightforward chorus mixture with a reedy timbre. Sometimes these stops were made to draw in bass and treble halves, the latter made to 12:15:17 and called *cornet*. It was not a true cornet being of diapason pipes instead of, as is correct, flute-toned ranks.

The *Tertian* has the composition 17, 19, the minor third interval with a function similar to that of the II rank Sesquialtera.

The Furniture (Fourniture, Fr.) or 'plein jeu' is a mixture voiced fairly boldly where a powerful effect is needed. It often contains four or more ranks and should not be too grave in composition. A typical IV rank might be:

19	22	26	29	breaking back every octave to—
15	19	22	26	
12	15	19	22	
8	12	15	19	
8	12	15	15	

The doubling of the 15th in the top break reinforces the fundamental and avoids introducing sub-fundamental harmonic series.

Very large mixtures tend to be unwieldy in registration, and are best broken up into grave and sharp groups.

The mixture known as *Harmonics* was used in some romantically conceived organs. Normally of four ranks, voiced softly with pipes of small, almost dulciana scale, it was principally a colouring mixture with a reedy tone. A usual composition was 17:19:$^\flat$21:22 in the bass.

A mixture of relatively high pitch, as the names indicate, is the *Sharp Mixture*, *Scharf* or *Acuta*. It may have two or more ranks. Inevitably

GROUP 6

such high-pitched ranks must break many tunes in the compass. A II rank might be 26:29, 22:26, 15:19, 12:15 breaking back every octave except the top one.

The highest pitched mixture of all is the Cymbel, the ranks breaking back at least once per octave and sometimes more often. Some have been rudely described as sounding like a cypher on a top note of the fifteenth! Indeed one rank Cymbels have been made presumably on the principle that at such high pitches the breaks are inaudible! The Cymbel should add a tingling glitter to whatever combination includes it, and, because of its extreme high pitches need only be voiced relatively softly. It may or may not include tierces, according to the designer's judgment. A typical *Cymbel III* would be 29, 33, 36 in the bass.

Shape of pipes: Open flue pipes with cylindrical bodies as for diapasons.
Scale: Depends on the overall design of the organ. In romantic instruments with soft mixtures the pipes were made up to eight notes smaller than the 8-ft. diapason. On the other hand in the organs of Smith, Snetzler and Schultze they were made the same scale as the 8-ft. unison. The famous 'Armley' Schulze has every 2-ft. pipe in diapasons, principals and upperwork, near enough 2 in. in diameter.
Material: Preferably in spotted metal (50 per cent tin content) but 70 per cent tin alloy is used by continental builders.

OPEN METAL FLUTES

Open Flute	Hellpfeife	Flute ouverte	Flute Octaviante
	Flautino	Block Flute	Blockflöte
Wald Flute	Waldflöte	Flageolet	Sifflote
Clear Flute	Piccolo—Corno Flute		

(See Fig. 38.)

The group comprises open metal pipes of all scales, ranging from dulciana size up to and larger than diapason. They are all voiced with the open pipe series of upper partials much suppressed in power relatively to the fundamental, resulting in flute tones mostly of a non-imitative character.

Power levels run from the gentle *Corno Flute*, a fluty dulciana, to the firm and slightly horn-toned *Wald Flute*. The 2-ft. tones are *Flautino* in the medium scale and when a little larger as *Flageolet*, or *Piccolo* when

GROUP 7

smoothly fluty. A further increase of scale near to maximum, and with flue regulation voicing, it becomes the *Blockflöte*.

Flute ouverte covers plain Wald Flute to almost principal depending on the designer's intentions as to use.

It is usual to make the low octave (and sometimes up to seventeen notes) of closed wood or metal pipes, not for economy as sometimes mistakenly assumed, but to obtain some tonal definition and ameliorate the cloying flutiness that would otherwise result from the lower notes. Many stops in this group may be often preferably be made of wood.

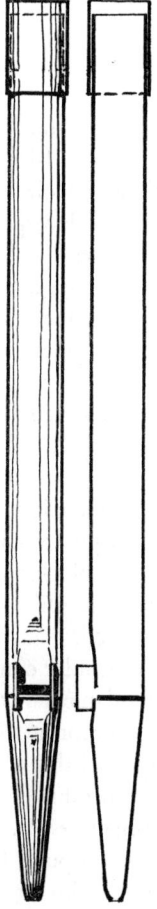

FIG. 38. Open flute. Group 7

Shape: Open flue pipes with cylindrical bodies.

Scale: These stops form part of the 'wide scale' family of the 'werk' principle and are normally larger in scale than the diapason-toned stops. The scale is arranged on a slow progression so that diameters are relatively large in the treble pipes, but may be of small diapason scale in the bass. Commonly the scale is 2 in. at 2-ft. C pipe for a metal Waldflöte and up to $2\frac{1}{2}$ in. for the Blockflöte.

Flageolets are usually smaller, sometimes only $1\frac{1}{2}$ in. and relying on a high cut-up to achieve a flute quality. The mouth is usually of one-fifth circumference in width. Many of these stops can be made with tapering bodies with advantage.

Material: Generally plain metal (20–30 per cent tin) is good enough and spotted metal confers no particular advantage.

Voicing: The cut-up is kept fairly high, often at least $\frac{1}{3}$ in. at the 2-ft. pipe. The smaller scale stop are cut-up higher and the top lip arched,

GROUP 7

but need not be bevelled. The speech is deliberately made 'quick' as this encourages a fluty quality. If the cut-up or scale is insufficient for the power required they tend to 'cough' on speaking.

Tone: Fairly pure flute tone, with weakened higher harmonics. Not as pure as harmonic flutes.

Musical Uses: Generally as non-imitative flute tone used in many pitches as part of a flute chorus.

OPEN WOOD FLUTES

GROUP 8

Clarabella			
Clear Flute	Claribel Flute		
Hohl Flute	Hohflöte	Melodia	Flute Triangulaire
Suabe Flute	Wald Flute	Waldflöte	Holzflöte
			Holzpfeife
Pedal Open Diapason	Open wood Bass	Tibia plena	

(See Figs. 39 and 40.)

Wood as a material for pipes naturally suppresses some of the higher harmonics. This accounts for its popularity for bass pipes and also for very pure-toned flutes.

Not all wooden flutes are, however, the same, as variations in block shape, lip shape, rates of depth to width, as well as the usual factors of scale and mouth cut-up, greatly influence the tone-colour obtainable.

The first common open wood stop was the *Clarabella*, invented early in the nineteenth century. It is made like an open-pipe version of the wooden stopped diapason, with flat-faced English block and normal lips. The tone is fluty but not entirely pure, sounding like a wooden diapason. The two low octaves are usually stoppered.

The familiar English *Pedal Open Diapason* is of similar construction. Its prime purpose, to provide great weight of fundamental 16-ft. tone, is achieved by large scale, 12 in. × 14 in. being common at 16 ft. CCC. It is a flute and not a diapason. Upward extension of this scale gives a very pure and powerful flute, the *Tibia Plena*, introduced by Hope-Jones it became a fundamental part of theatre organ design.

Reducing the harmonic development to produce a purer flute tone, the *Claribel Flute* has an inverted top lip that is flush with the pipe front and bevelled on the inside. A still purer sound is obtained by a German

GROUP 8

type block having a recessed space below the flue level. This is the *Wald Flute* or *Melodia*. In 4-ft. pitch it is sometimes called *Suabe Flute*, and in 2-ft. as *Flageolet* or *Piccolo* but usually with many top notes in metal.

The great power required of a prominent solo flute stop, is partly obtained by increase of scale and partly by a wider mouth obtained by making the pipe wider than its depth. This is the *Hohl Flute* [40] although some stops of this name are identical to Wald Flutes. The extreme wide mouth stop is the *Flute Triangulaire*, the three-sided wooden flute. Occasionally these stops have open pipes down to the

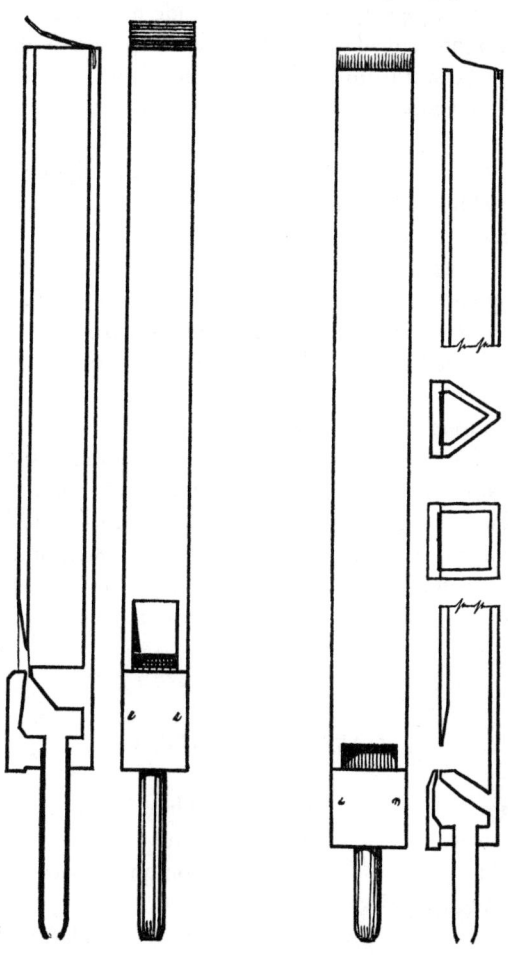

FIG. 39. Open wood flute   FIG. 40. Hohl flute. Group 8

GROUP 8

lowest note but it is more usual to use stoppered wood for the lowest twelve or seventeen and avoid the cloying fullness of the open-pipe bass.

Shape: Wooden flue pipes of rectangular (or occasionally triangular) construction.
Scale: Clarabella and Wald Flute 2 ft. pipe $1\frac{1}{4}$ in. × $1\frac{1}{2}$ in. inside measure.
Hohl Flute 2 ft. pipe $1\frac{3}{4}$ in. × $1\frac{1}{4}$ in. inside measure.
Tibia Plena 2 ft. pipe $2\frac{1}{2}$ in. × $3\frac{1}{8}$ in. inside measure.
Material: Straight-grained soft wood of fair thickness. Wald Flutes and Hohl Flutes benefit from hardwood front planks.
Voicing: The Clarabella has a fairly low-cut mouth, $\frac{1}{2}$ in. at mid. C, and moderate nicking. The Wald Flute and Hohl Flute have high cut-ups at $\frac{3}{4}$ in. at mid. C, and arched. With even higher cut-up and leather-faced lips is the Tibia Plena. Heavy nicking is necessary to get good speech.

All these pipes are cut slightly short of correct length and tuned by the shading effect of an adjustable metal flap at the top.
Tone: Varies from sweet quasi-flute, quasi-diapason in the case of Clarabella to the hard, forced flute tone of the Hohl Flute. The latter is best placed under expression, as the swellbox rounds out and modifies its tone in a useful way.
Musical Use: Intended as a solo stop on the great organ the Clarabella was frequently fitted in the nineteenth century as a middle C compass stop in place of a discarded cornet. The Claribel Flute is usually a great organ stop as is the Wald Flute, in either 8-ft. or 4-ft. pitches, but in Victorian and Edwardian instruments, they can all appear on almost any manual in 8 ft., mainly for general accompanimental use.

HARMONIC FLUTES

GROUP 9

Concert Flute	Orchestral Flute	
Flauto Traverso	Traverse Flute	
Harmonic Flute	Flute Harmonique	Harmonic Piccolo
Harmonic Clarabel (Wood)		
Zauberflöte	Magic Flute	Harmonic Twelfth
		(See Fig. 41.)

GLOSSARY OF STOP NAMES

GROUP 9

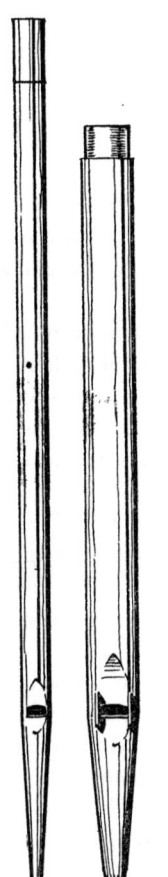

FIG. 41. Harmonic flutes. Group 9

An open flute pipe is made double length and overblown to speak its octave and omitting the fundamental. The speech is made secure by piercing the resonator at about the nodal point around half of its length. These harmonic length pipes are only from tenor G—middle C upwards, the bass being of plain length, high cut-up flute pipes simulating the tone well enough at the matching point.

Stops of this construction yield a bright dainty imitative flute tone. The strong fundamental and weak upper partials peculiar to this form are highly suggestive of the traverse orchestral flute hence the name *Flauto Traverso*. Larger scaled examples, usually on higher wind-pressure and with high-cut mouths, produce a loud solo tone sometimes described as 'creamy', and named *Concert Flute*. This evocative orchestral sound can be made more closely imitative by the use of triple-length resonators blown to sound their third harmonic as prime tone, however, this is rare.

Occasionally a stop of this class is made of wood, notably the solo *Harmonic Claribel,* usually in 8 ft. The bass is usually made of stoppered wood pipes, some old wooden harmonic flutes and piccolos have slightly tapered bodies.

Stoppered Harmonic Flutes

As stopped pipes when overblown sound the quint as the prime tone, the resonator length must be three times normal stopped length. Perforation on the nodal point holds the note and eliminates the overlength

GROUP 9

ground tone. This is the Zauberflöte, a solo stop in the larger concert organ.

Sometimes this form is used for the *Harmonic Twelfth* intended for solo tone synthesis, however the difference between stopped and open harmonic pipes at this pitch is so small as not to justify the manufacturing trouble.

Shape: Open flue pipe with cylindrical body of twice nominal length, or stoppered flue pipe with cylindrical body one and a half times nominal length.

Material: Plain metal (20–30 per cent tin) of medium to full thickness.

Scale: Scaling is on a very slow progression giving relatively narrow-scale basses and wide-scale trebles. The scale normally breaks back five or six notes larger at the first harmonic pipe. Depending on power, required scales run $2\frac{1}{2}$ in.–$2\frac{3}{4}$ in. at 4 ft. C and $1\frac{7}{8}$ in.–2 in. at 2 ft. C.

Voicing: The mouth is cut-up $\frac{1}{2}$ in.–$\frac{5}{8}$ in. at mid. C and is generally not flattened, but arched and rounded to the contour of the body. The languid needs to be well nicked and kept low to prevent the pipe from speaking the octave below and then flying up to its intended prime tone. One, sometimes two, small holes are pierced in the resonator about half-way up (two-thirds in the stopped pipe) to hold the desired prime tone. These stops thrive on ample wind-pressure.

Tone: More or less resembles the Orchestral Traverse Flute being very pure and having negligible harmonic development.

Musical Use: Though an excellent solo stop, the harmonic flute blends poorly except with other open flute stops. It is commonly found at 4-ft. pitch in many British organs built between 1875–1925. It has fallen almost completely from musical favour outside the solo organ.

TAPERED PIPES

GROUP 10

Nachthorn	Cor de Nuit	
Blockflöte	Block Flute	
Spitzflöte	Spitz Flute	Flute conique
Waldflöte	Wald Flute	
Gemshorn	Spitzprinzipal	Spitz Principal
Viola Pomposa	Spitzgamba	

GLOSSARY OF STOP NAMES

GROUP 10

Erzahler	Harfpfeife	Erzahler Celeste
Koppelflöte	Koppel Flute	Coppel Copula
Spindle Flute	Spillflöte	Flute à Fuseau
Spitz gedeckt		

(See Fig. 42.)

This group is a whole family of stops with conical tapering bodies. They all share the tonal quality this introduces, but otherwise vary greatly in scale and use. The amount of taper is also variable from a ratio of 2:3 up to 1:4. The steeper taper increases the tonal colouring but reduces the power of the stop.

The *Nachthorn* is the widest scale pipe normally made. A taper of 2:3 is usual but may have parallel bodies. A very narrow (¼th) mouth is characteristic. Slightly smaller is the *Blockflöte*, 2½ in. at 2 ft. C tapered 2:3, but is quite often made parallel. The *Spitzflöte* is given a more marked taper, generally 1:3, an average scale at the mouth is 2¼ in. at 2 ft. C. These are most useful non--imitative open flutes, the tapered form introduces certain harmonic emphasis particularly the 'seventeenth', which assures its blend with other voices besides flutes. They can be used on the pedal in 4-ft. pitch and on great organs in 4 ft., 2¾ ft., in Positive at 2 ft., and in swell organs in unison. The metal Wald Flute is often now made with a slight (2:3) taper.

The *Gemshorn* or *Spitzprinzipal* is a stop in the normal diapason series having a tapered body, generally 1:2 but sometimes 1:3. The scale needs to be a few notes larger to counter the power reducing effect of the taper. The bright clean tone is especially good as a second 8-ft. diapason on the great or as a 4-ft. swell stop.

Viola Pomposa or *Spitzgamba* is a mild string-toned stop relying on the

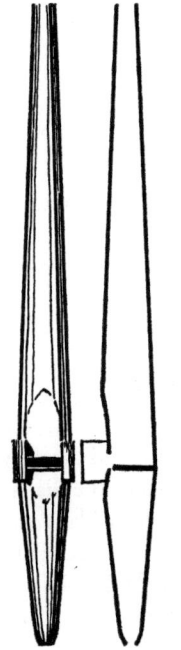

FIG. 42. Tapered pipes (Gemshorn) Group 10

GROUP 10

taper to produce a tone rich in harmonics instead of the small scale used in conventional parallel-bodied stops. The *Erzahler, Harfpfeife* and soft *Spitzflöte* are tapered stops of dulciana power and bright flute tone. They make excellent Celeste stops, as *Flute Celeste* or *Erzahler Celeste*.

The *Koppelflöte* family have conical tapered tops to the parallel lower half. The tone is similar to the chimney-flute type in the bass but becomes more like the Spitzflöte as the scale ascends. This compound construction seldom extends below tenor F or above top F, 8 ft. It is most often used in 4-ft. pitch. Tuning is either by mouth shading with flexible ears or by length adjustment, the straight portion having a sleeve joint. The stop is troublesome to make and voice. Normal scale at 2 ft. C is about 2 in. The *Spillflöte* is of similar construction but of smaller scale yielding a brighter tone.

The *Spitzgedeckt* is seldom seen outside Germany. The pipe is tapered almost to a point and a tiny stopper is placed in the top. The tone is very soft and strongly coloured with marked emphasis on certain harmonics.

STOPPED PIPES, WIDE SCALE

GROUP 11

Sub-bass	Sub-bass	Gedeckt	Choral Bass
Cor de Nuit	Nachthorn	Choral Bass	
Doppelflöte	Doppel Flute		
Bourdon	Sub Bourdon	Bass Flute	
Stopped Diapason	Nason	Nason Flute	
Quintaten	Quintade	Quintadena	Gedeckt Pommer

(See Figs. 43 and 44.)

Organ flute tone pervades all stoppered pipe stops, the virtual elimination of the even-numbered upper partials, and the emphasis on the fundamental, marks the tone as the antithesis of the diapason.

Large-scaled plain-stoppered wood pipes yield a bland foundation tone of little upper harmonic content. This is characteristic of the weighty Pedal *Sub Bass* and its octave the *Gedeckt*. In higher pitches a brighter but still firm flute tone of solo quality is the *Nachthorn* or *Choral Bass*. When built with a mouth back and front, the *Doppel Flute* gives a flood of organ flute tone, but of limited musical interest hardly justifying its complex construction.

At more modest scaling is the *Bourdon* in 16-ft. and 8-ft. pitches

GROUP II

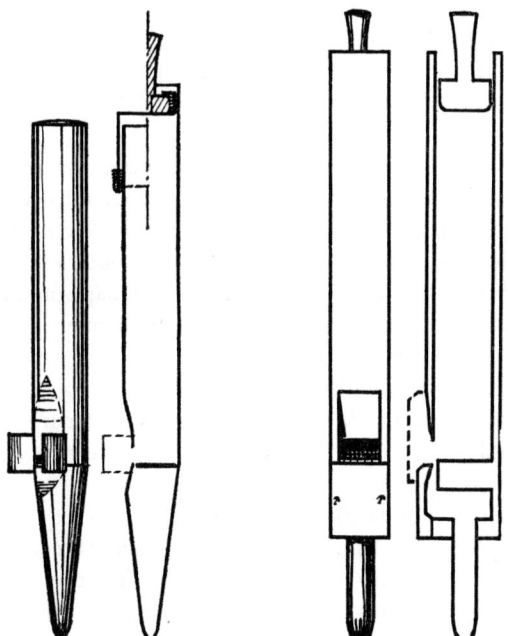

FIG. 43. Stoppered metal flute and three tuning methods. Group 3

FIG. 44. Stopped wood flute

ranging from a dull drone to a soft purring foundation upon which choruses and tone-colours can be built. A manual version with rather more of a quinty chirrup in its speech is the *Stopped Diapason* and its octave the *Nason Flute*.

Without structural differences but with an entirely different voicing technique comes the *Quintadena* family, they are good mixers without smothering with an excess of cloying fundamental. Good also as solo tones in all pitches.

Shape: Cylindrical flue pipes capped or stoppered and half the nominal pitch length, or rectangular wood pipes with stoppers, also half length.

Scale: Normal Gedeckt or stopped diapason pipes are in the range $2\frac{1}{2}$ in.–$3\frac{1}{4}$ in. at 4 ft. C. Quintadena pipes are slightly smaller $2\frac{1}{2}$ in. at 4 ft. C being almost the maximum.

Material: Gedeckt & stopped diapason are normally of plain metal (20–30 per cent tin). The bass octave may be made with the pipes' upper

GROUP 11

half of zinc to withstand the stress of the tightly fitting stoppers or tuning canisters. The 8-ft. octave can be in wood pipes and the 16-ft. octave is almost invariably of wood. Alternatively the entire stop may be made of wood, such as the preferred straight-grained spruce. This is a peculiarly English form.

Quintadena pipes are usually of spotted metal (50 per cent tin) but otherwise similar to Gedeckts. Again, a wooden version is an English form, common as Nason Flute 4 ft. in old organs.

Voicing: Normally the cut-up for Gedeckts is about $\frac{1}{2}$ in. scant at 2 ft. C or slightly higher for pedal stops. Stopped diapasons are generally cut-up rather less at about $\frac{3}{8}$ in., and may alternatively be voiced with a perforated stopper or chimney.

The prominent twelfth or quint in a Quintadena is obtained by a very low-cut mouth. A box-type mouth or a frein is required to obtain stable speech in the bass. It is not an easy stop to voice successfully.

Wooden rectangular pipes in this group have an English type block, with a flat top and a flat face, the windway being recessed in the cap.

These wooden pipes are always tuned with stoppers, but metal ones may have stoppers, canister sleeves or fixed tops. In the latter case tuning is by mouth shading flexible ears.

Tone: Basically flute-like with strong fundamental. The even-numbered harmonics are suppressed entirely by the stoppering, giving a clarinet-like tone in the bass, and a colourful flute-tone in the treble.

The Quintadena is similar but more highly coloured, with a weaker fundamental and a prominent quint. It cannot be properly considered a flute stop as the intensity of the upper harmonics approaches that of the diapason or even mild strings.

Musical use: Stopped-pipe tone is a fundamental organ sound and an important constituent of the wide-scale chorus. Owing to its compact length it is much used in the pedal organ. Quintadena is useful in 8 ft. as a solo tone yet it blends very well with the diapason chorus and especially as a manual 16-ft. stop.

STOPPED PIPES, NARROW SCALE   GROUP 12

Lieblich Bourdon   Lieblich Bass   Echo Bourdon
Lieblich Gedeckt   Lieblich Flute   Lieblichflöte   Lieblich Piccolo
(See Fig. 45.)

GLOSSARY OF STOP NAMES

GROUP 12

These have the least assertive tone of all organ flutes, being almost pure sine wave with but the merest trace of upper partials, and completely innocent of any articulation, transient sounds or chiff. The pipes are readily identifiable from the very high cut-up, never less than half the mouth width and often up to square.

Shape: Cylindrical flue pipes, stoppered, or rectangular wood pipes stoppered, and both only half the nominal pitch length.

Scale: Generally 2 in. at 4 ft. C, but occasionally smaller. A two-ninth of the circumference is the usual mouth width.

Material: Usually plain metal (20–30 per cent tin content) but the 8-ft. octave may be made of zinc or, as more commonly, of wood.

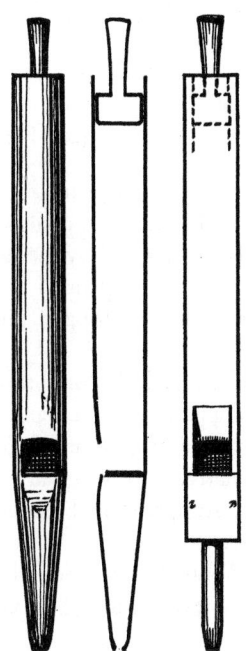

FIG. 45. Stoppered pipes narrow scale (Lieblich flutes)

Occasionally English builders have made the entire stop of wood.

Voicing: The top lip is arched and cut-up about ⅝ in. at the 2 ft. C. It is not flattened but retains the cylindrical curve of the body. There is no bevelling. Quite heavy nicking is required and the languid is set low for good speech. When of wood the blocks must be of the German type, having a sloping front, and sunk top, used with a plain cap. The power tends to fall away in the bass and the speech 'coughs' if forced too hard.

Tone: A distinctive hollow sound, sometimes described as 'liquid', and harder than the Gedeckts.

Musical Use: This group of stops was introduced to England by Edmund Schulze in the 1850's. Often better as solo stops than the wide-scaled Gedeckts, they blend less well, however, with stops of other tonalities. These stops are largely confined to swell organs often in 16-ft., 8-ft. and 4-ft. pitches. Also used in nineteenth-century choir organs.

PIERCED-STOPPERED PIPES

GROUP 13

Rohr Bourdon   Rohrbourdun
Rohr Flute   Rohrflöte   Rohrgedeckt
Chimney Flute Flute à cheminee

(See Fig. 46.)

Bright singing non-imitative flute tone of great charm, standing midway between Gedeckt and Gemshorn, is the tone quality distinguishing this group. No special difference is indicated by the several names. The effect of the chimney is not readily explained but by appearing to reduce the normal quinty sound of a stopped pipe, it 'clears' the tone and makes it less intense.

Shape: Cylindrical flue pipes, stoppered and with a hole bored through the stopper, or capped and with an internal or external chimney. Alternatively rectangular wood pipes, stoppered and pierced as above.

Scale: As in the wide-scaled stoppered pipes, $2\frac{3}{4}$ in.–$3\frac{1}{4}$ in. at 4 ft. C.

The mouths being one-fourth circumference in width.

Material: Plain metal (20–30 per cent tin content). Occasionally of thin spotted metal, and in England sometimes of wood.

Voicing: Mouth cut-up is usually about $\frac{7}{16}$ in. at 2 ft. C with little or no nicking. The tone is bright if the pipe is capped and a metal chimney is fitted, in which case the tuning is made by mouth shading flexible ears. Stoppers are seldom pierced in pipes below tenor F as unless the chimney is very long the pipe is put off speech. Quintadenas cannot have pierced stoppers.

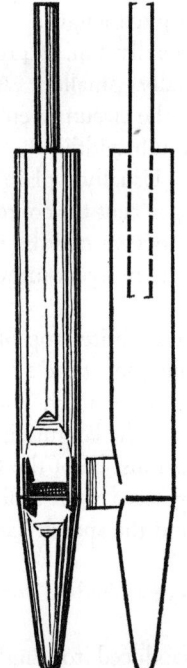

FIG. 46. Pierced stoppered pipes (chimney flute)

Tone: The chimney adds certain harmonics of the even-numbered series to those natural to the stopped pipe. The result is a characteristic 'clear', even perky sound. When voiced on the flue-regulation system without nicking, the stop has a not unattractive 'chiff' on speaking.

Musical use: A classical member of the wide-scale chorus, and as an alternative to the ordinary wide-scale Gedeckts. They are used in both 8-ft. and 4-ft. pitches and usually unenclosed.

MUTATION STOPS

GROUP 14

Twelfth $2\frac{2}{3}$ ft.   Seventeenth $1\frac{3}{5}$ ft.   Nineteenth $1\frac{1}{3}$ ft.

Gross Quint $5\frac{1}{3}$ ft.   Quint, Quinte, Spitzquinte, Nasat, Rohr Nasat, Nazard $2\frac{2}{3}$ ft.
Gross Tierce $3\frac{1}{5}$ ft.   Tierce $1\frac{3}{5}$ ft.
Larigot, Quinte $1\frac{1}{3}$ ft.
Septieme $1\frac{1}{7}$ ft.
None $\frac{8}{9}$ ft.
Cornet III ranks, Cornet IV ranks, Cornet V ranks
Mounted Cornet V ranks

Acoustic Bass   Resultant Bass   Harmonic Bass 32 ft.

This group comprises a number of stops not sharing a common tone or structure system, but having in common an off-unison pitch. Here the pitch of the stop does not bear an octave relationship to the unison, but involves some other musical interval, such as an octave and a fifth, or two octaves and a major third.

The addition of octave or super-octave voices to a foundation of the same tone family, makes the sound brighter but unchanged in tone-colour. This is not so when the added voice is of non-unison pitch e.g., $2\frac{2}{3}$ ft., 2 ft., $1\frac{1}{3}$ ft. or $1\frac{1}{7}$ ft. The addition of one or more of these to a ground tone causes an easily discernable tone-colour, change or mutation of the original sound, into something other than a compound sound. A liquid-toned Lieblich Gedeckt, on mutation by a Quint, becomes a pungent nasal sound evocative of the clarinet.

The *Twelfth, Seventeenth* and *Nineteenth* are simply the representatives of the diapason chorus in these pitches, the third, fifth and sixth harmonics respectively of the fundamental. Italian organs apart, only the

GROUP 14

twelfth is normally found as a separate stop. The others when present are usually incorporated with mixtures, which reduces the number of stop-controls to be handled, and permits early 'breaking back' of ranks to avoid shrillness in the treble. The twelfth adds a fullness to a diapason chorus and is found on the great in most organs but the smallest.

The *Quint, Tierce* and *Larigot* come into the category of flute-mutation stops. Their purpose is to blend singly or together, with a stop of 8-ft. or 4-ft. pitch, to create a very great variety of interesting and colourful sounds. When placed in enclosed expressive departments the flutes are made nearly pure toned, with the object of synthesizing tone-colours for solo use. The *Nazard* is then made of narrow scaled Lieblich-type stopped pipes. In Great or Positiv divisions they are made quasi-diapason toned to blend the better in chorus uses. Then the quint may be a wide-scaled stopped *Nazard*, or a *Rohrnasat* having a chimnied stopper. Alternatively it may be an open *Nasat* or tapered *Spitzquinte*. The higher pitched mutations are generally made of open pipes, sometimes of tapered form.

In general the *Quinte* $2\frac{2}{3}$ *ft.* adds colour and fullness, the *Larigot* $1\frac{1}{3}$ *ft.* adds colour, the *Tierce* $1\frac{3}{5}$ *ft.* adds reediness. The *Septieme* $1\frac{1}{7}$ *ft.* and the *None* $\frac{8}{9}$ *ft.* intensify reediness. Mutations other than the Twelfth, normally break back to the octave below at some point in their upper octaves as they approach that limit of practical pipemaking and tuning, the top note 2 ft.

The use of flutes of 8 ft., 4 ft., $2\frac{2}{3}$ ft., 2 ft. and $1\frac{1}{3}$ ft., together produces a powerful reedy sound known as the *Cornet V ranks*. While it may be synthesized from independent stops where available, it is better presented as a separate stop. If this is of III or IV ranks, the missing pitches are added by drawing 8-ft. and 4-ft. flute stops. The V rank cornet is the only compound stop that can be played on alone without other stops. Its chief function is as a fairly loud and colourful solo stop, sounding more like a reed-stop than a chorus of flue pipes. In the past this stop had a secondary purpose, to make up for the weakness of the trebles of early reeds, but this is now not necessary. Below middle C the tone-colour tends to break up into its constituent pitches and is therefore less successful as a solo tone, in consequence cornets are short-compass stops seldom going below middle C or tenor G at most. In order to make the stop as powerful as possible, and also because of the amount of sound-board space required by five ranks of large-scaled pipes, the stop is often mounted on an elevated soundboard fed by conveyances from the main chest beneath. It is then referred to as a *Mounted Cornet* (Plate 30).

GLOSSARY OF STOP NAMES

GROUP 14

There is another type of mutation stop, though not normally thought of as one, the not uncommon pedal *Acoustic Bass* 32 ft., featuring the difference tone between a pipe of 16-ft. pitch and a mutation of $10\frac{2}{3}$-ft. pitch sounding the G above. The ear is only deceived in this way at very low pitches hence it is usual to confine this device to generating the low octave. Often the required quint pitches are obtained by derivation from a unison stop, but better results are always obtained using independent quint pipes whose power can be accurately set for this use without compromise to any other.

REED STOPS

Unlike stops of flue pipes, reeds do not by their shape and outward appearance give certain indication of the tone-colour to be expected. Less visible features have more significant effect, nevertheless some broad classification by external form is possible.

There are two main and easily recognizable groups, those with simple flared resonators and those having cylindrical tubes half the nominal length. The latter correspond somewhat to stopped pipes in flue stops, in that odd-numbered harmonics tend to prevail, imparting a basic colouration of non-imitative clarinet tone. There is a sub-group of fractional length reed-stops with resonators of many varied shapes.

Unlike the flue stops, the effect of lighter or heavier wind-pressure is all important and plays a large part in determining the final tone.

The groups are:

	Full length	*Half length*	*Fractional length*
1. Trumpets	a. Bassoon	3a. Clarinets	4a. Vox Humana
	b. Trumpet	b. Rohr Shalmey	b. Ranketts
	c. Horn		c. Regals
Heavy-wind	{ d. Tromba		
	{ e. Tuba		
2. Oboes			

TRUMPETS

REED GROUP 1

a. Bassoon	Fagotto	Fagot	
b. Trombone	Trumpet	Clarion	
Double Trumpet	Trompette	Clairon	Cornopean
			Posaune

		REED GROUP I
c. Horn	Waldhorn	Closed Horn
d. Tromba	Harmonic Trumpet	Ophicleide
e. Tuba	Tuba Mirabilis	

(See Fig. 47.)

Inverted conical tubes of narrow scale encourage harmonic development at some expense of the prime tone, and allow the production of the quieter voices. These sounds lie between the trumpet and woodwind tones and merit the derivative names of *Basoon* and *Fagotto*. The manual sub-unison octave in those stops is often of half-length tubes to retain the tone-colour in the bass, and to thin the tone to assure polyphonic clarity thereon.

A plain inverted conical resonator, medium-scale and open-topped, typifies the trumpet family, which stands in middle range, all others being either smoother, louder or both, or on the other hand brighter and looser-toned.

FIG. 47. Trumpet mid C 8 feet

The organ *Trumpet* has a restrained brassy clang, evocative if not strictly imitative of its namesake. It should be capable of assimilation into any full organ chorus. In its octave pitch as *Clarion* the tone is usually a little louder and more intense, while in sub-unison pitch the *Double Trumpet* is commonly made a shade smaller-scaled to sustain the tone-colour in the bass. When made as a pedal stop, the dynamic level is maintained without roughness and then merits the name of *Trombone*.

When French type parallel shallots are used, with corresponding lighter tongues, the brassy quality is intensified and merits the name *Trompette*, or in octave pitch *Clarion*. When used on narrow-scaled resonators and quite modest wind-pressures, with the pipes disposed horizontally to project their voices directly out of the organ, the tone

GLOSSARY OF STOP NAMES 169

REED GROUP I

can be highly imitative of the herald's trumpet hence the descriptive names of *Fanfare Trumpet, Trompeta Real* and *Trompette en Chamade* (Plate 31). Short flared or belled ends assist tonal production and improve appearance.

A further widening of the scale and other proportional changes imparts a fullness to the brightness and is characteristic of the *Cornopean*. When set a little less 'close' and in consequence somewhat louder, the popular Edwardian stop the Posaune emerges, some examples were almost of tuba power.

Differences in shallot and tongues to suppress some of the higher harmonics gives the *Horn*, not really imitative, but a name for a closer toned cornopean. When the pipe-top is covered and the tube has perforations around its top edge, a refined mildly assertive chorus reed tone is developed and called *Waldhorn* or *Closed Horn*, but today it is regarded as too lacking in tonal transparency to be acceptable in normal instruments.

The use of higher wind-pressure, as a general rule, either allows greatly increased power for solo purposes or permits smoother firmer tone without loss of power. When coupled to full-scale and thick, well-loaded tongues on closed shallots, there emerges the *Tromba* tone family, also represented on the pedal in the *Ophicleide*, a smooth, close, intense tone, yet in good examples with more than a trace of 'clang', it is now little regarded and rarely found in new instruments unless of romantic design.

With even higher wind-pressure and the use of double-length or 'harmonic' resonators down well below Middle C, the power and smoothness is further intensified, to yield the dominant voice of the *Tuba Mirabillis*. The *Tuba* or *Harmonic Trumpet* is only slightly less in sonority and power, representing the ultimate effect of pressure on trumpet pipes.

OBOES

REED GROUP 2

Oboe
Hautboy   Hautbois
Orchestral Oboe
Cor Anglais   English Horn
Shalmey   Schalmey   Schalmei   Shawm
                                     (See Figs. 48 and 49.)

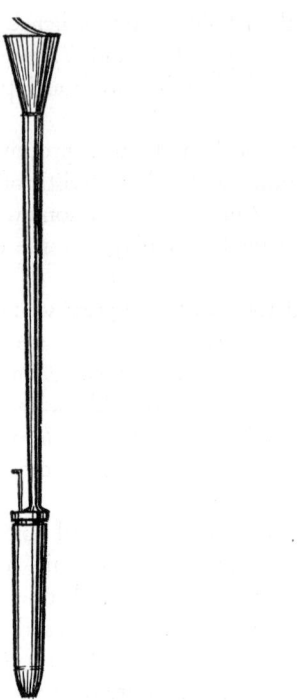

FIG. 48. Oboe mid C 8 feet.   FIG. 49. Cor anglais

Flares or 'bells' topping inverted conical resonators have a marked modifying effect on the tongue-generated tone, giving added fullness to the natural harmonic richness.

Narrow-scaled tubes surmounted by short wide 'bells' having either lift up covers or solid tops with side vent holes is typical of the commonest of all church organ reed-stops, the *Oboe*. Voiced with half-closed shallots, stiffish tongues set for low wind-pressure the tone is at best a nasal echo horn, an effective romantic solo voice but a poor mixer. A more musical form is that giving echo trumpet tone, sometimes defined by naming it *Hautbois*. This has valuable qualities as a soft manual double reed, wherein the bass tone approaches that of the bassoon, indeed the half length pipes of that stop are often used for the low octave.

Even narrower scales of this shape, produce thinner plaintive orchestral sounds reminiscent of the *Orchestral Oboe*, a purely solo stop of no chorus pretensions.

GLOSSARY OF STOP NAMES

REED GROUP 2

By increasing the bell diameter and mounting a further section of truncated cone to form a bulb-like resonating chamber we have the pipe shape for the *Cor Anglais* (Fig. 49). Fractional length tubes are often used for the lower octaves to maintain the thin sweet tone that usefully blends with most flutes.

The above stops are basically romantic in conception and find little place in neo-classical designs. The *Shalmey* is, however, an acceptable stop of this form with a tone derived from the precursor of the oboe, the *Shawm*. It is of similar construction to the organ oboe but the bells are larger and the shallots are of the open variety so that the tone is louder, brighter and less refined. It is often used as a higher pitched pedal stop.

CYLINDRICAL TUBE REED-STOPS

REED GROUP 3

a. Musette
Cromorn   Crumhorne   Krummhorn
Cremona
Basset Horn   Corno di Bassetto
Clarinet
Dulzian
Cinq   Zink
b. Rohr Shalmey

(See Figs. 50 and 51.)

These stops have a parallel tubular body as a basic shape. This may be joined to the block by a short conical section. The resonators are half the nominal pitch length and emphasize the odd-numbered harmonics, as in a stopped flue pipe. Considerable wind-pressure is not required even for romantic stops. The general power level is less than that of stops of the trumpet family.

The narrowest scale is the *Musette*, of thin acid tone, which is not now greatly used. Of medium small scale and voiced with open, beak-shaped shallots is the classical *Krummhorn*, its highly distinctive tone blending well with minor diapason choruses, yet making an appealing solo voice. Its traditional home is the positiv manual division.

The *Cremona* is a typically English compromise between Krummhorn and the *Clarinet*. The latter is a romantic stop of full scale, voiced with closed shallots in deliberate imitation of its orchestral namesake. The top of the body is capped and slotted to assist in obtaining the

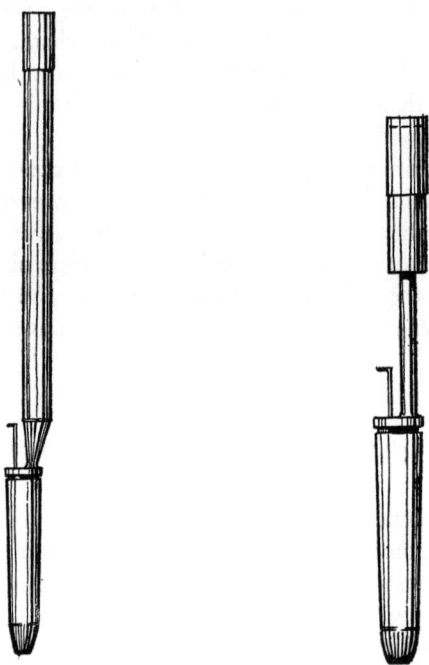

Fig. 50. Clarinet mid C 8 feet   Fig. 51. Rohr Shalmey mid C 8 feet

desired woody tone. The *Corno di Bassetto* is very similar, perhaps slightly thinner toned. Sometimes it has a double-belled top as for the cor anglais.

Next in scale above the Krummhorn is the classical *Dulzian*. It differs in having the lower conical section lengthened to about one-third of the body length which makes the tone less colourful and assertive, but one with good blending qualities.

The *Zink* or *Cinq* is of larger scale still, it is sometimes used in 2-ft. pitch on the pedal organ. It has a loose-toned Oriental trumpet sound.

The *Rohr Shalmey* has the main cylindrical part of the body separated from the block by a long thin stalk (83). There is no conical section. The tone resembles the oboe-type Shalmey but is more pungent and less trumpet-like.

GLOSSARY OF STOP NAMES 173

REED GROUP 4

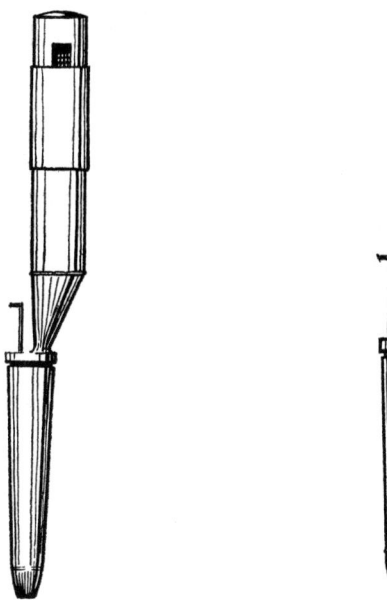

FIG. 52. Vox humana   FIG. 53. Ranket

FRACTIONAL LENGTH REEDS
a. Vox Humana   Bärpfeife
b. Rankett   Sordun
c. Regal

(See Figs. 52 and 53.)

The resonators of these stops are of various shapes but all have the common factor of being only a fraction of the nominal pitch length. Their tone is soft and buzzing.

The *Vox Humana* is the only romantic stop in this group and has resonators similar to a very short capped clarinet. Other stops bearing this name have double-belled resonators. A wider scaled version is found in Continental Europe and is known as the *Bärpfeife*.

The very softest of reeds is the *Rankett*. The resonator consists of a small chimney leading from the block and covered by a chamber, closed except for some holes near the lower end. This smothers the tone, allowing only a frog-like rattle to escape. The resonators are frequently made of wood. In some classical instruments it appears in 16 ft. on the manuals.

THE ORGAN TODAY

REED GROUP 4

The pedal organ counterpart of the Rankett is of considerably larger scale and known as the *Sordun*. Neither stop is found in England but there is a growing interest in these sounds.

The *Regals* are a group of reed-stops made with such short resonators as to have little effect upon the tongue. They are often of fanciful shapes. The tone is a bright but soft buzz. The few antique examples known in England are all believed to have been imported from Holland or Germany. An example can be seen in the picture of the rear view of the Carisbrook Castle organ (Plate 8).

13

The Organ-Case

A WELL-DESIGNED organ-case gives a purposeful and finished appearance to what is usually the largest single item of church furniture, but it should be something more than a mere ornamental facework. Some enclosing cabinet work of seemly appearance is normally necessary, at least to guard the smaller pipes from interference. It is usually a help to enclose the mechanism against an excess of dust and to confine mechanical noise. Such an organ-screen provides a convenient mount for the larger bass pipes, whose tones lose 'bloom' if muffled by interior placing.

Many organ-cases meet these needs admirably and may be impressive in design and craftsmanship, and yet pay no more than a casual respect for the principle that the organ-case should be a real part of the musical instrument, serving an acoustic need and should indeed be part of the tonal design. An organ without enclosing casework skilfully devised, lacks not only visual appeal, but also elements leading to tonal cohesion. An uncased organ in a small and acoustically good building, poses a fastidious voicer or tonal-finisher great difficulty in setting the final balance between voices and in note to note regulation. No amount of time and artful skill can overcome the seemingly wilful insistence of some notes to sound overloud or off-tone depending upon the position of the listener. This is not to denigrate open display of pipework, but to be musically successful this calls for designing skill beyond mere orderly arrangement.

Organ-screens or cases fall clearly into definable types of design:

A. Simple grille screens, usually across an organ chamber tone-opening.

B. Unencased pipework displayed in an orderly arrangement that emphasizes the natural progression of sizes and lengths.

C. Ranges of the larger bass pipes massed as a screen, sometimes in interleaving planes and usually without visible staying.

D. Bass pipes of natural or manipulated length, in functional groups, simply framed to give a unity of composition, which in some degree may and should reflect the internal layout.

E. Facework of timber and organ pipes, many often sham, in a stylized architectural composition ranging from utter simplicity to the lushly enriched. Too often these designs bear no relation to interior layout or acoustical considerations and are just a façade, on the other hand the best examples and they are all too few, are technically and artistically admirable.

There may be places where the anonymous and sterile quality of an organ chamber grille is appropriate or even unavoidable. Designing a grille of acceptable acoustic quality is far from an easy task. Usually about 60 per cent open space is essential for freedom of tonal egress. The other 40 per cent of structural area should not be of sound-absorbing material, form or finish. The extremes are roughly finished fibrous plaster at one end of the quality scale and wrought iron at the other.

Most organ grilles cover organs of such irregular appearance that they demand some fabric hanging to obtain obscuration which incidently assures a sterile appearance. These fabrics can seriously impair the tone unless selected for low weight and open texture. Materials that attract and hold muffling dust must be avoided or at least arranged that they may be vacuum cleaned *in situ*. An example of grille screening, possibly the largest in the country, is that covering the large four-manual instrument in Holbrook School Chapel (Plate 32). Of teak, this one is efficient because of its great effective area, but the appearance reveals nothing of the riches within.

Those case designs that come into the next category display a completely opposite approach to the all-obscuring grilles. They seek to display openly the pipework in all its wide range of sizes, lengths, shapes and materials. This involves careful organization of a good acoustic and structural layout of the interior parts, to make them acceptable to the eye in an unscreened form. This form relies on attractive outlines and textures arising from pipes of natural length, orderly arrayed on their supporting windchests (Plate 33). It is by no means as easy to do as the appearance of good examples suggests.

This open display treatment is advocated by those who believe that there should be no avoidable intervening screening between the pipes and the listeners' ears. Certainly in the right acoustics, the musical voice of pipes so placed has a special quality (Plate 34). A precision of intonation and a crisp brightness of sustained speech are marked characteristics.

While these are good and generally accepted reasons for avoiding the obstructive screening too often found in elaborately cased organs, these completely open layouts are rarely ideal in practice. Fine regulation of pipe-speech becomes extremely difficult in mildly resonant small buildings. Instead of the sounds coalescing within a sympathetic resonant surrounding before dispersing, as in a competently designed organ-case, each pipe tends to have its own series of reflective sound paths to the ear, these varying to listeners in other positions. When instruments are of the sort that are merely set up, perhaps this is not noticeable, but serious tonal artists are often troubled by this acoustically naked display. Some care and experience can minimize this difficulty, but as rules of layout they are too complex to be gone into here.

From an architectural view-point, this style has a strong vertical emphasis and a smallness of scale that results in a spikey impression, that is too competitive in most Gothic surroundings, unless it is kept well away from enriched details. It is best in a plain building. Examples are not numerous in England, Hyde Park Chapel, London, S.W., is a treatment of a concert hall instrument in a small auditorium of low musical reverberation.

Next we have an arrangement of the larger bass pipes, as a plain screen from impost level upwards. It has the attraction of low cost, as these pipes usually stand off the main windchest anyway. In the nineteenth century the stay posts and rails were exposed, either plain or elaborately moulded and pierced. Truly these were functional arrangements, containing nothing but essential parts in orderly array, but too often this was their artistic downfall, the resulting unselective coarseness of scale and the aggressive outline being uncritically and unfortunately accepted as the ordinary look of an organ.

In examples where the staying woodwork is arranged out of sight, where attention has been paid to selection of diameters and pipe foot-length proportions, and where necessary, a reasonable use of over-length, together with wide spacing, a lively and satisfactory screen design is achieved. Within sensible limits this is a reasonable and artistic manipulation of basic organ parts as elements in a composition forming a necessary screen. An example of this style, dating from 1956, is Giffnock South Church (Plate 33). A simple and effective use of available bass pipes to form a small functional screen. This is not to defend those where complete 'fronts' of dummy organ pipes, often of preposterously unnatural scales and size progressions are presented as 'design for organ-case'.

A related casework form is the same basic pipework arranged as interleaving screens, usually asymmetrical and two and sometimes three ranks deep in places. This is much practised by some continental European builders. The use of differing metals and finishes gives interest, but a curiously rigid, even blind quality results. One cannot believe, looking at such screens, that the organ can sing. Such double ranks of large metal pipes are quite a formidable tone barrier.

An interesting hybrid, that anticipated the current interest in open display, was that of the Royal Albert Hall, London (and to a lesser degree the Alexandra Palace, London) by Willis in the latter quarter of the last century (Plate 35). Here bass pipes and their stays form a boldly proportioned composition framing intriguing glimpses of unenclosed pipework in natural array. It is curious that these two organs had so little impact on design at that time.

Now we come to those cases in which bass pipes are framed in timber surrounds. In the earliest times in England, the casing of the organ, then a free-standing item of church furniture, was an exercise in the cabinet makers' art. Directed with an eye (and an ear too) to the acoustic values of carefully placed slim shafting and panelled surfaces, these cases undoubtedly had a tonal function, that is now coming to be appreciated again. Some seek to explain this as merely protection from dust, which it certainly was, but the nature of the early voicing style was such that a tone-cabinet form was beneficial. The North European 'werk prinzip' organs and cases still have this quality.

These cases by past masters, have grace and dignity. The displayed pipes always dominate the mouldings, encirclements and classical detail of the architectural composition. So many modern examples never quite attain this quality, this right balance of wood and metal, whereby the instrument acquires a visible personality, that can wear unfunctional enrichment without falseness. An ancient example illustrating this quality is that in St. Mary-the-Great, Cambridge (Plate 36), and a modern composition, which has also faint overtones of 'werk prinzip' is the choir face of the pulpitum organ of Norwich Cathedral (Plate 37).

Organ cases that reflect the 'werk prinzip' underlying the design and layout of the instruments, in both ancient and modern examples, are to be found in Germany, Holland and Denmark, but are all but unknown in England. In these instruments the external architecture is dictated by the strict relative positions and shapes of the manual and pedal divisions of the structure, and the tonal and acoustic concept of shallow depth, and the avoidance of any smothering by purely decorative woodwork or by pipes other than those of the immediate stops. The example illustrated, the New Kerk, Doetinchem, Holland, shows the basic form, in this case charmingly treated with embellishments that in no way disturb the musical functioning of the instrument (Plate 39).

These organ-cases almost always grace transept or west gallery sites where there is ample height. The smaller churches and crowded chancels in England that drive organs into restricted, former chapel organ-chambers, is infertile ground for this spacious and characteristic style.

While we have no typical example in the United Kingdom, the influence of its form and treatment has been and is being felt where new cases for new churches are being designed. Lighter framing, avoidance of pipe body overlength, the inclusion of smaller pipes in the façade and shaped top profiles are characteristic (Plate 40).

In the small, almost 'portative' organ field there has been a remarkable advance in external design. Formerly, with few exceptions, these had a fussily cheap look, and indeed some still have, but in the 1950's Mander's 'Denham' was a brilliant break-away, light, buoyant, functional and decorative (Plate 41). It reflected some Netherlands influence artfully scaled down to size. Another is the H.N. & B. 'Quintet' deliberately incorporating a tone-cabinet form that acoustically complimented the straight five-stop chorus, the whole form deriving from strict functional requirements (Plate 42), as in their functionally shaped free-standing one-row with a strong traditional flavour, the 'Bridgetown'.

Some attempts at uncased miniatures of minimal pipe content are less happy, offering no protection from interference or accidental damage, yet it cannot be denied the low height achieved has much to commend it. There is a need for a modern design of cabinet-organ of compact plan and low height, suited to country church chancels. Designs are known to exist but are slow to get off the drawing-board while most of the craft is so busy with larger projects.

The Royal Festival Hall organ in London has an exterior treatment that does not readily fit into any of these broad classifications. The bold unmannered structural expression has dignity from its sheer size so that the symbolic composition of freely treated pipe-forms seems almost impudent. It is a unique treatment that seems unlikely to lend itself to imaginative repetition.

Another contemporary attempt that avoids traditional forms no matter how well founded, is the organ screen in the new Coventry Cathedral. The result is an insensitive and unexciting use of bass pipe groups of pedestrian proportions that lack grace of form and tell nothing of the exciting contents behind them. A personal view perhaps, but we feel here a lost opportunity.

There is in these islands a slowly growing appreciation amongst organ-builders, musicians and enlightened churchmen, that the organ case is a functional entity with the organ, as something more than a tidy enclosure of the mechanism or an exercise in monumental composition with an organ flavour. Our younger architects are coming to realize that treated three-dimensionally, the organ offers a plastic medium for functional sculpture, that also pays musical dividends. However, this cannot be achieved without the closest co-operation with the organ-builder-designer as an equal. Indeed we have an opportunity, even a duty, to lead in our own spheres, as do our allied artist craftsmen in stained glass and church furniture. It is we who must show the way to integrity in organ-case design.

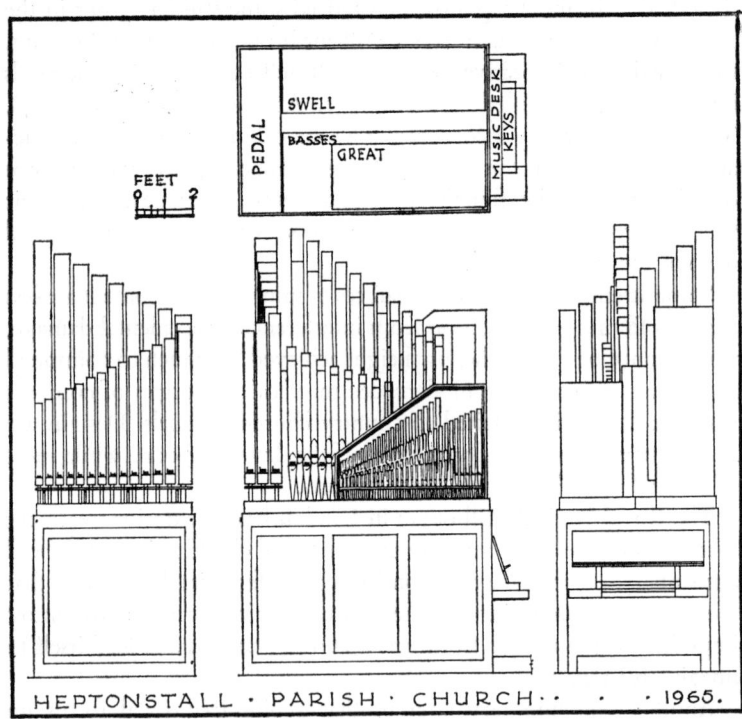

Fig. 54

14

The placing of the Organ

THE position of an organ and its surroundings in a building, can make or mar the instrument's musical success. Therefore this aspect of organ-design deserves more consideration than it usually receives. Architects in general are not well informed on this and it is rare that they are adequately briefed by church committees, who are often uninformed in the matter anyway.

Careful site planning with attention to complementary acoustic conditions, will assure a satisfying musical quality and the greatest effect from the tonal resources that can be afforded or accommodated. When favourably placed and planned, a smaller instrument can have adequate accompanimental power, and because of the lesser need for wide dynamic levels, it yields better blending to give a wider range of compound tones. This is a saving which could easily pay for a worthy organ-case that the open position may demand.

The introduction of power blowing, giving relatively unlimited volume and pressure of wind-supply, allowed organs to be voiced more loudly and coarsely, and so to be placed in crowded and almost detached organ chambers. This sort of Gothic organ kennel was beloved of nineteenth-century Tractarian architects for its tidyness in relation to the introduction of chancel choirs, and as affording an opportunity to design a woody screen. Unfortunately it drove organ-builders to yet higher pressures and more strident tone to overcome the stifling effects of this mistaken planning. It still persists where advice is sought too late.

For centuries the organ was developed as a free-standing instrument, often on elevated rear galleries, as may be seen and gloriously heard in many continental churches. Its relegation, in England, to confining organ chambers, undoubtedly started the artistic decline that deprived the organ of the support of serious musicians for so long.

It is all very well to advise that the organ should be set up free standing in a rear gallery because it is demonstratively the most effective position musically, but traditional practices and liturgical forms are not readily adapted to this position in buildings of traditional shape. Many galleries are not lofty enough and in small modern parish churches it would be much too close to some of the congregation. Because there can be no universally ideal arrangement, each case must be considered, following some basic rules. It may well be that these rules cannot all be fully satisfied, but at least a practical compromise should result.

In churches and chapels where the choir is taken seriously and is not merely a hang-over of Victorian tradition, it is there to sing the music of the service and to lead the singing of the congregation. For this latter purpose it needs almost as careful positioning as the organ. In this task it needs the support and lead of the organ, which should therefore be *near it* and be *heard as one with the singers*. The accompaniment of choirs of normal accomplishment by organs at a distance, lacks their need for attack and definition, as well as depriving them of the encouragement of a sense of corporate music-making.

The difficulty of a rear gallery organ sixty feet distant from a chancel choir is easily imagined. Some listeners would be too close to organ or choir, with unavoidable loss of balance and lack of synchronization. The difficulty can still be there at half the distance, if the sound is strongly directional as a result of building shape and organ placing.

The next consideration is the relative position of the player to instrument, choir singers and congregation. Here we must take into account some physical factors that cannot be ignored. They are the action response rate and the time sound takes to travel through air. There are clearly very practical limits to the distance from an organ to a detached console when set up near to the choir stalls. Well designed and adjusted electro-pneumatic actions and windchests have a response rate of around 30 milliseconds from key touch to pipe speech. All makes of action are by no means as good as this. The average is probably around one-twentieth of a second. To this must be added the time sound needs to travel say 60 ft., another one-twentieth of a second, making a total of about one-tenth of a second. From experience this has been found to be the utmost that can be tolerated, and even that involves conscious anticipation on the part of the player. Added to this is a loss of definition caused by loss of power and by hearing multiple reflections of sound when heard at a distance from its source.

It is sometimes proposed that the player be placed with the distant organ. Here we must allow not only action response and sound lag time, but also for its return in the form of the singers' audible response. Simple calculation suggests a total around one-sixth of a second. With such a time-lag, the player had better not try to listen, if in fact he could hear them. In such an arrangement no sensible control of balance is possible, and anyway both balance and synchronization would vary according to the position of a listener relative to organ and distant choir, a hopelessly unmusical arrangement. When there is no choir, and organ and congregation form the musical unit, different considerations apply and it then has some merit.

Clearly no amount of art or science can overcome the shortcoming of wide division of organ and choir. With the player placed so as to hear and command the accompanimental balance, they should form a spatially and acoustically closely related group.

All this does not detract from the advantages that can be derived from a detached console placed where it gives good hearing and choir command. There is no inherent superiority in detachment over attached positions, indeed the first consideration should always be the possibility of an attached position that could give good hearing. More than mere economy should dictate this, that is, expenditure on a good attached position is better than money spent on detachment.

Where detachment seems necessary, there is much in favour of a slightly elevated loft position. Consoles set up within or behind choir stalls at the same or at sunken levels rarely allow good hearing and become doubtful vantage-points.

So much for position, what about organ space and arrangement? With the reawakening of taste for warm bright unforced tone and the use of lower wind-pressure to that end, comes a re-emphasis on an old rule that no organ is the better for being buried. Historically the organ was developed as a free-standing instrument, standing openly in the building and only in the past hundred years have debasing influences tended to banish it to tone-muffling organ chambers. Reappraisal shows that higher wind-pressures, heavier pipes and larger stop-lists are not satisfactory compensations. It is probably true that a totally enclosed and expressive design in a building devoid of any noticeable reverberation would lose nothing by burying in a small recess, but such designs are largely at a discount with our revived taste in clear, precise tone.

Natural laws and the differing response of our ears to frequencies at either end of the musical scale, result in a more rapid decay in the loudness of high notes compared with low-pitched sounds as the distance from the source is increased. Try walking away from an organ while a full organ chord is sustained. No matter how brilliant the registration it is the left hand and the pedal that is heard in the churchyard. Furthermore reverberant surfaces nearly always more efficiently reflect the graver tones and tend to filter out brightness. Therefore directly heard speech of unencumbered pipework tends to be bright and of definite intonation. Reverberant sound tends to be duller, warmer and imprecise.

As a general rule, the pipes of unenclosed divisions, and that should include pedal upperwork, should be placed *as much as possible in the same open space as the listener.* Where this is not possible, at least two sides of the organ should be wide open and as little encumbered with woody casework and large front pipes as it is possible to contrive. In such cases a generous space above the pipes can help a lot, but this must not be a pocket of poorly reflecting roof structure. This just absorbs and confuses. For similar reasons an unavoidably chambered instrument should not be crowded, and the temptation is great; it should be as open and spacious as possible. This not only helps to assure good tone and ensemble but make possible effective maintenance.

The prominent and open position for the organ can often pose questions of taste and considerations other than acoustic and musical. There are sight lines, structural stresses and questions of architectural balance and appearance. All these are important but they should not, as too often, be lightly used to dismiss the organ to some sound-damning dungeon, unfavourable, inartistic and in the long run uneconomic and poor value for money. The answer should be sought in a conference, on site between clergy, musician, architect and organ-builder on equal terms. The admitted dangers of mediocre design by committee, are in our experience, well offset by the creative atmosphere brought about by wide diversity of interests and goodwill to the project.

A good building for sound has often been described as the best stop on the organ, everything blends well with it. Indeed without a favourable acoustic condition, every aspect of the organ-builder's art is called upon in an endeavour to obtain acceptable musical tone qualities and a semblance of blend between the voices of the instrument. In flattering acoustic surroundings an admired instrument has often on critical examination been found to be less than the best, in material, form and voicing, underlining the value of care in the acoustic design of an organ's surroundings.

What do we mean by 'a good building for sound'? and how can this be recognized at the planning stage? An important requirement is a high cubic content or volume in relation to the seating capacity, because all else being equal, this controls the reverberation time. As floor areas are usually closely related to seating capacity, a high ratio must mean a lofty building.

An old rule of thumb, well founded on observation of good examples was the 'double-cube' as a basic shape, that is a building as high as its width and twice the width in length. Of course other layout considerations demand other shapes and proportions, but it is an interesting thing to observe that the further the basic shape departs from the double-cube rule, the more musical and acoustic problems arise.

A contemporary trend to neglect the acoustic 'bloom' in favour of a 'dry' quality achieved by a very short reverberation time at all pitch levels, has some appeal in chamber ensembles, but it robs the organ tone and the choir singing of warmth, so that the virile definition of modern, or for that matter antique, upperwork, becomes tiring and tiresome to listen to for long.

Long buildings, like our larger parish churches and cathedrals, present problems of attenuation of sound. In these cases the position of the accompanying organ in relationship to the more distant members of the congregation needs special consideration. Sometimes it is not possible to satisfy these requirements from one single source, and an antiphonal section, placed nearer those distant from the main instrument is then the only practical solution. Bradford Cathedral contains a very recent example of this form (Plate 38). Of course such antiphonal sections are essentially accompaniment supporting, for some special effects and processional accompaniment. They have no place in the solo performance use, at least in the classical repertoire. Long auditoriums tend to emphasize a phenomena that plagues pedal organ low notes, known as 'standing waves' whereby the weight of bass notes is either excessive or negligible in patches throughout the building. There is little that can be done to overcome this, other than to avoid dull tones of little harmonic content.

Leaving the theories of acoustic design of buildings to the many excellent, if not unanimous books now available, let us concentrate on those aspects of detail that affect the organ in significant ways. We should first have regard to the ceiling or roof in general, and particularly immediately above the instrument. The roof area is usually a very large part of the reflective areas by which the sound is driven around the building, to some extent it is important in countering the normal loss by attenuation with distance. In very general terms, the bright treble notes need hard smooth surfaces for their efficient reflection, whereas the bass notes are much less critical of surface texture and require weight and rigidity of structure to resist penetration and throw their sounds back to the listener. Thus a smooth stone vault has ideal properties, but a lightweight suspended ceiling would result in tones lacking warmth and the bass lacking gravity. A rigid framed and panelled roof is again excellent, indeed probably the best. But substitute open rafters, brackets, beams and trusses, and then the higher frequencies, exposed to so many diffusing reflective surfaces, are weakened, leaving the bass tones in excessive proportion.

Boarding-over open rafters can brighten the tone of an organ and give much encouragement to a choir. A modern practice of ceilings panelled in soft thin building board, acoustic tile or thin hardboard is regrettable, in this context. Rarely are these buildings so lofty or large that there is really a need to dampen sound reflected from the roof. The ill effects on singing and its accompaniment for the next fifty years surely questions the wisdom or economy of such low cost or misconceived construction. Plain boarding or well-secured plywood is much to be preferred. Should an unfortunate focus occur, its correction is possible with a strategically applied and limited amount of acoustic absorbency.

Wall surfaces come in for much the same observations as for roofs and ceilings, but of necessity they are usually strong and massive and acoustically unobjectionable unless deeply recessed.

Carpeted floors, cushioned seating and screening curtains are all highly sound absorbent, as is also the listener's clothing, hence the tone-dulling effect of a large audience. Moderation in carpeting and hangings is essential if satisfying musical 'bloom' is desired.

What should be the reverberation time of a building in which good organ music is required? This is nearly always necessarily a compromise. Whereas there may be differing tastes as to musical quality, speech must be intelligible or it is useless. This latter consideration is, however, less of a problem in the smaller building. Often acoustic design leans heavily towards the safety of shorter reverberation times—which clear speech seems to demand. For organ music with an audience present, the ideal is of the order of two and quarter seconds between stopping the source of sound and its decay to inaudibility. A reverberation time of less than one and a quarter seconds results in a loss of 'tonal bloom' that leaves a musical gap between the higher pitched partials and the more readily reverberant low frequencies. The sound thus tends to lack warmth and appeal. A skilful designer and perceptive voicer-finisher can make good some of these deficiencies but never wholly recover what has been lost. Good design and prudent spending clearly go hand in hand.

15
Buying an Organ

THE purchase of something as costly as a new organ or the rebuilding of an old one, not unnaturally presents a worrying problem to most church organ committees. Often they will admit their perplexity and lack of understanding so it is not surprising that they resort to what they imagine is businesslike procedure—and call for 'competitive tenders'.

There is of course nothing basically wrong in calling for tenders except the absence of a common comprehensive specification. Without this the resulting bids cannot be compared readily and indeed they may well be so contradictory in objective and recommendation that the committee find themselves baffled and quite unqualified to make a wise choice.

Much of the reason for all this is to be found in the old-style structure of the organ-building industry, in which the master is consulted on one hand as a professional artist taking full responsibility for the integrity of his advice, and on the other hand he is expected to be a tradesman, tendering prices and undertaking contracts in a strictly commercial way as though working under professional supervision. This combination works well enough in practice, and at its best it confounds those who quite understandably believe they require competitive tenders to get the best value.

Prices in organ-building, while ranging widely, are nevertheless a fair indication of the level of technical design and the structural standards that can be expected and which will be reflected in the durability of the projected work. Unless work is entrusted to untried practitioners in the particular style of work involved, you may be fairly sure of receiving at least fair commercial value.

Sometimes an organist committee man will draw up a brief list of organ stops and an outline of improvements or accessories required, but this is too elementary to be effectively useful in comparing tenders. No two organ-builders would interpret such a stop-list in the same way, it leaves so much room for commercial interpretation or imaginative treatment to suit the individual requirements of each case. Standards of detail design, material quality and durability vary very widely indeed, a low tender may assure no more than that the result will be a fair money's worth in material.

It is not uncommon practice to ask from four to six or more firms, often of a range oddly assorted in artistic esteem, to tender designs and specifications, with great detail as to alternatives and of course to call and discuss the matter, without obligation and at no cost to the inquirer. Certainly this is competitive. It is also very wasteful and it is certainly an illusion that it is at no cost. The requisite attention by competent specialists costs a considerable amount in time and expenses and all with the promise that only one in six can be a sale. This means that at the lowest estimate of cost of £30 per inquiry, an added cost on successful tenders of £200 or more is inevitable even if estimates are nominally free. Someone has to pay for it.

Not unnaturally many firms view invitations for competitive tenders with some well-founded scepticism. Too often between the lines, can be seen the hope to collect any design ideas cast on the receptive ears of the inquirers, and all without cost. Can this really be the right way for ethical bodies such as our churches to negotiate, a way that loads the overheads against other buyers? The increasing practice of requesting a consultation fee of a nominal value is a reflection of this dilemma, and a way of sorting out the serious inquirer from collectors of information who in the end are all too often, ill equipped to assess its value.

In some countries the solution is found in engaging the services of an organ architect to function in much the same way as his counterpart in the building construction industry. In these islands this is not practical as there are no professional qualifications possible that can assure integrity and the responsibility that such a title implies, although there are some would-be practitioners. They should not be confused with organ consultants whose useful function is quite different.

How is this dilemma to be resolved? How can full professional advice be enjoyed without reserve, and wasteful expense be avoided? It is important to appreciate that no organ specification can be sufficiently detailed to define, in an artistic creation, the finer and important differences of imaginative interpretation, design and musical finish; to specify responsiveness of mechanism or to assure durability of adjustment. Even if it were possible to do so adequately there is no competent independent professional supervision available, so that *the choice of an organ-builder is in the first place more important than the price*. This principle is being accepted in industries far removed from organ-building, where also the competitive tender approach has been found inadequate and a source of serious disappointment.

We believe that the best work has always been the outcome of the stimulation from the interplay of ideas of those technically concerned with the project, organ-builder, organist, Minister and architect or organ consultant working together as responsible equals. But how does one choose an organ-builder?

The only safe way is to rely on reputation; and to view, examine and compare costs of instruments by different builders who have met similar design demands as may be involved in one's own requirements, and then to select and invite one, or at most two, to discuss the project and prepare an estimate of costs.

When an organ committee is in doubt as to what is required to meet their musical standards and practices, the paid professional services of an organ consultant of repute can be most valuable and a sound investment. He can study the musical needs, advise on basic requirements and select typical instruments for examination. He can help in the preliminary discussions with the selected builder, advise on the fairness of cost estimates and consult with the builder during the final voicing and tonal finishing. In this way the organ committee can be guided to both quality and suitability, and in the avoidance of any misguided extravagance arising from misunderstandings, easily afford the fees involved.

Who should be the organ consultant? Well preferably, a musician well versed in the service music of the denomination and, possibly by recital experience, one who is familiar with the contemporary products of many builders. This need not rule out the presiding organist, but he should be paid fees for this special service. However well intentioned, free advice is rarely worth very much and proper fees induce a responsible attitude to those being served.

Do not expect the organ consultant to specify technical details outside the musical considerations, it will almost certainly be outside his experience and master organ-builders of repute not unnaturally object to technical direction by amateurs who in the end bear no responsibility. It is the builder's name that is borne by the instrument, he alone stands or falls by its performance during the next thirty years or more. A church committee may benefit from professional music experience but certainly not from amateur organ-building advice.

When the problem is planning a new building and providing an organ to suit, the procedure least likely to end in disappointment and unnecessary expense, is slightly different. The first step is most important and cannot be taken too soon, certainly it should be at the architect's sketch-plan stage, but better still at the drafting of his brief for the whole of the accommodation required.

The emphasis here is on the wisdom of having an organ-builder, in his professional capacity, assisting at this critical time. The architect will appreciate it, his work is made easier and better if his brief is firm and complete, and if he is not later asked to make changes that involve inefficient compromises.

Very few architects have sufficient experience of organ planning to make adequate and effective provision unaided which means the most economical way in any circumstances.

Most organ-builders recognize the importance of early conference to ensure effective results not marred by mis-conceived planning, and are ready to advise and go to considerable trouble to do so. But who should be consulted? Someone who has recently been associated with an outstanding example in a particular denomination could be a good choice.

The use of a consultant organ-builder at this early stage need not hamper the final choice, but it is not fair to expect free advice of a professional standard and then to impose competitive buying based on his advice and, quite probably, original ideas. Freedom is preserved by paying a professional fee, it is often little more than to cover expenses involved, and it can save money tenfold, besides avoiding a disappointment realized too late to amend the cause.

It is sometimes claimed on behalf of self-styled organ advisers that by employing their judgment, superior work may be obtained at lower cost from organ-builders of otherwise lower-grade work. It could be true that following their advice, specification and even planning errors arising from inexperience or misconceived cost-cutting ideas, might be avoided, but they cannot substitute for the lack of an experienced specialist, or the imagination and artistic knowledge that distinguishes the work of the reputable builders. It is easy to be a critic but real knowledge and experience is essential to constructive criticism. They cannot assure the design and material quality that alone promises durability and trouble-free working. Better-class work at lower-class prices is an illusion, a dream that could turn into a nightmare and nearly always does.

Planning to buy an Organ

What are the main considerations to be kept in mind when planning? The keyword should be effectiveness. In the long run effectiveness means economy achieved by fitness for purpose and a high musical value for money spent.

The first step is to draft a basic stop-list, designed to meet the musical needs relative to acoustic conditions and not just to fill the organ space, large or small as it may be. There are no rules of thumb for this, the size of the building and the extent of the seating have important bearing on the number of full organ stops needed to achieve adequate accompaniment, and, if there is a liturgical service, a sufficient variety of quieter stops. After that it becomes a matter of just how complete a recital instrument can be afforded.

With the basic musical resources decided, space requirements can be assessed—a necessary step towards physical planning in an effective location with an acoustically efficient interior layout. Too much compromise at this stage may involve unsuspected waste, as the instrument may then need to be larger to assure tonal range and volume because of unfavourable placing resulting in ineffective tonal egress and distribution.

Burying the organ in a close-fitting organ chamber or detaching it at a distance from the choir may seem architecturally convenient but it is musically wasteful. Local considerations should take into account a position relative to choir singers *and* the congregation, and the position of the player relative to all three. It should also have regard to any acoustic correction treatment, a buried organ in an unresponsive building needs to be much larger and needs the best professional attention to achieve useful results.

Cost is increased by crowding into a small space, or by the special construction of a divided instrument. The latter often doubles casework costs as well and this treatment should be regarded as a last resource and avoided unless the alternative is acoustically less advantageous.

An effective open position may almost certainly need more frontal casing, usually on one or both sides besides the front. This might seem to be a telling disadvantage, until it is appreciated that casing need cost no more than the bricks and mortar, tiles and timber of an organ chamber and those extra stops that this accommodation would make necessary.

Organ-cases are part of the technical structure of the instrument and not just screens over the less sightly parts. Effective casing today must avoid those woody architectural edifices of the past sixty years. While impressive of appearance they are often acoustically obstructive. The light shafting and well-spaced frontal pipes of eighteenth-century examples should be our models though we need not copy their mouldings and enrichments.

A very important part of any organ work is the final voicing or 'finishing' as it is called. This should be highly personal craftsmanship of a high order, yet it defies adequate contract specification, indeed in many contracts we have seen it is not even mentioned. It should involve well-paid tonal artists of cultivated taste and experience in weeks of painstaking detail adjustment to create a unique musical instrument from that which would otherwise be run-of-the-mill and of no distinction. In choosing an organ-builder, inquire about this aspect of his work, who does it, and how long does he spend at it, for it is the mark of creative organ-building and essential to effective musical value for your money, and there are no short cuts to it.

As in all fields of artistic endeavour, there is the inspired creation, the dull mediocre, and the indifferent that is not art at all, and so it is in organ-building. The commercially successful is not necessarily inartistic, but it too often reflects rather less than the mean of taste and quality in its search for material value.

16

Organs and Organ-builders— the future?

WHAT does the future seem to hold for the organ and the pipe-organ master's craft? Twenty-five years ago this question usually brought answers predicting slow death by suffocation from quantity produced electronic substitutes, and from the poverty of the main customer, the churches. But it has not happened that way at all. Most 'electronics' have become cheaper to buy, a few have got better, but critical standards have advanced in a way unimaginable years ago and this challenge the pipe organ has won on artistic grounds. Some of the money of our affluent society has rubbed off into the offertory plate, along with a new sense of responsibility on the part of church supporters to hand on in good order, that which they have enjoyed from past benefactors. The interest in the pipe organ has never been so active as now.

A quarter of a century has produced a revolution and a revelation. Or perhaps it is that a revelation has brought about the revolution. Broadcasting, hi-fidelity recordings and opportunities for international travel have lead to a rediscovery of the classical tone-colours and choruses of historical instruments on the European continent. It has been possible to savour the creative artistry arising from close partnership of composer, player and builder so evident in Denmark today, and to some extent also in Holland and Germany.

By comparison, the great bulk of British twentieth-century work now seems to make a dull showing in solo performance so that a startling reappraisal has occurred. Serious musicians have a new evaluation of the instrument, while students, quick to respond to new approaches have, and are spreading, dissatisfaction with some of the older concepts of British organ-design. So wide is the impact of this that it can now be observed affecting the thinking of some who are otherwise unwilling to accept that a period of artistic degeneration has come to an end.

The pipe organ of the future is being developed from the new concepts based on, but not blindly copying, the new realized qualities of the admired old instruments. Inevitably in artistic circles a degree of austerity tends to accompany new thinking resulting in the discarding of earlier developments, at least temporarily and the organ is no exception to this trend. Already, some players are demanding tonal schemes suitable for the registration of a wider literature than is possible with the narrow resources and minimal playing aids that some advocate, and which derive sincerely from impeccable historical sources. This demand can only be satisfied by designer, voicer and player in creative partnership and the best work today is largely due to such inspiration. This can assure a lively future for the pipe organ and its makers.

Future historians may see more clearly the impact all this is making on the whole of the organ-building craft. Already a new generation of designers and voicers is succeeding those who in weathering the pressure of change not unnaturally sought to combine old with new, thus creating unhappy hybrids. These new men of an ancient craft will resolve the artistic problems demonstrated in some of the forward-looking and occasionally unhappy instruments that have lately passed as classical revivals. Theirs will be the task to remould the native improvements of the last century with the time-tried best of the ancient models. All the indications are there that they will produce instruments of music superb in their ecclesiastical function of mass accompaniment, as well as being majestic but articulate vehicles for solo interpretation.

Perhaps the combination of pipes with electronic generation of pedal bass notes which many anticipated thirty-five years ago may yet be achieved. Given a good standard of tonal production and pitch control it could make big and significant savings in bulk, that at least would allow many organs to be more effectively placed. It could be a major break-through for the smaller church organ otherwise condemned to tonal suffocation while hiding their unsightly bulk in some small organ chamber. However, at present the artistic and technical problems involved have prevented any wide adoption.

Progress in the mechanical design of organs, is today almost breathless compared with the second quarter of the century. Electric action is reliable and now the least costly. The gradual elimination of pneumatic aids and the possibilities in adaptations of the products and techniques of the electronics industry, is leading to much needed mechanical simplicity. Already circuitry is being successfully adopted which gives action movements that are virtually without time-lag, that are noiseless, and are astonishingly compact and durable.

Even with the revival of tracker-action, new materials are giving greater reliability. Mass produced parts of uniformly high quality are available to all builders, making possible unconventional designs or a uniformity of performance that was unthinkable in earlier days. As the new-found skills are perfected, direct mechanical actions superior to the admired models and resistant to man-made climatic conditions, are surely promised.

The new sheet materials with their uniform quality and durability, with more scientific application, will continue to oust even further the old-fashioned solid natural products with all their whims and uncertainties. With them less of the rare skilled craftsman's time will be wasted in mere laborious preparation.

The organs of the future will increasingly reflect the growing understanding of the importance of open acoustic conditions in determining placing and layout. This in turn will markedly affect the appearance. Casing will be required to enhance tone production and projection, as well as provide a graceful face to its surroundings. The trend is already away from traditional architectural compositions, often woody and reflecting little of the contents, and this will develop as lighter forms of functional screening, depending upon grace of proportions with little or no reliance on ornament. Success on these lines should make possible the replacement of many clumsy and smothering organ screens, to the delight of eye and ear.

But what will be the effect on the craftsmen? Will they still be available? Will they be necessary? I believe there is now and will be more than ever, a need for that expression of personal experience and integrity in a personal product, that is true craftsmanship. Economic pressures however, may mean the passing of the comprehensive tradesman.

As mechanization, volume production and automation reduce the real cost of commercial products, so personal craftsmanship which is helped little by these aids, seems to become more and more costly in proportion, although the real cost of organ-building has changed little in sixty years. Perhaps the best work is even better value for money having regard to the higher standards and the many playing aids now furnished as a matter of course. The answer to the preservation of craftsmanship, is in lowering costs by greater efficiency in design and building, and in the efficient and rewarding use of craftsmen.

Too much of a craftsman's time is taken up in operations calling for a little skill that is easily acquired and is uninteresting in performance anyway. An all too small proportion of his time calls for the exercise of skill, judgment and manipulative dexterity. Management and trade union opinion seem to support this situation. This is a pity for it deprives the skilled man of adequate financial reward and the incentive to acquire greater understanding and consequent advancement in his craft.

As the specialist production of well-designed, volume-produced parts increases, the past ten years has seen a tremendous change. More and more the organ tradesman will become an assembler with the laborious part of his work increased. Yet well-paid and highly skilled foremanship and technical supervision are and will be necessary more than ever before. That is where real craftsmanship will be exercised. It will call for much new thinking by all who work in this craft industry. There will be a need for willingness to accept division of skills as between easily acquired dexterity, and studiously acquired judgment and objectivity, as mechanics, or as masters of the craft. I believe that only in this way will craftsmanship be adequately rewarded and so preserved. Already we can see moves in this direction in continental Europe and the results there leave no doubt as to the benefits to all concerned.

There is an alternative, a development of perhaps limited possibilities, in which small co-partnership groups of artist-craftsmen, of complementary abilities and specialities, work as partners under a leader. Given the right inspiration, such a group could be both creative and productive because of a commonly shared objective. It would involve a change in the structure of the industry as we know it, as its operations would be small scale and necessarily limited to new work, apart from the guarantee servicing of their own creations. This would leave the ordinary repair, rebuild, maintenance and tuning to local men or firms. Such co-partnership firms already exist on the American continent and have high reputations in their localities. We may yet see this in these islands.

How will the future of the pipe organ be affected by the electronic instrument, will these advance to a level that could present artistic competition? There seems little reason to suppose that this is not possible, but will anyone want to do so? The compactness possible in electronic organ construction makes it advantageous to design it for volume production and sales, at a quality and low price to meet an undiscriminating popular market of home music-making. In this market, so much wider than offered by places of worship, so much money can be made that it leaves little incentive to compete with the pipe organ on its own ground.

The extra that could raise the artistic standard, that could make each instrument unique to its use, costs so much more as to be commercially incompatible and unattractive. Certainly, quality will improve from sheer competition within its present field, and then it will be the purely commercial pipe-organ-builder who will need to worry because it is his market they will be after.

One aspect of the future of the organ craft needs much more championing by players than it gets at present and that is the tuning and regulation service. In common with all services involving personal attention it is becoming relatively costly as it is not susceptible to mechanization or time-cutting techniques. In this, more than ever the best is really the cheapest, as an indifferent man costs as much to transport, feed and assist, as a highly skilled and attentive one, and this is a significant part of the whole cost. Good tuning at adequate fees and reasonable frequency is urged as an insurance of continuing good performance. This could go a long way towards encouraging what could be a dying service. Assure good work by adequate heating, a minimum of interruptions and help to keep costs down by avoiding wasted time in travel by co-operating with a neighbouring place of worship.

It will surely be agreed, that the extent of support given by contemporary composers to the literature of an instrument must eventually affect the artistic health of a musical instrument for good or ill. Fortunately there are already examples of creative partnerships between composer players and imaginative organ-builders existing in Europe. We could have new organ music, making demands on designers and voicers, calling for new voices and new concepts of balances. The all too common injunction to 'go back 200 years and all will be well', is hollow advice if it produces only sterile copies. We believe it could be, and will be otherwise.

The late Dean Cranage was conducting a distinguished Oriental visitor around the many points of interest and beauty in Norwich Cathedral. They came at last to the vista down England's longest Cathedral church. Seeing the high pulpitum supporting the great width of the 1898 organ the visitor commented 'I did not know you worshipped a God of many voices!' To the many enthusiasts, students, players and organ-builders, it is indeed almost a God, impressively regal in voice and case and dazzling in the display of its genius. With so much absorbing interest in it, critical and constructive, may it always be so.

o

Appendix

Appendix

Appendix

Stop-lists

Some stop-lists from recent works to illustrate range and diversity of style to meet particular usages. A five-stop chorus, the Hill 'Quintet', having surprising versatility, any two stops combine as a musical sound.

One manual CC–A, 58 notes
Open diapason 8 ft. (derived bass)
Gedeckt   8 ft.
Principal   4 ft.
Nasat   2⅔ ft. Mid. C
Fifteenth   2 ft.

254 pipes voiced on low wind-pressure (1¾ in. wg.)
Internal electric blowing with plug connection
Tracker action

Developed and spread over two manuals, with liturgical service accompaniment in mind, as at St. James' Bridgetown.

Great organ
(CC–A 58 notes)

	feet	pipes
Open diapason	8	52
Stopped diapason	8	58
Gemshorn	4	58

Swell organ
(CC–A 58 notes)

	feet	pipes
Salicional	8	58
Nason flute	4	58
Principal	2	58

Pedal organ
(CC–F 30 notes)

	feet	pipes
Bourdon	16	18

and remainder derived
Swell to great ⎫
Swell to pedal ⎬ couplers by catch pedals
Great to pedal ⎭
Tracker action throughout
Bar and slider windchests
2¼ in. wind-pressure

Designed for the same purpose, but using electric action to derive useful octave voices outside the 'straight' chorus, is King's Park Catholic Church, Glasgow.

Great organ

	feet	pipes
Open diapason	8	61
Stopped diapason	8	73
Viola da gamba	8	from swell
Principal	4	61
Stopped flute	4	derived
Swell to great		
Swell octave to great		

Swell organ

	feet	pipes
Viola da gamba	8	derived
Hohl flute	8	61
Viola principal	4	66
Mixture	III	(15.19.22)
		183
Contra oboe	16	61
Tremulant		
Octave		
Sub octave		
Unison off		

Pedal organ

	feet	pipes
Sub bass	16	12 remainder from great flute
Bass flute	8	
Octave flute	4	
Bassoon	16	from swell
Swell to pedal		
Swell octave to pedal		
Great to pedal		

A little larger with marked classical leanings but still an accompanimental organ. Tracker action discipline requires independent completeness of every stop at Holy Trinity Church, Cookridge.

Great organ
(CC–A 58 notes)

	feet
Stopped diapason	8
Principal	4
Quint	2⅔
Fifteenth	2
Swell to great	

Swell organ
(CC–A 58 notes)

	feet
Quintadena	8
Salicional	8
Spitz flute	4
Principal	2
Larigot	1⅓
Crumhorn	8
Tremulant (fan)	

Pedal organ
(CC–F 30 notes)

	feet
Bourdon	16
Spitz flute	8
Nachthorn	4
Great to pedal	
Swell to pedal	

Between the foregoing basic church organ designs and the major instruments is a wide field for the development of their principles and the exercise of personal preference and taste. First a small concert organ in the Mormon Hyde Park Chapel, London. You may be able to identify some of the displayed ranks in Plate No. 10, from this stop-list.

APPENDIX

Great organ
(8 stops, 11 ranks, 671 pipes)

	feet
Quintaten	16
Open diapason	8
Gedeckt pommer	8
Octave	4
Octave quint	2⅔
Super octave	2
Mixture IV (19, 22, 26, 29)	
Trumpet	8

Choir-positif
(10 stops, 10 ranks, 610 pipes)

	feet
Rohr flute	8
Dulciana	8*
Gemshorn	4
Principal	4
Nazard	2⅔
Nason flute	2
Tierce	1⅗
Sifflöte	1
Krummhorn	8*
Schalmei	4*
Tremulant (adjustable)	

Couplers

	feet
Swell to great	8
Swell to great	16
Swell to great	4
Positif to great	
Swell sub octave	
Swell unison off	
Swell octave	
Swell to choir-positif	8
Swell to choir-positif	4
Swell to pedal	4
Swell to pedal	8
Great to pedal	8
Positif to pedal	8

Swell organ
(13 stops, 16 ranks, 974 pipes)

	feet
Wald flute	8
Viola pomposa	8
Viola celeste (FF)	8
Spitz flute	4
Spitz flute celeste (AA)	4
Octave geigen	4
Lieblich flute	4
Fifteenth	2
Quint mixture III (15, 19, 22)	
Scharf II ranks (26, 29)	
Contra fagotto	16
(73 pipes)	
Trumpet	8
Clarion	4
Tremulant (adjustable)	

Pedal organ
(11 stops, 8 ranks, 280 pipes)

	feet
Principal	16
Sub bass	16
Quintaten (Great)	16
Octave	8
Bass flute (Sub bass)	8
Spitz flute	4
Rauschquint II (2⅔ and 2)	
Fagotto (swell)	16
Trombone	16
Clarion (Trombone)	8
Dulzian	4

All ranks are complete and of full compass unless otherwise indicated

Compass: Manuals CC–C
61 notes
Pedals CCC–G
32 notes
Electro-pneumatic action
Discus Blower

Grand total: 42 stops, 38 voices, 45 ranks and 2,535 pipes.

A modern major church design, in which service accompaniment use and considerable solo performance potential, is reflected in the carefully balanced design as between the several departments, in the instrument in Wigan Parish Church.

Great organ	feet
1. Quintaten	16
2. Open diapason	8
3. Principal	8
4. Hohl flute	8
5. Octave	4
6. Block flute	4
7. Twelfth	$2\frac{2}{3}$
8. Fifteenth	2
9. Quint mixture, 3 ranks	
10. Trumpet	8
Swell to great	
Positif to great	

Swell organ	feet
1. Bourdon	16
2. Open diapason	8
3. Stopped diapason	8
4. Salicional	8
5. Vox angelica	8
6. Geigen principal	4
7. Lieblich flute	4
8. Super octave	2
9. Mixture, 3 ranks	
10. Scharf, 3 ranks	
11. Contra fagotto	16
12. Cornopean	8
13. Oboe	8
14. Clarion	4
Tremulant	
Swell sub octave	
Swell super octave	
Swell unison off	

Positif organ	feet
1. Rohrflöte	8
2. Prinzipal	4
3. Flöte	4
4. Nazard	$2\frac{2}{3}$
5. Octave	2
6. Terz	$1\frac{3}{5}$
7. Larigot	$1\frac{1}{3}$
8. Sifflöte	1
9. Rohr schalmei	8
10. Tuba	8
11. Octave tuba	4
Swell to positif	

Pedal organ	feet
1. Sub bass	32
2. Open wood	16
3. Open metal	16
4. Bourdon	16
5. Principal	8
6. Bass flute	8
7. Gemshorn	4
8. Nachthorn	2
9. Mixture, 3 ranks	
10. Trombone	16
11. Trumpet	8
12. Clarion	4
13. Krummhorn	4
Swell to pedal	
Swell octave to pedal	
Great to pedal	
Positif to pedal	

APPENDIX

Lastly, a concert organ rich in tonal resources, matched to all periods of the literature and fit to grace a seat of learning. The Bute Hall Organ, University of Glasgow.

Great organ	feet	Solo organ	feet
Double open diapason	16	Quintade	8
Open diapason I	8	Viole de gambe	8
Open diapason II	8	Viole celeste	8
Spitz principal	8	Concert flute	4
Dulciana	8	Nasat	$2\frac{2}{3}$
Stopped diapason	8	Piccolo	2
Clear flute	4	Tierce	$1\frac{3}{5}$
Octave	4	Cor anglais	16
Gemshorn principal	4	Krummhorn	8
Twelfth	$2\frac{2}{3}$	Hautbois	4
Fifteenth	2	Unenclosed	
Mixture IV (19, 22, 26, 29)		Tuba	8
Cornet III (12, 15, 17)		Tuba clarion	4
Trumpet	8	Trompette en chamade	8
Clarion	4	Tremulant	
Solo to great		Octave	
Swell to great		Sub octave	
Positif to great		Unison off	

Swell organ	feet	Positif organ	feet
Geigen principal	8	Quintaten	16
Hohl flute	8	Chimney flute	8
Echo salicional	8	Principal	8
Voix celeste	8	Koppel flöte	4
Stopped flute	4	Octave	4
Octave	4	Wald flöte	2
Super octave	4	Quint	$1\frac{1}{3}$
Plein jeu III (15, 19, 22)		Principal	1
Scharf III (26, 29, 33)		Zimbel III (29, 33, 36)	
Contra fagotto	16	Trumpet (Great)	8
Cornopean	8	Clarion (Great)	4
Oboe	8	Solo to positif	
Clarion	4	Swell to positif	
Tremulant			
Octave			
Sub octave			

Pedal organ

	feet	pipes			
1. Harmonic sub bass	32		13. Quartane II	$2\frac{2}{3}$ and 2	64
1. Great bass	16	44	14. Trompette en chamade (Solo)	8	
3. Sub bass	16	44	15. Contra trombone	32	68
4. Contra gamba	16	32			
5. Lieblich bourdon	16	32	16. Ophicleide (No. 15)	16	
6. Octave (No. 2)	8		17. Trumpet (No. 15)	8	
7. Principal	8	44	18. Clarion (No. 15)	4	
8. Violoncello	8	32			
9. Bass flute (No. 3)	8		Solo to pedal		
10. Nachthorn	4	32	Swell to pedal		
11. Fifteenth (No. 7)	4		Great to pedal		
12. Sifflöte	2	32	Positif to pedal		
			Swell octave to pedal		
			Great and pedal pistons coupled		

Index

Index

Index

Action systems, 31
Acoustics (for organ), 184–6
Acoustic Bass, 167
Acuta, 148–52
Aeoline, 142–3

Bärpfeife, 173–4
Basset Horn, 171–2
Bass Flute, 160–2
Bassoon, 167–9
Bell Gamba, 147–8
Block Flute, Blockflöte, 152–3, 158–60
Bourdon, 160–2
Bradford Cathedral, 185
Bridgetown, St James, 179
Brüstwerk, 5
Buckingham Palace Chapel, 89

Cambridge, St Mary the Great, 178
Carisbrooke Castle Organ, 8
Casework, 175–80
Celestes, 6, 142–3
Cello, 143–5
Chimney Flute, 164–5
Choir, Chayre organ, 5, 13, 21
Choral Bass, 160–2
Cinq, 171–2
Clarabella, 154–6
Claribel Flute, 154–6
Clarinet, 171–2
Clarion, Clairon, 167–9
Clear Flute, 152–3, 154–6
Closed Horn, 168–9
Combination actions, 106–7, 109

Compass keys, 10, 96–7
Concert Flute, 156–8
Cone Gamba, 147–8
Consoles, 96–111
Console dimensions, 98–101
    Layout rules, 108–9
Contra Bass, 140
Cookridge, Holy Trinity, 300
Coppel, Copula, 159–60
Cor Anglais, 169–71
Cor de Nuit, 158–60, 160–2
Cornet, 165–7
Corno di Bassetto, 171–2
Como Flute, 152–3
Cornopean, 167–9
Cremona, 171–2
Crescendo pedal, 106, 109
Cromorne, Crummhorn, 171–2
Cymbel, Zimbel, 148–52

Detached console, 182–3
'Denham' organ, 179
Diapason, open, 140
    Bell, 147–8
    Cantabile, 140
    chorus, 117
    Echo, 142–3
    Geigen, 140
    Horn, 140
    Pedal Open, 141, 154–6
    Phonon, 141
    Violin, 140
Doetinchem, 178
Dolcan, 147–8
Dolce, 147–8

INDEX

Doppel Flute, Doppelflöte, 160–2
Double Trumpet, 167–9
Drawstops, 3, 16, 104–5
Dulciania, 11, 142–3

Echo Bourdon, 162–3
Electric action current supply, 86
Electro-magnetic action, 28, 53
Electro-pneumatic action, 27, 28, 46–57
En-charmade, 7, 132, 137
English Horn, 169–71
Erzahler, Erzahler Celeste, 159–60

Fagotto, Fagot, 167–9
Fifteenth, 140
Flageolet, 152–3
Flautino, 152–3
Flauto Traverso, 156–8
Flue stops, 112–27, 139–67
Flute à Cheminèe, 164–5
Flute à Fuseau, 159–60
Flute à pavillon, 147–8
Flute Conique, 158–60
Flute Harmonique, 156–8
Flute Octaviante, 152–3
Flute Ouverte, 152–3
Flute Triangulaire, 154–6
Fugara, 143–5
Full Mixture, 148–52
Furniture, 148–52
Fractional Length reeds, 173–4
Frequency range, 17–18

Gamba, Gambette, 153–6
Gedeckt, 160–2
Gedeckt Pommer, 160–2
Geigen Principal, 140
Gemshorn, 119, 158–60
Giffnock, South Church, 177

Glockengamba, 147–8
Glasgow, the Bute Hall, 203
Kings Park, 199
Grave Mixture, 148–52
Great Organ, 20
Gross Quint, 165–7
Gross Tierce, 165–7

Harfpfeife, 159–60
Harmonic Bass, 165–7
Harmonic Claribel, 156–8
Harmonic Flute, 156–8
Harmonic Piccolo, 156–8
Harmonic Trumpet, 168–9
Harmonic Twelfth, 156–8
Harmonics, 19
Harmonics (Mixture), 148–52
Haupt-orgel, Hauptwerk, 5
Hautbois, Hautboy, 169–71
Hellpfeife, 152–3
Hohlbrook School, Chapel, 176
Hohl Flute, Hohlflöte, 154–6
Holyflöte, 154–6
Holypfeife, 154–6
Horn, 168–9
Hydraulus, 2.

Keraulophon, 143–5
Keyboard, manual, 96–98
Pedal, 10, 12, 21, 98–102
Koppel Flute, Koppelflöte, 119, 159–60
Krummhorn, 130

Larigot, 165–6
Lieblich Bass, Lieblich Bourdon, 162–3
Lieblich Flute, Lieblichflöte, 118, 162–3
Lieblich Gedeckt, 118, 162–3

INDEX

London, Alexandra Palace, 178
    Mormon, Hyde Park Chapel, 15, 177, 200
    Royal Albert Hall, 178,
Long compass, 10

Magic Flute, 156–8
Magnet valves, 46–47, 53–54
Major Bass, 140
Melodia, 154–6
Mixtures, 148–52
Musette, 171–2
Mutation stops, 19, 20, 165, 167
Mounted Cornet, 165–7

Nachthorn, 158–60, 160–2
Nasat, 165–7
Nason, Nason Flute, 160–2
Nazard, 165–7
Nineteenth, 165–7
None, 165–7
Norwich Cathedral, 178, 197

Oboe, 169–71
Octave, 140
Octavin, 140
Open Diapason, 140
Open Flute, 152–3
Open Wood Bass, 154–6
Ophicleide, 168–9
Orchestral Flute, 156–8
Orchestral Oboe, 169–71
Organ Architect, 188
Organ case, functional, 15, 175–7
Organ chambers, 13, 24, 27
Organ Chamber heating, 87–8
Organ Consultant, 189–90
Organ metals, 120–2

Pedalboard, historical, 10
    radiating & concave, 12
    compass, 21
    dimensions, 98–102
Pedal Organ, 21, 24
Piccolo, 152–3
Pitch notation, 17–19
Plein Jeu, 148–52
Pneumatic actions, 26–27, 39–45
Posaune, 167–9
Position of organ, 24, 181–6
Positive, Positiv, 4, 5
Principal, 140

Quartane, 149–52
Quint, 165–7
Quintaten, Quintade, Quintadena, 118–9, 143, 160–2
'Quintet,' 179, 199
Quint Mixture, 149–52

Rankett, 173–4
Rauschquinte, 148–52
Reed stops, 12–**13**, 167–74
Regal, 4, 131, 173–4
Resultant Bass, 16, 165–7
Rohr Bourdon, 164–5
Rohr Flute, Rohrflöte, 119, 164–5
Rohr Gedeckt, 164–5
Rohr Schalmey, 171–2
Rückpositive, 5

Salicional, Salicet, Salicetina, 142–3
Schalmey, Schalmei, 130, 169–71
Scharf, 148–52
Sesquialtera, 148–52
Septieme, 164–7
Seventeenth, 165–7
Sext, 148–52
Shallots, 129, 133, 168
Sharp Mixture, 148–52
Shawm, 169–71
Sifflöte, 152–3

Solo organ, 21
Sordun, 173–4
Soundboards, *see* wind chests
Spindle Flute, Spillflöte, 159–60
Spitzflöte, 158–60
Spitz gamba, 120, 158–60
Spitzgedeckt, 159–60
Spitzprinzipal, 158–60
Spitzquinte, 164–7
Stop control systems, 102–5
Stop-Keys & stoptablets, 102–5
Stopped Diapason, 160–2
Stopped pipes, 160–3
Suabe Flute, 154–6
Sub Bass, Subbas, 160–1
Sub Bourdon, 160–2
Swell-box, 11, 89–95
Swell-box action, 93–4, 105–6
Swell organ, 11, 12, 21
Sydney, Town Hall, 35

Tapered pipe stops, 158, 160
Tertian, Terz, 148–52
Tibia Plena, 154–6
Thumb pistons, 108–9
Tierce, 165–7
Tracker action, 26–29, 30–38
Traverse Flute, 156–8
Tromba, Trombone, 167–9
Trompette, en-chamade, 7, 132, 168–9
Tuba, Tuba Mirabilis, 168–9

Unit-extension system, 23
    windchests, 73
Unda Maris, 142–3

Viol, Violina, 145–6
Viola, Viola da Gamba, etc., 143–5, 158–60

Viole, Viol d'amour, etc., 145–6
Viole Celeste, 145–6
Violone, Violoncello, 143–5
Voicing, fine stops, 112–3, 122–7
    reed stops, 127–38
    scales, 114–20
Voix Celèstes, 142–3
Vox Angelica, 142–3
Vox Humana, 173–4

Wald Flute, Waldflöte, 152–6, 158–60
Waldhorn, 168–9
Werkprinzip, 5, 22
Wigan, Parish Church, 202
Windchests, bar & slider, 58–61, 66–7, 74
    choice of, 66–67
    direct electric, 66
    off note, 70–73
    pitman-pouch, 64–65, 69–70
    sliderless, 62–65, 67–70
Wind pressure, 26, 29, 81
Wind supply, fan blowing, 78–81
    feeder blowing, 76–78
    Humidification, 87–88
    regulators, 83–85
    steadiness, 83–85
    Tremulant, 85–6
    Wind trunks, 84–85
Wooden pipes, 122, 154–6
Wymondham Abbey, 89

Zauberflöte, 118, 156–8
Zinc, 171–2